Flight

Genevieve Mckay

Chapter One

"Easy, boy." I laid a steadying hand on Quarry's shoulder as his sturdy legs swished effortlessly through long grass so high it brushed my bare toes. The morning sun was warm on my back, the whole meadow alive with bird-song. I inhaled deeply, delighting in the smell of fresh, spring grass and wildflowers.

Quarry mouthed the bit gently, the movement travelling up the reins and translating his question to my fingers: *can we go faster?*

I kept my hands feather-light on the reins, sending a whispered message back in the most tactful way I could. *Never interfere with impulsion*, Claudia would say, *always channel forward energy; never stifle it.*

Be patient, I told him, shifting my weight back slightly.

His grey mane fluttered in the breeze, silver strands catching the sunlight so they glowed with an otherworldly light. One ear flicked toward me, reading my seat, my hands, my mind perfectly. He compressed his steps, arching his neck and floating into that powerful lofty trot that always felt like flying.

"Good boy," I said as he slowed, trotting nearly in place, each footfall lasting an eternity. And then he sat, rocking back on his hocks like a pendulum, elevating his powerful shoulders until he'd risen into a perfect levade. I sat motionless, legs draped around his sides like I'd been painted there, smiling from ear to ear with the astonishing perfection of it all. The good horse, the sun, the meadow—all blended together in one moment of harmony that was as close to magic as I'd ever get.

"Astrid?"

No. I opened my eyes reluctantly, the disappointment of being pulled from the dream a physical pain in my chest. *No.* I sighed and stared blearily out the widow, squinting in the late afternoon light.

Brown, sunburnt hills whooshed past our rig; an endless line of dry slopes, dotted with dead trees, their blackened trunks scorched like there'd been a recent fire.

I rubbed at the goosebumps rising on my good arm, the one not encased in a cast, and held back a shiver. Despite the oven-like heat outside, inside the cab felt like winter.

"Are we here?" I asked, looking at the shrivelled countryside. For some reason, I'd imagined my aunt's ranch would be all lush green grass and rolling hills. I hadn't thought the heatwave crouched over Vancouver Island like a suffocating blanket would follow us north across the ferry and way up into the interior of British Columbia. From the looks of it, things had worsened the further inland we'd driven. The fact that it was mid-September meant nothing at all to the weather gods.

"Yep, almost there." Allan smiled so his tanned face crinkled into a hundred laugh lines. "You've had a long sleep."

"Sorry about that," I said, yawning. "It's the pain medication; I sleep all the time."

My phone beeped faintly, and I reached down to fish it out of my backpack.

Hey, are you there yet? How's Folly?

I glanced at the large monitor above our heads, the one trained inside the trailer we pulled behind us. There was only one horse left in the cavernous space: Folly. She leaned her big shoulder against the wall like it was the only thing keeping her upright, her head held low, almost dozing.

She's okay, I typed back to Hilary, *it looks hot here.*

Like, full of hot cowboys?

No. I laughed. *Definitely not, more like a hot desert.* I pressed send but an error message flashed up. *Message unsent.* I frowned and poked a few buttons.

"Yeah, cell service is hit or miss in these hills. It comes and goes," Allan said, glancing over at me.

"Great." I sighed and flopped back in my seat then looked up at the monitor again. "How has she been?"

"Oh, she's hanging in there. She'll be glad to get on solid ground, though. She's probably ready for some grass under her feet."

"Is there grass?" I asked doubtfully, staring at the brown hills dotted with charred-looking trees. "It looks...scorched."

"Oh no, those trees are from the pine beetle kill." He looked over at me and frowned, registering my confusion. "We lost millions of acres of forest to it. You must remember; it was all over the news. The trees turn black like that once they die. The lack of grass is just from the drought, it will be back once this heatwave ends. Your aunt's place has that big lake, so it fared a little better."

I nodded and rubbed my eyes, still not fully awake. I didn't remember anything about beetles on the news, but I wouldn't insult him by telling him that.

We turned left off the highway, tires crunching onto a narrow gravel road that cut between two sunburnt hills. Rickety fence posts held together by strands of barbed wire lined the road beside us; I couldn't imagine something that flimsy could contain an animal wanting to escape. Folly would barge right through in a heartbeat. I hoped my aunt's fences were more substantial.

Ten minutes later we slowed, the rig swinging wide to make a left-hand turn into a broad driveway.

I gulped and wiped my damp hand on my leg. This was it; my new home.

There wasn't an impressive gate with a horse statue like at Claudia's. Instead, a huge wooden arch spanned the driveway, made from the curved, polished trunks of two dead trees. At the top of the arc where the trees merged together, hung a large, bleached-out cow skull topped with a set of long, twisted horns.

I leaned sideways to get a better look as we drove underneath, shivering with the ridiculous impression that the empty eye sockets had blinked at me.

A red mailbox shaped like a miniature barn stood on one side of the driveway and on the other hung a large cryptic wooden sign; no words, just a series of symbols burned deep into the wood—three wavy lines stacked horizontally one above the other.

"What does *that* mean?" I turned to Allan. Was my aunt part of some sort of cult?

"Well, that's the name of the place: Triple Hills Ranch. It's been called that for over a hundred and fifty years. The triple hills symbol is the brand they used to mark the cows and horses for identification."

"Oh." It all sounded so wild and strange. A wave of homesickness hit me, and I wondered again if I'd made the right decision to come here.

It had been an easy choice at the time. My dad and Marion had practically begged me to come and, once I'd agreed, all the arrangements had been made at lightning speed. I'd been so busy saying goodbye to everyone, getting packed for the move, and worrying about Folly, that I hadn't given much thought to what it would be like when I arrived at the ranch. I didn't know if Aunt Lillian even *wanted* me and Folly, or if she'd been pushed into the visit just like I had.

It was too late now to turn back.

The driveway was in better shape than the road, gravel packed so smooth it was almost pavement. Allan slowed again as the road split in two. A wooden sign stood at the fork, two words branded at either end: 'Homestead', the scrolled word pointed uphill to the left, and 'Barn' read the other side, heading downhill to the right.

Allan steered the big horse trailer in the direction marked 'Barn' and I hummed nervously under my breath, glancing again at the trailer cam.

We're almost home, Folly, I thought, *don't worry.*

She didn't look up, just swayed tiredly on her feet with the motion of the trailer.

The driveway curved around a low hill and the view opened

all at once to a huge sweeping valley, unfolding as far as I could see.

"Oh," I said breathlessly, taking it all in as fast as I could. Beneath us lay miles of undulating hills and, far off to the right, shone a huge, dark lake shimmering in the late afternoon sun. Green grass radiated out from the lake like the arms of a gigantic starfish, five green fingers poking into the browner grass further up the hills.

"Look at them all," I said in excitement; craning my head to take in the hills dotted all over with horses. There were way too many to count.

"Yep." Allan nodded. "Those there are some of the finest minded horses put on this earth. Your aunt has a talent for mixing beauty with brains and athleticism. People come from all over the world to buy them. Or at least, they used to."

I twisted around to watch the valley until it disappeared. We went through a patch of woods and then came to a wide clearing where a huge barn stood. I could just make out rows of paddocks behind it.

"This is the training and sales barn, and where the indoor is. Your aunt gave me orders to take your horse further up to the broodmare barn. It's a bit quieter there this time of year."

I turned to look at the stable as we passed. The big wooden barn was the polar opposite of Claudia's stable, Mud Lark, but was just as striking in its own way.

"Oh," I said, turning to Allan excitedly, "it's beautiful. It's all wonderful."

"I thought you'd like it," he said, smiling. "Triple Hills is one of the nicest properties in this area. There was once over ten thousand acres of pristine farmland here. Of course, most of that has been sold off over the years but it's still a good spread."

"It's beautiful," I said again, feeling glad for the first time to have made this long trip.

Allan kept talking. "This next barn here was built by your aunt and your Uncle Trent before he passed away. There are suites upstairs for staff or working students."

"I don't remember my Uncle Trent," I said, frowning. "I heard he'd passed away a couple years ago, but we didn't come up for the funeral. I haven't been here since I was a kid."

"Is that so?" Allan maneuvered the truck carefully up to another wooden barn. This one was smaller than the first, but still impressive. "Well, your uncle was a good man. His death was a blow to the community and it hit your aunt especially hard. It hasn't been quite the same around here since, but it's still a fine place. They had a few upheavals with staff recently, but I'm sure that's all been worked out."

He shut off the truck and stared thoughtfully out the window. "You'll get on just fine here, Astrid. Your aunt went through a rough patch, but she's smart as a whip and a fine horsewoman. Any horse I've ever picked up from Triple Hills was in mint condition. Your mare will do fine."

On the video screen, I saw Folly raise her head slightly and let out a half-hearted whinny. Somewhere, far off, another horse responded, and then another.

I stretched the stiffness out of my muscles as best I could and slowly pushed open the door. Heat poured inside the cab, closing around me so thick I nearly choked. I clambered down as best I could, gravel skidding under my boots as my feet hit the earth with a thud.

"Astrid? Is that you?"

A woman I recognized only from faded photographs strode toward me. She wore a grey cowboy hat pushed back on her head, tendrils of silver hair curling out underneath. The rest of her hair was plaited into a long braid that trailed over her shoulder.

She stopped a couple of feet away and took a deep breath, frowning at the bandages still covering half my face. When her gaze slid down to the cast on my arm, her eyes widened, and she put a hand over her mouth.

"Your father ought to be shot," were her first words and, before I could form an answer to *that,* she reached out and pulled me into a tight hug that made me wince.

She stepped back and held me at arm's length, searching my face as if she were looking for something. "Sweetie, I'm so glad to see you. But I'm shocked at how badly you're hurt. I had no idea."

"It's no big deal." I shrugged and looked at the ground, not sure if my dad or Marion had told her the important details about the accident; mainly that it had been my fault and that I'd nearly killed my horse. "They had to do surgery to fix my nose and cheekbone but it's healing now. There shouldn't even be much of a scar. I have to go to the doctor to get it checked in a couple days, and then hopefully they can take off the bandages and put on a splint."

"Oh, well," she said, sucking in a deep breath. "We'll get one of the boys to drive you to town; I don't do doctors anymore." Her eyes trailed back down to my cast and she frowned again. "That arm will take time to heal. You won't be up to much riding or farm work for a while. That's disappointing; I'd hoped you could ride some horses."

"Sorry," I said in a small voice, feeling my face flush. Maybe she'd expected a farm hand that could earn their keep by shoveling stalls and stuff right away. And here I was; hardly able to dress myself let alone do heavy farm work.

I must have looked miserable because my aunt touched my cheek softly with the tips of her calloused fingers. "Astrid, you took me by surprise. You remind me so much of your mother and I wasn't prepared for that. I am so sorry I haven't been in your life all these years. I blame myself. If I hadn't been so stubborn…if I hadn't fought with your father—"

"Sorry to interrupt"—Allan came around the side of the trailer with a lead rope in his hand—"but we should get this horse settled. She's sweating up a storm in there."

Aunt Lillian straightened, her expression business-like again. "Yes, of course, by all means bring her inside. I have a stall set up."

Please don't attack anyone, Folly, I thought, trailing nervously after them, *please be good.*

Allan swung the door open and Folly lifted her head and then dropped it back down again as if the movement had exhausted the last of her strength. Her coat was patchy with sweat and her eyes had a vacant look in them like she'd withdrawn somewhere far inside herself. She hobbled after Allan slowly, ears pinned flat, nostrils flaring and tail swishing in discomfort with every step.

"Oh, that poor horse," my aunt said under her breath, "the poor creature."

I looked away sharply, my throat so tight I could barely

breathe. I knew it was my fault Folly was in this condition, she was living evidence of what an idiot I'd been. I would do anything to make it up to her.

The cooler air in the barn was a welcome relief to the relentless baking oven outside. Immediately, some of my tension melted away and I could breathe freely.

There were no chandeliers lining the ceiling like at Claudia's place; instead, beautiful wooden beams crossed overhead and pigeons cooed gently in the rafters, wings rustling softly. Light shone in from dusty cob-webbed windows set high in the wall. Instead of concrete aisles lined with rubber mats, there was a wide dirt aisle someone had raked into an intricate criss-cross pattern that my boots disturbed as soon as we walked on it.

"Oh, don't mind that." My aunt laughed when I looked back guiltily at my foot prints. "I always rake when I get nervous. It's a compulsion, but it does look nice afterward even if it doesn't last."

The oversized stalls we passed stood empty, doors gaping open to reveal smooth, dirt floors bare of sawdust. I wondered where all the horses were.

"The girls stay out in the fields until the snow comes," my aunt said, reading my thoughts. "They like it better and that's less work for us. That will make it nice and quiet for your mare in here."

Aunt Lillian led us to a roomy double-sized stall bedded in knee-high, yellow straw, and ushered Allan to lead Folly inside.

Folly took a small nip at Allan as he unclipped her halter and then swung abruptly away. She lurched around the stall, checking every corner and pushing at the unfamiliar straw with her nose. She ate a few pieces before opening her mouth wide and spitting out the stalky, yellow strands in disgust. She stumbled over to the waiting pile of hay, lipping at it half-heartedly before moving restlessly on to inspect her water bucket. She snorted at it and wrinkled her nose but didn't drink, just glared around her stall unhappily; a picture of discontent.

"We'll have to keep a good eye on her, Astrid. We don't want her to colic," Aunt Lillian said, shutting the stall door and frowning at the mare's sweat-soaked sides.

I leaned my good elbow on the stall door and looked inside dolefully. There was no way around it; Folly looked awful. Her coat was damp with sweat, she had deep hollows over her eyes and her untrimmed mane stood up roughly in all directions. She kept shifting off her front leg to take the weight off it, clearly uncomfortable.

Aunt Lillian and Allan unloaded the trailer, hauling feed, blankets, and medication into the feed room while I leaned over Folly's stall door, feeling miserable.

"You'll be okay, girl," I whispered to her. "Look at your nice, big stall; it's like a palace compared to your stall at home. This is a great place to recover."

Folly raised her head slowly and flattened her ears, shaking her head wearily at me in warning.

"Astrid, where's your tack?" my aunt called. "Did they forget to pack it?"

"Uh, I don't have any," I said, turning in her direction. "All her stuff belonged to Cole. I have her halter and Liza sent her blankets along, so I guess I own those."

"Oh?" Aunt Lillian opened her mouth like she wanted to say more, but Allan interrupted.

"All right, we're all unloaded, kid. I have three horses to pick up in Prince George, so I have to go. It was nice meeting you."

"Thanks, for taking care of Folly, Allan," I said. "Have a good trip back."

"See you in a few weeks for the foals," my aunt said, giving him a wave.

Aunt Lillian and I stood in silence while Allan rumbled the big truck back to life and pulled carefully out of the driveway. I looked at the ground, not sure what to do with myself. Aunt Lillian was practically a stranger and I had no idea what to say to her.

"Well, show me what Folly gets for food. We'll get her tucked away and then I'll take you up to the house and get you settled."

"I could give her her medication," I said suddenly, "she has stuff to help with the pain. She's not due for a few hours, but maybe she can have it a bit early?"

"Probably a good idea," my aunt agreed, "the trip was hard on her."

I followed Aunt Lillian to a big room that was a combination of feed and storage. Dusty halters and blankets hung from metal racks on one wall, and opposite was a low counter and sink with a pile of buckets stacked beside it. Every other bit of exposed floor was piled with Rubbermaid storage tubs, each labelled with a strip of masking tape.

Folly's supplements had been stacked haphazardly on the counter next to the sink; her bag of pellets on the floor beside it.

"This is pretty high-test food, Astrid," my aunt said, frowning at the ingredients on the feed bag. "You might want to have her on something less exciting while she's on stall rest. She doesn't need all this protein and sugar right now; you can feed her some of the maintenance food the horses here get."

"Oh," I said, "but she's a dressage horse, can she eat what western horses eat?"

Aunt Lillian covered her mouth, making a choking, sputtering sound that most definitely was a supreme effort not to burst into laughter.

I looked down at the counter, my lips curled politely into a smile I didn't feel. *Ha ha, stupid Astrid, asking the wrong questions again,* I thought wearily. It had been a long, exhausting day; the pinnacle of a long, exhausting month, and I was bone tired. So what if I knew nothing about horse food. How was I supposed to learn anything if I didn't ask questions?

"Oh, Astrid," my aunt said, recovering herself a little and wiping a tear from the corner of one eye. "Yes, dear, that will be fine. Horses are horses."

"Fine," I said, focusing on lining up the little tubs of Folly's supplements neatly next to the sink and then unpacking the Ziploc bag of her medication. She was on antibiotics, anti-inflammatories, and an additional pain control and she needed everything twice a day. There wasn't any beet pulp to soak so I dissolved her medication in water like the vet tech at the hospital had showed me and stirred it up with the pellets and chunks of carrot. I hoped she would eat it.

We walked back to the stall and my aunt pointed inside. "There you go, feed tub's up there in the corner," she said, waving at the rubber bowl directly in striking distance of Folly's front feet.

She clearly expected I was capable of feeding my own horse.

Well, I was not going to be the one to let her know how incapable I was. She'd find out on her own soon enough.

"Sure." I gulped, somehow keeping the quaver out of my voice.

"Hey, Folly." I gingerly slid open the stall door, prickles of nervous sweat already prickling my back the closer I got to the sullen looking mare. "It's just me with your dinner. You like your dinner, don't you? Nice girl."

Folly didn't bother to look up from rooting through the pile of coarse hay; searching for softer, greener bits to eat. But she flattened her ears and swished her tail in warning. Taking a deep breath, I inched closer to the rubber feed tub and then, in one swift move, dumped the bucket contents inside and sprang for the door. The second the latch clicked shut, Folly barged over to the food with surprising agility for someone who was supposed to be injured and greedily ate everything, hunching over her feed tub like a panther mauling its prey. She glared up at us, wet food dripping from her mouth, shifting from foot to foot like she was about to charge. Even from this side of the door she looked terrifying.

"Whoa," my aunt said, raising her eyebrows, "is she always so…aggressive?"

I shrugged, thinking this had actually been low-key for Folly. "Sometimes," I said evasively, "she probably just needs to settle in."

There was a low wheezing noise next to my elbow and I peered into the stall beside Folly's to see a small, grey face peering up at me. "Oh, he's adorable!" I said, looking in at the fat, fuzzy donkey. "What's his name?"

"Donkey," my aunt said with a laugh. "We aren't a very imaginative bunch around here. He usually stays out to guard the foals, but he was due for a hoof trim anyway, so I brought him in to keep Folly company."

"Well," she went on, brushing her hands together in a business-like way, "now I suppose it's time to get you settled. We'll come back and check on Folly after dinner."

Allan had stacked my small pile of belongings just outside the barn door. All my worldly possessions were squished into a backpack, a large hard-sided black suitcase, my laptop bag and, most importantly, a large carrying case that held both my old practice bow and my competition bow.

The entire past summer I had technically been banned from archery and, now that I had my bow back, I didn't plan to let it out of my sight again. I lifted the bow case with difficulty and my aunt scooped up the rest and carried them to an ancient, battered blue farm truck that was parked nearby with the passenger-side door already ajar.

"Sorry about all the dog hair, Jake likes to sleep in here sometimes. He thinks it's his truck. Don't mind that door, Astrid, the latch doesn't work."

Aunt Lillian tossed my stuff into the backseat on top of about an inch of grey, wiry dog hair and a pile of smelly saddle pads. With a herculean amount of effort, I hoisted the oversized bow case on top, trying not to wrinkle my nose at the overpowering smell of dog.

I crawled into the front passenger seat and used my good hand to heave the door shut only to have it bounce immediately back open again. Aunt Lillian got in on her side and then leaned right across me, her elbow digging painfully into my leg, to attach a complicated bit of wire between my door handle and the seat. She gave it a good twist and then sat back, satisfied. "There, good as new. That should keep you from falling out."

"But it's still open," I said, looking nervously at the inch of daylight between the door and the truck.

"Bah, the wire will hold it. It's been that way for years."

The door rattled ominously when she started the truck and I clutched the seat, double checking my seatbelt to make sure it was clicked tight.

"I do keep meaning to fix it," Aunt Lillian said apologetically, "but we're so busy here in the summer that some things get put off until the slow season. Unfortunately, that season never seems to arrive."

We passed a sign that read "Private Property—No Entry" and bumped along a dirt track with pot holes so deep my teeth rattled in my head whenever the tires lurched into one. The truck had no shocks to speak of and I clung to my seat with my one good arm to keep from bouncing around. The door clanged loudly with every bump, and I squeezed my eyes tight, sure I was about to die at any second.

"Sorry, Astrid, I probably should have taken the main driveway. This is the short cut."

"It's okay," I squeaked, bouncing so high my head came inches from hitting the ceiling.

Pain meds, I thought weakly, *I will have to double up on those as soon as I get to the house. If I even survive that long.*

"Well, here we are. Oh look, there's Jake on the porch waiting to meet you. Don't mind him; he looks tough, but he's a big teddy bear."

I opened my eyes carefully, gaping as I took in both the oversized log house and the most gigantic dog I'd ever seen in my life. I couldn't decide which was more intimidating.

The house was a sprawling honey-coloured, two-story log structure matching the broodmare barn in style. A wide porch wrapped around the front and sides, scattered with wooden tables and chairs, and even a large porch-swing. Massive wooden beams ran upward and were topped with carved eagle heads that stared out across the parched, brown lawn like baleful sentries.

Sauntering down the porch steps was a shaggy, grey dog the size of a small pony, wiry hair falling over his eyes. He woofed low under his breath and wagged his tail stiffly before coming to stand at the passenger door. He was so tall he didn't even have to look up; he just rested his chin against the glass and watched me intently, his beady black eyes peering out from under a grey fringe of fur, teeth glinting wickedly.

"Go away, Jake," my aunt commanded, hopping out of the truck and coming around my side to push him out of the way. She wrenched open the back door and hauled out my suitcase and backpack, carrying one in each hand as if they weighed nothing and slinging my laptop bag over her shoulder. "Not everyone wants to see you, you big galoot. Get going."

He trotted ahead, and she strode after him, not even looking back to see if I was okay. I stared after her with my heart sinking. She'd forgotten to undo the wire that held my door shut.

"Seriously?" I said out loud, staring down at the complicated twist of metal trapping me inside. "Why does everything have to be so difficult?" After poking myself twice on the sharp ends and a few minutes of awkward fumbling, I was finally able to work myself free.

I sighed and slid out of the truck carefully, rescuing my bow case from the backseat where it had partially slid to the floor. *Ack,* I thought, brushing at pieces of wiry dog hair sticking to the case, *what sort of place is this?*

I walked slowly up the porch stairs, feeling irritable and out of place. My whole body throbbed, and I needed to take my pain medication badly.

I passed a large porch swing and a group of carved wooden chairs and tables arranged at one end. A round, fur-covered dog bed sat right next to the front door and on it sat the massive dog, watching me intently.

"Um, hello, uh, Jake," I said, edging past him. "Nice doggy, don't eat me. I'm family." His pink tongue lolled out and he slowly lay down, still keeping an eye on me.

"Aunt Lillian?" I called, pulling open the outer screen door and then shouldering past the heavy wooden door behind it. "Hello?"

I stood in the front foyer looking up in amazement at the vaulted, beamed ceiling overhead. The room was wide open; a sunken living area to my right and, beyond it, a huge gleaming kitchen with a big wooden table that looked like it could seat dozens of people. Directly to my left was a long hallway lined with thick wooden doors on one side; they were all closed.

Straight ahead was a wide, wooden staircase that led to the second level.

"Hello?" I called out uncertainly, "Aunt Lillian?"

"Up here, Astrid," my aunt called from somewhere upstairs.

I pulled my boots off with difficulty and dropped them at the front door before moving cautiously up the stair case, socks slipping on the overly-polished wooden steps.

I paused at the top, looking around in awe. Directly in front of me was a large nook with couches and end tables and heavily-laden bookshelves set between two huge windows. There was even a fireplace in the corner.

"Wow," I said out loud. I could easily picture myself spending the whole winter curled up here with a good book. It was a wonderful spot.

"There you are, Astrid." Aunt Lillian appeared beside me. "I see you've found the reading nook. It's a little pretentious, but the guests always seem to like to congregate here. Come on, I'll show you your room."

I followed her down the hall, past three or four closed doors until we came to one that was open.

"This will be your room. I hope you like it. I didn't have time to do much decorating, but I suppose you'd like to personalize it yourself anyway."

"Oh," I said, looking around in approval. "It's nice, thanks."

It wasn't a huge room, but the polished log walls and the picture window made it beautifully cozy. There was a big wooden bed with a small table beside it, a desk and a closet for all my stuff. The bed was covered in a red plaid duvet that matched the curtains. On one wall was an open door that led to a small bathroom. It was everything I needed.

"Feel free to put up posters or decorate however you like. As long as you don't nail holes in the wall to hang up your bras like our last working student then you're free to do what you please."

"Uh, no problem." I sat down on the bed and smoothed the wrinkle out of the heavy cover, the texture rough against my hand. This room was so different from my cold, sterile room back home. This one felt warm and inviting, like somewhere you could just curl up in and… I yawned, covering my mouth quickly so my aunt wouldn't think I was being rude.

"Well, you've had a long trip, so you must be exhausted. Would you like to rest before dinner?"

"Yes, please," I said, stifling another yawn. "If that's okay."

"Of course. I'll call you for dinner at seven. I invited our farm manager, Bryce, and his girls over to meet you, and I know they're looking forward to it. I hope you and Casey become friends. She's about your age, I think, but she's going through a rough patch right now. It would be nice for her to have a friend." She hesitated as if she was going to say more and then turned away instead. She was gone before I could ask her anything else.

I rummaged through my bags until I found my bottle of pain meds. I downed two of them without even getting a glass of water; I needed them to start working quickly in the worst way.

I was too exhausted to shower, but I changed out of my grungy travelling clothes and flopped down on top of the bed with a sigh, feeling the tension drain out of my body. There was just one thing I needed to do first, before I did any napping. I hauled the bow case from the floor to the bed and flipped open the lid. I'd deconstructed the limbs of both bows for travel, but, even with one hand, it didn't take me long to put my old practice bow back together again. The competition bow I'd leave safely tucked away for now.

I looked around the room and found a good spot over the door where someone had stuck nails in just the right places. Balancing precariously on top of the desk chair I'd pulled across the room, I was just able to carefully prop my bow across the two nails. I stepped down and surveyed it with satisfaction. Now the place felt more like home.

Chapter Two

"Astrid, dinner's almost on the table. You come on down when you're ready."

"Okay," I groaned and rolled over, sleep tugging heavily at my limbs. I could easily sleep for a thousand more years. "I'll be there in a minute."

"Take your time," my aunt said, her voice moving away from the door, "but supper will be on the table in five minutes."

I heaved a sigh and sat up, swinging my legs slowly over the side of the bed and waiting for the room to stop spinning. When I was reasonably sure I wouldn't fall over, I stumbled to the bathroom to wash up and convince my wild curls, which were already out of control, to stay in a ponytail. I hadn't been able to manage hair elastics one handed yet, so Marion had found these big clips that I could use to clumsily scoop the hair up and snap it into some sort of order. Usually it left me with a few pieces straggling outside of the clip, but it was better than nothing.

I studiously avoided looking at my face in the mirror. I knew how awful the bandages made me look by the way people stared at me. On the ferry ride from the Island that morning I'd been unable to avoid the questioning looks, some sympathetic and some just openly curious, as Allan and I ate our breakfast in the cafeteria. At least I didn't have to start school until I looked more human.

I guess I should get this over with. I straightened my shoulders and moved reluctantly from my room to the hallway. As soon as I opened the door, I sniffed appreciatively, hit with the delicious smell of cooking food.

Voices floated up from the kitchen and I peered over the carved wooden railing to the open room below, hoping to catch sight of them before they saw me. No luck, there was only Jake, lying on his gold-coloured cushion by the front door, staring at me balefully.

"Nice dog," I said encouragingly, walking slowly down the stairs toward him. "You don't need to bite me."

"Oh, don't worry about Jake," my aunt said, appearing at the bottom of the landing. "Honestly, he's a big softy. Come on and meet him properly. Here, give him a cookie and he'll never leave your side." She came to meet me and shoved a bone shaped biscuit into my hand, giving me a slight push toward him.

The big dog rose to his feet, eyes glued on the cookie in my hand and his tail making a few tentative sweeps through the air. I held it out in front of his nose and he curled his lips back to take it ever so gently from my fingers with his big, white teeth.

"Aunt Lillian, what type of dog is he? He's gigantic."

"Irish Wolfhound. Well, he's supposed to be purebred, but I've never seen one shed as much as he does. We usually have a pair of them, but his sister died last year, and I didn't have the heart to replace her so soon. He's not real friendly to other dogs anyway. He loves people, though. You probably don't remember this, but you came up and spent the winter here after your…well, after your mother died. You were just tiny, but you spent nearly all your time running around with our last pair of wolfhounds. They'd trot around all day watching over you while you played."

I had a sudden dim memory of snow crunching under my boots as I waded up the long driveway, plunging purposely into drifts as high as my waist and my breath pluming up like dragon smoke in front of my face. Two big dogs, my friends, trailed after me like watchful guardians as I plowed through the snowbanks.

"I think I remember it, a little bit." I reached out tentatively and touched the wiry fur on Jake's cheek, right below his ear. Instantly, he groaned and leaned his head into my hand, telling me to scratch that spot right there and not stop.

I laughed, and Aunt Lillian put a hand on my shoulder. "Now you have a friend for life. He lives for food, ear scratches, and truck rides. Come on, I want to introduce you to Bryce and the girls."

I left Jake reluctantly and followed her into the cavernous dining room attached to the kitchen, where a huge wooden table big enough to sit twenty people took up most of the room. There were only three other people at the table tonight, though, all seated at one end.

The first to look up was a tanned, blond man wearing a green hat with a yellow tractor on it. His face crinkled into a smile when he saw me, and he took off his hat, pushed back his chair, and came to meet me.

"Astrid, this is Bryce, our farm manager. We couldn't run this place without him and his family. His boys are wonderful hands with the horses; talented riders and trainers both. The girls help out, too, of course. They live in our original homestead right here on the ranch."

Bryce took my good hand in his big, warm, callused one and beamed at me, bright blue eyes full of kindness. "Welcome to Triple Hills, Astrid. These are my daughters, Casey and Olive. Say hello, girls."

A sturdy, little girl maybe around eight years old, sat closest to me. She had her long blonde hair pulled back in a messy ponytail. She stared at the bandages crossing my nose and cheek, her eyes widening. "What…what happened to your *face*?"

"Ollie," Bryce said warningly, "we talked about this. Astrid had a riding accident."

I smiled at her weakly, trying not to be insulted. She was just a child and probably couldn't help sounding rude. "I go to the doctor in a few days and then the bandages should come off. I guess it looks scary now, though."

"Does it *hurt*?" she asked, wrinkling her nose.

"Sometimes. I have medication to make it feel better, though."

"Oh." She frowned thoughtfully. "Your horse is a chestnut, right? Mine's a bay named Salsa. We're going to California to live with my mom. Do you want to sit beside me?"

"Hey," Bryce warned, "don't pester Astrid on her first day here. She's probably exhausted."

"I'm not *pestering*," Olive stated, glaring at her dad. "I'm just telling her about—"

"And this is my other daughter, Casey," Bryce interrupted quickly, waving toward a serious looking girl with dark brown hair cut just below her chin. She had on a pair of large, black-rimmed glasses and a bulky, oversized cardigan that made her look like miniature librarian.

"Hi," she said shyly, glancing up from the table with a quick smile and looking away again. She had mint green eyes with dark lashes and a constellation of freckles splashed across her nose and cheeks. Her nose was strange, though; it looked swollen and a faint greenish bruise curved up over one eye. I wondered if she'd hurt herself on a horse like I had.

"All right," my aunt said, clapping her hands together briskly. "Now that we're all introduced, let's sit down before dinner gets cold. Astrid, I'm afraid we're still short a cook right now so you'll have to make do with my kitchen messes."

She didn't have to tell me twice, I'd been secretly eyeing up the huge basket of fried chicken at the head of the table. That was the sort of food that would have never crossed the threshold of our condo back home. There was more fat on each of those drumsticks than I'd normally see in a week. My stomach rumbled, and I sat down beside Olive, waiting impatiently for my aunt to pass the basket down.

Fried chicken, creamy mashed potatoes dripping with butter and chives, baked beans, creamed corn, and gigantic biscuits. It was like food-lover heaven at that table. While everyone else loaded their plates, I had to literally force myself to take just a small helping of everything. My dad would kill me if I gained any weight. He was big on self-control. He'd even instructed the hospital to make sure I had low-carb meals while I was healing. He'd ship me off to the Windy Shores health spa the second I got home if I tipped the scale in the wrong direction.

"Dig in, Astrid. We don't stand on ceremony here," Aunt Lillian ordered, biting into a crispy drumstick. "Take as much as you like; there's more than enough to go around."

"Okay, thanks," I said, practically melting at my first bite of chicken. I cleaned my plate in about five minutes.

I looked up guiltily, but everyone was too busy eating their own meals to even pay attention to how much I ate. The mashed potato bowl had conveniently ended up just in front of me, so it was easy to just reach out and covertly scoop another spoonful onto my plate. And it wasn't very far to reach the chicken again, either. I closed my eyes while I ate, savouring the delicious flavours.

Dad is thousands of miles away, I reasoned, *you'll have plenty of time to diet later.*

There was a horrific, loud buzzing noise and I jumped half out of my skin, looking around shamefully as if someone were about to leap out from behind a potted plant and shout at me about my lack of will-power.

"Oh, sorry, Astrid." My aunt laughed. "That's that darn landline. Cell service is almost non-existent out here, so I keep it as a back-up. It's loud as sin, though."

She rose and went to a faded yellow box on the wall that had a handle sticking out of it. "Hello," she answered. "Triple Hills. Who's this?"

There was a short pause and then her face lit up. "Marion! Good to hear from you. Yes, she's here, she's fine. Yes, terrible cell service. I'll put her on right now."

She held the phone out to me. "It's for you, Astrid."

I slid back my chair and walked slowly toward the phone,

wishing it wasn't attached to the wall so I wouldn't have to have a conversation with everyone listening to me while they ate.

"Hi, Marion," I said as quietly as possible.

"Sweetheart, you arrived safely. We didn't hear from you, so we were worried."

"I'm sorry." I pressed the funny receiver to my ear, happy to hear her familiar voice, even if it was so many miles away. "I fell asleep and then it was time for dinner. There's something weird about the cell reception here."

"Well, the main thing is that you're okay. Are you settling in, darling? How's Folly?"

"She's fine, I think." *As fine as she can be under the circumstances.*

"That's good. I wish I could have come along to get you settled in, darling. I hate to think of you all by yourself."

Suddenly a volley of high-pitched, hysterical barking echoed through the line, making me wince.

"I'm fine," I said, raising my voice. "Everyone seems nice."

The barking escalated until I could hardly hear a thing.

"Darn it, Caprice is barking at the float planes landing in the harbour again. Thank goodness, the trainer is coming tomorrow to work with her. Astrid, I wanted to let you know the good news; thanks to your old principal at Sacred Heart we were able to secure you a last-minute spot at a good, private school, after all. Remember, we looked it up online: Redmond. It has an excellent reputation."

"Wait, what?" Despite all the noise, I pressed my ear to the receiver, certain I must have misheard her.

"I know we'd settled on you going to the public school, Astrid. But this is an opportunity we couldn't easily pass up."

I stared at the wall, trying to comprehend what was happening. When I'd agreed to come live here, the three of us had sat down and had the first real family discussion we'd ever had in living memory. It was the very first time I'd ever been asked for my input on anything important. I'd actually felt *listened* to.

This had to be a mistake. "Marion," I said slowly, raising my voice to be heard over Caprice's yapping, "we looked at that school, but it didn't have any archery at all. The public school has a team—"

"Oh, I know, darling," Marion said, her voice sounding tight with nerves, "but this is a great opportunity and with your arm being hurt—"

"But it won't take a whole *year* to heal!" I interrupted, forgetting to be polite. "The public school has a club and they go to meets regularly. You said that I could go there; we had a whole conversation about this."

"I know dear, but your father's therapist has convinced him that he's been pushing you much too hard. This whole incident with Folly shook him up and he doesn't want to make the same mistake again."

"No!" I said, desperation kicking in. "That's not true. Well, with Folly it was true but not with archery. It's the one thing I'm okay being pushed at. I love it; it's all I want to do."

There was a long silence at the other end of the line, and then Marion sighed. "But maybe there are *other* things you'd like to do once you're not being pushed so hard, Astrid; you never had a chance to try other sports."

"I *hate* sports," I spat. "I love archery and horses. Period."

There was another silence. "Astrid, your principal at Sacred Heart spoke to the principal at Redmond and we were able to get a last-minute scholarship for you, free of charge. We can't afford to turn down a good placement like this, Astrid; who knows if we'll be able to give you this opportunity again. And it's only temporary. Once your arm heals and this silly court case is over, you can come home and start archery again. It won't hurt you to take a break and you can focus on your school work this year instead."

"Marion, you have to change his mind," I said miserably, swallowing hard in my effort not to burst into tears.

Another volley of hysterical barking crackled down the line and it was another minute before Marion was able to speak again.

"I'm sorry if this is not what you wanted, Astrid, but we're trying hard to make the best decisions for you. I'll talk to your father again and see if there are any other options, but he's under a lot of stress right now. Now, darling, I do have to go and stop Caprice before the people downstairs complain. Be good and help your aunt; your father sends his love, too. I'll call you this week with an update. Take care, sweetie."

"Bye," I whispered, hanging up the phone extra carefully. I stood there in shock, not able to process what had just happened. After all that time spent getting to know my dad again, after we'd almost become *friends*, this felt like the ultimate betrayal. They'd pretended to listen and then literally the minute I was out of earshot, they'd changed everything to suit themselves. Again.

I took a deep breath and turned around to find everyone at the table eating purposefully, eyes fixed on their plates as if they hadn't sat there listening to every word I'd said.

I walked woodenly to my spot and sat down hard.

"Eat up dear," my aunt said, her voice warm with sympathy.

I obediently picked up my fork, my hand shaking as I forced down a lukewarm bite of mashed potato.

"So, Astrid," Bryce said after a few minutes, clearing his throat a couple of times to break the growing silence, "tell us about your mare. What are her bloodlines like?"

"Lines? Oh, she's a warmblood, I guess" I said, smooshing the edge of my biscuit until it was a pile of crumbs.

"I know." Bryce laughed. "But what type of warmblood?"

I looked up at him blankly, struggling to remember the few details I knew about Folly. "She's imported from Germany," I said finally.

There was another long silence while everyone stared at me with their forks halfway to their mouths. Even Olive looked like I'd said something wrong.

"You don't know her bloodlines?" Casey asked incredulously. "Well, who is she registered with? What's on her paperwork?"

"I don't *know*," I said abruptly, irritated at the way everyone was looking at me. "I never bothered to look."

It came out sounding all wrong, like I was a spoiled brat who didn't care about my horse when really all I did was worry about Folly practically every waking moment of the day. But it was too late to take the words back.

"Oh," Casey said, raising an eyebrow. "Okay."

Aunt Lillian cleared her throat. "Astrid is fairly new to horses, Casey. She didn't grow up with them like you did, so you'll have to give her some slack. Folly's a new horse for her, too."

"Sure," Casey said, but she sounded doubtful.

"Salsa is a Quarter Horse." Olive turned to me with a knowing expression on her face. "Her great-great-great-great-great grandfather was Poco Bueno, and that means 'pretty good' in Spanish. Casey *sold* her horse and she didn't even cry; she doesn't like riding anymore." She raised her eyebrows dramatically. "All she wants to do is *study*."

"Don't be stupid, Olive," Casey said quickly, "of course I like riding; I just don't want to spend my whole life doing it. And Dinah went to a good home so why would I be upset?"

"Well, I'm *never* selling Salsa," Olive declared, "and mom said we'll go to lots of shows in California and I'm going to win everything." She fell silent, dreamily contemplating all her winnings.

"That's enough, Ollie," Bryce said, sending her a pointed look across the table. "Astrid, if you're interested, you should talk to my wife, Celeste, when she comes to visit next time. She's crazy about genetics and tracing bloodlines, she could probably tell you your mare's history back to the Roman Empire. She should be home around Christmas."

"*Ex*-wife," Casey said quietly, not looking up. "And this isn't her home anymore. She left, remember?"

"Yeah, she already has a *boyfriend* and everything," Olive added, popping a heavily-buttered biscuit into her mouth.

Bryce's smile slipped from his face and he reached up to rub a hand wearily across his eyes, looking sadder, older and very tired.

Aunt Lillian pushed her chair back so the legs slid sharply over the wooden floor. "Hope you have room for pie, everyone," she said with forced cheerfulness, moving around the table to pick up our dirty plates. She stacked them together loudly and then set them on the counter with a bang. "It's almost out of the oven. So, Astrid, when were you planning on starting school?"

"I'm supposed to start in the middle of October, I guess," I said unenthusiastically. "The doctor said to wait until I'm off the pain medication."

"October? But that's weeks away. Are you sure it's wise to wait that long, dear? You'll fall behind in your school work."

"It'll be fine," I said, not caring at all at this point. I'd almost been looking forward to school before tonight's phone call, but now it was just a looming prison sentence. "I was in an accelerated program at home so I'm probably ahead. And I especially don't want to go while I look like this."

"Oh, Astrid, you look fine. Casey here is quite the little scholar, too. Maybe you girls could study together. At least you can ride to town together in the mornings; that will be fun."

Casey looked interested in me for the first time. "You're going to Triple Hills with me? What year? I'm doing some advanced courses, so we might have a few of the same classes together."

Tears threatened, but I held them back. "No, my step-mom said it was called Redstone or something like that. A scholarship spot opened there, I guess, so they got me in last minute. All I know is that it doesn't have archery."

My stomach roiled, and I looked down at the table, feeling miserable. It took me a long time to realize that another heavy silence had descended over the table.

I looked up to find Casey staring at me as if she'd turned to stone, her already pale face draining a ghostly white. The mottled bruises over her nose stood out starkly.

"You got into *Redmond*?" she whispered, pressing her hands against the tabletop as if it were the only thing holding her up.

"Yeah, I guess so," I said, sniffling in my effort to keep from crying. "The principal at my old school pulled some strings and got me in. I guess they had an opening."

"Oh, of *course*," Casey said hollowly. "Of course they did. Why wouldn't *you* get a last-minute scholarship?" She stood up slowly, breathing rapidly through her mouth as if she had just finished running a race. She fixed her sharp gaze on me; eyes glittering in the dim light.

"What's wrong, Casey?" Olive asked, sounding worried.

"Olive, leave it. Casey, sit down," Bryce said, his voice was firm but gentle. He sounded sad. "Be reasonable."

"Yes, Casey, sit down and have some pie with us. I'm sure we can talk everything through." Aunt Lillian stood and laid a sympathetic hand on Casey's shoulder before moving to the oven to pull out a delicious smelling blueberry pie, still bubbling in its pan.

Casey dragged her gaze reluctantly from me, glanced grimly at the pie, and slowly sank back into her seat.

I stared at her in bewilderment, completely clueless as to what was going on.

Aunt Lillian piled our plates with mouth-watering pie and vanilla ice cream, but I could hardly eat when mine was passed down to me.

"Don't you like pie?" Olive whispered, nudging my elbow. "I can have yours if you don't want it."

She stared up at me winningly, tendrils of blonde hair floating around her heart-shaped face.

I smiled down at her hesitantly. "No, it's okay. I'll eat it."

Everyone ate in silence, but part of that was because the lava-hot pie was amazingly good. The berries exploded with bursts of flavour, and the crust was so light and flaky it practically melted in my mouth. Aunt Lillian was the most amazing cook I'd ever met.

I was only halfway through when Casey stood up abruptly, chair legs scraping across the wooden floor. "I'm done. Thanks for dinner, Lillian. Come on, Ollie. You have to get ready for bed. Goodnight, everyone."

"But Dad drove us in the truck and I want to see Astrid's horse. Dad said—"

"We'll walk. Come on, it's late and you have school tomorrow."

"Dad, she's being bossy—"

"I know, but this time she's right. It's getting late. You can see Folly tomorrow."

"Fine," Olive said, stomping her feet a few times in protest as she followed her sister outside. "Bye, Astrid, bye, Lillian. Thanks for dinner, it was delicious."

"You're welcome, sweetie," Aunt Lillian said, "any time."

Casey left without a backward glance, Olive trailing along behind her.

"Ugh, sorry about that," Bryce said, rubbing a hand across his face tiredly. "It's like she hit her terrible teens overnight. To her credit, she's had a terrible summer, what with everything going on between her mother and I, and well, the things happening here. But getting in trouble at school, starting fights with other girls, being disrespectful at home, that type of behaviour isn't like her at all. She even came home with a bloody nose last week. I'm sure you never give your parents this kind of grief, Astrid."

I stared down at the table, not knowing what to say. My dad would have easily tossed me off the balcony if I'd ever spoken to him with any sort of *tone* and, despite all the crazy stuff that had gone on in my life, I certainly wasn't the type of person to cause trouble and get into actual fist fights. I mean, who does that?

"She's having a hard time adjusting to this business with her mom. Celeste and I are on a bit of a break, but Casey is taking it hard."

He trailed off and looked down at the table while I sat there uncomfortably, not exactly thrilled with all the sharing.

"Well, now I'm sure Casey will work it out," Lillian said briskly, "everything is going to be just fine. Let's go make sure Folly is tucked in for the night."

"How about I drive?" Bryce said. "I'd like to meet her."

I was glad we took Bryce's truck down to the barn. There were no mounds of dog hair coating everything and the doors actually shut properly. He avoided the short cut and stuck to the smooth road, so I didn't have to clutch my seat for dear life.

The outside barn lights came on automatically as we pulled up and I squinted against the glare. The barn was totally silent as the three of us walked in. Aunt Lillian flicked a switch so just a dim light over the aisle came on. It was enough to see by, but not enough to wake up the animals.

Folly had her head hanging over the stall door. She blinked sleepily, and then wrinkled her nose in disgust when she saw us, her eyes closing into two, narrow slits.

"Hey, girl," I said encouragingly, but my only reward was

more flattened ears and the sound of her grinding teeth as she reached out to grab the top of her stall door, biting deep into the wood.

"Hey," Aunt Lillian commanded, flapping her arms near Folly's face, "you stop that, horse."

Folly grudgingly drew her head back a few inches inside the stall and stood there, nostrils flaring in disapproval. I carefully peeked over to check that she had hay and water. Besides being her usual cranky self, she seemed well enough.

Bryce stood back a few feet from her door, arms crossed over his chest while he studied her carefully. "Well, despite her attitude, she's a looker, Astrid. You know, if the bloodlines are there and if you can't get her sound again, she might make a nice broodmare. It's something to consider anyway."

"Uh, maybe," I said, choking at the thought. No matter how pretty or talented she was, I couldn't imagine breeding more little clones of Folly and sending them out to unsuspecting buyers. How many killer horses did the world really need?

"See that mark on her hind-quarters, the brand?"

"Yeah, it looks like moose antlers."

"That means she's a registered Trakhener. Now you know what type of warmblood she is when people ask. Some of them have a reputation for being hot and feisty, but that's the case in any breed. Half of it is just how they're handled. Bet she's athletic and brave, though."

Too brave and athletic, I thought, thinking of all the times she'd nearly tossed me; riding her was like piloting a loaded missile.

Folly was done with company. She pulled back into her stall

and went to stand in the far corner, turning her quarters at us.

"Goodnight, Folly," I said, just in case she cared, but there was no response. By that time, I was practically asleep on my feet anyway. Despite my earlier nap, it had been a long, long day. I almost nodded off on the short drive back to the house and, after saying goodnight, I had to practically drag myself up the stairs to my waiting bed.

But the second my head hit the pillow, my mind switched into overdrive. Would Marion actually talk to my dad and convince him to change his mind about that stupid school? Or was I stuck with a long, boring, archery-free winter away from the range, away from Rob and Hilary, and my other friends at the barn; away from everything I loved back home.

I fumbled for my phone on the bedside table and looked at it glumly; still no service. When I was in the hospital, Rob and I had gotten into the routine of texting for a few minutes every night before bed, and I'd grown to depend on it. He was usually the last person I talked to before I went to sleep and the first person I said good morning to when I woke up. Without our night-time routine, I felt lonelier than ever.

How did Artimax go today? I texted, even though I knew the message wouldn't go through.

Are you nervous about your event coming up this weekend?

Delivery error. Message unsent.

I miss you.

Delivery error. Message unsent.

I sighed and opened my photos instead, scrolling through them slowly one by one. I hardly ever deleted anything until I ran out of space so there were hundreds in there. The view from our condo balcony just as the sun was coming up, a million shots of Quarry doing cute things like lying down in his stall or yawning or rolling, and dozens more of the other horses at the barn. There were a couple of older ones from the range and then a few from that first horse show with Quarry; silly shots of me and Rob and Hilary, and some of the other ladies at the barn. One of Rabbit sticking his big head through the fence to reach some tempting grass, a bemused look on his face.

As I flicked through them, it dawned on me that I didn't have a single shot of Folly; not one. The photos stopped at almost the same time I'd started riding her.

There must be something, I thought, scrolling through them again. I finally found a far-off shot of the mist rising over the lower pasture. The fact that Folly had gotten in the photo at all was probably an accident; I'd most likely just been catching the sunrise.

She stood with her head up; ears pricked at something in the woods on the opposite side of the pasture. The sun had just come up and her copper coat was tinged with pink. She looked majestic, but sort of untouchable, too, like she wasn't a real horse so much as something mythical and out of the reach of regular humans. Definitely out of my reach.

"I'm sorry, Folly," I murmured and finally drifted into an uneasy sleep.

Chapter Three

The next morning the world looked much brighter. I brushed my teeth and got dressed with the usual difficulty and made my way downstairs.

The smell of frying bacon and eggs met me before I reached the kitchen, and I could hardly believe my luck. More real food!

"Good morning," I said shyly as I came into the kitchen.

Jake sat with his big body pressed up against the stove, staring up adoringly at Aunt Lillian's fork suspended above the frying pan, just inches over his nose.

"Pull up a chair, sweetheart. Breakfast is almost ready. I hope you're hungry."

"I am, thanks." I eyed the food up eagerly, my stomach growling.

"Well, I'm no Florian," she said, slapping an overflowing plate down in front of me, "but, until she gets back, I'll have to do. I do make a mean bacon and eggs. Here's some toast, too, darling. Butter and jam is there on the table."

I looked down at my heaping plate, unable to hide my happiness. It would be rude of me to not to eat everything Aunt Lillian had piled in front of me. My dad was always going on about how important it was to be polite (for everyone but himself, that was), so it was my duty to eat all the food on my plate, just so I didn't insult my aunt, of course.

I picked up my fork and dug in, taking great gulps of the coffee and orange juice she placed in front of me in between bites.

"Now, honey, that food's not going anywhere and we're not in a rush this morning. You just slow down and enjoy yourself."

"Oh, I'm sorry," I said, sitting back to gasp for air. "It's just all so good. I don't get to eat like this at home."

"Well, we work hard here and there isn't much time to stop for snacks, so we need food that will keep us going all day. Our cook Florian was always so good at keeping us fed and organizing the house. I'm finding it hard to adjust to her being gone."

"She's on vacation?" I asked to be polite, before stuffing a giant piece of bacon into my mouth.

Aunt Lillian straightened and frowned. "She went back to her family in Spain, no explanation. I always assumed she'd come to her senses and come home, but I'm afraid I'm going to have to accept at some point that she's probably not coming back."

"The place looks great, though," I said, "and you're an amazing cook. I've never tasted food this good in my life."

"Well," she clapped her hands together and jumped up from the table to grab more coffee, "that's because you haven't tasted Florian's food to compare it to. Anyway, enough of that, I guess we'll have to figure out a routine for you until you're in school."

"Sure," I said, "I'll help out however I can."

"Well, it's a darn shame you're hurt so badly. I was hoping you'd be up for practicing some of your dressage on a few of the horses here. I thought you could put them through their paces."

"Oh," I looked up, blushing, "I'm not a very good rider. Besides, I thought the horses were all trained western."

Aunt Lillian waved a hand dismissively. "A good horse is a good horse, Astrid. We breed versatile horses that are athletic and sound-minded. We like to think that they could do well for an amateur in any sport. But, the market isn't what it used to be, even for quality horses. I thought it wouldn't hurt to diversify. Florian was always telling me she thought some of them had potential for dressage; her family has a training facility in Spain. She'd come out here for a change in scenery but, no matter how much she dressed up as a cowgirl she couldn't quite shake her dressage roots. I didn't give it much thought at the time, but now, with your Uncle Trent gone, I'm interested in testing that market."

I chewed my food thoughtfully. I wanted to help, of course, but I was secretly glad I was hurt and wouldn't be able to ride Aunt Lillian's horses. Folly had taught me the hard way that I was pretty much the most incompetent rider on the planet. It was probably best if I stayed on the ground from now on.

"Astrid?"

I shook myself free of my thoughts and looked up to find Aunt Lillian watching me curiously.

"Sorry," I said. "I was just thinking."

"You looked far away there; I asked if you wouldn't be too lonely here until October without any kids around to keep you company? Casey will be in school all day—"

"No," I interrupted quickly. "Thanks, I'm fine." I would gladly put off going to this stupid new private school as long as possible.

"Aunt Lillian, do you think there's an archery club around here somewhere? I'm not sure if you heard last night, but Marion just told me…" I paused, searching for the right words, "well, I just found out the new school I'm being sent to doesn't have any archery at all. I need to find a place to practice; I couldn't shoot all summer and I'm missing it badly."

"Oh, that's a shame. You must be so disappointed. I've followed your progress since you started, you know. You're quite the accomplished archer. Marion kept me updated and sent me newspaper clippings from your tournaments. Did you know that?"

"No," I said, surprised. "I didn't."

"They've both always been so proud of you. Although, of course, your father shows that by being obnoxious and overbearing. That's just his way, I suppose."

"Yeah," I sighed, meeting her understanding smile with a small one of my own. "I know."

"Now, let me see, maybe the Fish and Game club has some targets set up at the gun range; we can certainly look into it. Do you think you can shoot with your arm like that, though, dear?"

"No, not yet. But maybe I can volunteer to teach the younger kids or something until I'm ready. Just *being* there is better than nothing."

"Well, I'm not much of an expert on the computer, but maybe you can use the Google to see if there is anything nearby."

Use the Google? I thought, stifling a laugh at the quaint way she said it.

"You probably noticed there is a bit of a connection problem. We have a land line up here and another in the training barn, so we can use the dial-up. It's slow, but it works. The kids go into town to do all their fancy texting and stuff on their phones."

Dial-up, what? Go into town?

I stopped eating, processing this startling information. What was I supposed to do without being able to talk to my friends back home?

"Well, if you can't ride, I guess we'll have to find another project for you," Aunt Lillian said. "We're a little short-handed right now. I know darn well that I should have brought on a few working students this year, but frankly I just don't have the energy to take on anymore new people right now. It's emotionally draining to have to train new people over and over and there's often a language barrier. Bryce is leaving next week to take Ollie down to her mom in California; he'll be gone a couple of weeks. Justin started school full time this year, and even though he *says* that he can do all his training and all his school work, I know how hard that will be for him. He'll have to do all his riding at night and he'll be exhausted. And Kade...well, he's a different kettle of fish."

She paused to collect my empty plate and load it in the dishwasher.

"If you don't mind, I'll see if I can work you into the schedule in the training barn, just brushing and cleaning tack, and maybe some feeding. Anything to help out."

"Oh, Aunt Lillian, that would be great. No, I don't mind doing that at all. That's what I've been doing all summer."

"You can ride any of the guest horses you like, of course, they're all safe to handle even for beginners, just take your pick. I imagine Kade or Justin can tell you more about them if you have one in mind you'd like to try out."

"Oh, okay, thanks, I guess," I said, "maybe in the Spring when my arm heals."

She looked at me sharply, registering the unenthusiastic tone of my voice.

"And, of course, you'll be responsible for taking care of Folly while she's here. Someone will do her stall and paddock for you until you're able, but you'll be in charge of keeping her groomed, fed, and exercised."

"Sure." I nodded, feeling heat creep up my neck. I rubbed my good hand nervously across my forehead and risked a glance at my aunt. I didn't want to be the one to tell her that I could barely handle my own horse. I had no idea what I'd do when it was time to start hand-walking her. The vet had said she needed to start light exercise in a couple weeks; the thought was terrifying.

"Great, well, if you're finished eating then let's get started. This ranch won't run itself."

*****

The temperature had dropped overnight into something almost breathable, but the sky overhead was clear, and I could tell already that it was going to be another scorching day.

I climbed carefully into the wheezing, rumbling truck where my aunt sat waiting; a newsletter of some sort spread open on the steering wheel. Jake was stretched out in the backseat, resting his pointy snout on my aunt's armrest and panting his hot, smelly dog breath onto my arm. I wrinkled my nose and shifted away from him, trying not to gag.

"Cattle prices are up," my aunt said, glancing up at me and

tossing the newsletter into the backseat beside Jake. "That's good, I have a group shipping out this week. I keep waiting for my opportunity to sell the whole lot of them."

"You don't like cows?" I asked curiously.

"No," she said, looking studiously out her window as I struggled to haul my door shut and wire it somewhat closed. "I do not. I hope a day comes when I never have to see them again. I'm thinking about replacing them with sheep or goats; anything would be an improvement. Bryce thinks I'm crazy, of course. There's good money in cows, but still…there has to be another way to make ends meet."

This time there was a definite gap between the door and the truck; I could clearly see over an inch of daylight. I clicked my seatbelt firmly in place and clutched the seat in preparation.

Luckily, Aunt Lillian didn't take the so-called short cut this time. She stuck to the main road and drove carefully down to the broodmare barn, so we hardly bounced around at all. The truck shuddered to a stop, and I unwired myself and jumped out. Jake whined and smacked the window nearest to me with his big paw, leaving a streak of dirt behind.

"Okay, you big baby," I grumbled. "Get out." I opened his door and he loped out, wagging his tail and following Aunt Lillian eagerly toward the barn.

Suddenly, the peaceful morning exploded with the sound of furious hooves cracking against wood like rapid-fire gunshots.

Jake let out an outraged bellow and lunged toward the barn, clawing at the big wooden door until it rolled aside, and he disappeared into the darkness.

Crack, crack-crack. Followed by the sound of wood splintering.

Oh no, Folly, I groaned inwardly, *what have you done?*

"Hey!" my aunt yelled, rolling the big wooden door fully open and striding into the barn. "You stop that, horse! Get!"

This last word was said in a deep, terrifying growl that would have scared a grizzly bear let alone a horse. I hurried after her, arriving just in time to see Folly kick out with both hind legs, her hooves connecting with a deafening crunch against the wood between her stall and the next. The board splintered, and I could see that the one above and below had already been cracked clean in two leaving a gaping hole into the stall next to her. Through the opening, a terrified Donkey cowered in the far corner of his stall.

Jake bounced up and down in a fury, lunging half-over the stall door at Folly, baying hysterically until my aunt grabbed him roughly by the collar and hauled him backward into the feed room. "That's enough of you, sir," she said sternly, pointing to the corner, "go lie down."

He slunk over to the corner and curled into a ball, muttering sullenly to himself as she slammed the door shut.

Ignoring Folly, who was now simmering in a quiet rage in the far corner of her stall, my aunt marched over to Donkey and threw his door wide open.

"Poor Donkey," my aunt crooned, letting him trot out into the aisle. He stopped as soon as he reached us, his sides heaving and a worried look on his face. He turned around to watch Folly nervously over his shoulder. "He must have had a terrible night. Look, his leg's bleeding and he hardly touched his hay. She must have been terrorizing him all night. Poor soul."

I looked guiltily at the small splash of blood running from

where his right leg met his grey furry chest. He rolled his eyes anxiously over to where Folly had started making some demonic snorting, grunting, squealing sounds in her stall. She sounded crazy and I had no doubt she would have hurt him badly if she'd managed to break through the wall.

"Folly," my aunt bellowed as there was another clatter of hooves. "You quit this nonsense, you hear me? Quit!"

Folly gave another half-hearted kick to the wall and then stood there, snorting angrily, sides heaving.

"Here, Astrid. I'll put his halter on and you lead him to the paddock just at the far end of the barn; it's directly on the left as soon as you go out that back door. We'll bring him his hay as soon as we figure out what to do with her majesty here."

I did what I was told. Donkey followed me placidly, his little hooves clip-clopping along on the concrete aisle floor, long grey ears swivelling around. I gave him a pat as I slipped off his halter and put him in the large, empty paddock. I hoped his wound didn't hurt him too much.

There was a sudden commotion back at the barn; wood crunching, angry squeals and a cry of pain or fear, and then silence.

I picked up speed, hurrying toward Folly's stall

Please don't have killed my aunt, Folly, please don't have done anything stupid.

Aunt Lillian leaned against the feed room door, panting breathlessly, her braid half-undone and her clothes covered in bits of straw. She turned to me with wide eyes and shook her head.

"*Who* in their right mind gives an animal like that to a child?" she said, sounding horrified.

"My dad," I said glumly. "I tried to tell him it was a bad idea."

"Your father…." She shook her head. "I'm going to have to give her a sedative, Astrid. I don't feel safe getting her out to a paddock when she's in this state, but she's not staying inside to ruin my barn. What on earth did you do with her at home?"

I cleared my tight throat with difficulty. "She wasn't always like this. The barn manager at Claudia's, Liza, just loved her. She was so good with her; she could get Folly to do almost anything. And Folly was fine in her stall. Even I could handle her…for a while."

My aunt blew out a deep breath. "Well, I suppose there's hope then. There's a small outside paddock with a shelter she can use in the meantime. We'll leave her out all this week and see if that helps her attitude. I'm sure the vet would say stall rest for a while longer yet, but we can't keep her drugged all that time; she's going to hurt herself in here. What do you think, Astrid? She's your horse."

I shrugged miserably, wishing I knew more about horse care. I'd always depended on everyone at Claudia's barn to tell me what to do; they were all so much more experienced than I was. "I don't know. But, I don't want her to hurt anyone. She had a bad reputation in Germany, she hurt a groom badly."

"Oh, that's just great," my aunt said grimly. "I wish I'd known that earlier. Well, let's get some sedation into her and then get her outside so we can fix this stall."

My aunt's plan to get a needle of sedative into Folly was quickly abandoned when Folly charged the door with her jaws gaping wide.

"Folly," I cried. "No!" To my surprise she screeched to a stop and looked at me for a second as if considering her options. Then she whipped around and fired both hind legs at the door. The wood shuddered under the impact, and for a second I envisioned her crashing into the aisle and killing us both, but it held, and she tucked herself back into the far corner of her stall to sulk.

"Okay, time for plan B." Aunt Lillian sighed. We trudged back to the feed room and added some water to a cup of pellets. She mixed up Folly's grain with the warped, wooden spoon hanging beside the sink and added a familiar looking powder.

"We just keep sedation on hand for emergencies," my aunt said sternly, raising one eyebrow at me pointedly. I wondered if she knew more of Folly's story, about the drugging, than she'd let on. We marched back to Folly's stall, with me fighting back tears the whole way.

"Stand back, Astrid." She slid the door open quietly, took a deep breath and shoved the feed tub inside, slamming the door shut before Folly could attack. I watched the mare glumly as she devoured her food, snuffling and snorting like a wild boar.

"Come on, let's go away and let her eat in peace. I'll show you the other barn while we wait for her to get sleepy."

"Okay." I sighed, following along in her wake.

We walked silently to the training barn with a newly-freed Jake padding along behind us. It wasn't a far walk, but the silence stretched out uncomfortably between us.

"Astrid," my aunt said finally, "please don't take this the wrong way, but I honestly don't think Folly is the right horse for you. I'm not sure she's safe for anyone. Are you sure you want to spend all your time and energy rehabilitating her, sweetie? She can't be much fun to ride. There are so many nice horses out there. I could find you something much more appropriate."

"Thanks, but I…I owe it her, though," I said thickly. "It's my fault she got hurt, or mostly my fault anyway, and I can't just abandon her. I know it's not going to be easy, but she wasn't always so terrible. Liza had her almost perfect at the barn, and I'm the one who ruined her, well, me and Cole did anyway. I don't want to ride her…not *ever*, but I promised Claudia that I would fix her and give her back to Liza."

Aunt Lillian nodded thoughtfully. "I see," she said. "Well, that sounds very noble as long as you don't get yourself killed in the meantime. Don't you want a horse you can ride, though? Marion said you loved it."

"I did," I said slowly. "I loved riding Quarry, but I think part of that was because he was so special, and he sort of took care of me. He was like my best friend. Without him, it's just not the same. Besides, I'm not that good a rider."

"Well, it doesn't sound like you had much of a chance to develop your skills, dear. But I saw the show video that Marion sent me; I'd say that your Claudia gave you an excellent foundation. Once you've healed physically, I think you could pick up where you left off."

I looked at the ground, not wanting to admit that it had been Quarry who'd made me look good in that video. I hadn't known it at the time, but he'd been babysitting me every step of the way, he and Claudia had made me feel like I could do anything, when actually, I was the most basic of beginners. Folly had shown me how little about riding I knew.

The front doors of the barn stood wide open, pungent smells that had become so familiar and loved to me over the summer wafted out. Horse, hay, leather, cleaner, earth, and wood all mixed together into a scent that meant 'home' to me.

"This is our training barn," Aunt Lillian said, a note of pride creeping into her voice. "All the horses here, except the stallions of course, are either for sale, sold, or in training. We have a backlog of young horses this year so we're trying to keep them moving on to new homes. And sometimes, that's like pulling teeth.

"Bryce and Casey fed and mucked out these guys already. The boys will be back this afternoon; they had a much-deserved week off after this hectic summer but, knowing them, I bet they can't wait to get back to it. Those boys are both most at home on a horse."

I nodded, trying to take in everything she was telling me while my focus had already moved to the horses.

I stopped in front of the first stall, leaning over the door to get a better look at the rich, cream-coloured horse inside. He brought his head up to look at me thoughtfully, hay trailing from his mouth. His eyes were ice blue, a striking contrast against the black forelock. He had black tiger-striped legs and a flowing black mane and tail. He looked like something out of a movie.

"Wow, he's beautiful."

"Well, he should be." My Aunt laughed. "Astrid, meet Doc. He's one of our stallions. Here, come say hello to him properly. He loves attention."

Before I could argue she slid open the stall door and ushered me inside.

"Hey, Doc," I said softly, holding out my hand.

He swung his big head around slowly and bumped the tips of my fingers gently with his velvety soft nose, blowing warm breath across my hand. I gently ran my palm down his incredibly silky shoulder and smoothed the fine, black mane flat against his neck.

"He's amazing," I whispered, "he's like a fairy-tale horse."

"He is certainly special. Some people are intimidated by stallions, Astrid, but ours are big softies. You can come visit him anytime. He has perfect manners and he loves attention."

I nodded as he gently ran his soft muzzle over my arm, his whiskers tickling my skin.

"The horses at the Spanish Riding School are all stallions," I said, remembering the first horse book I'd ever been inspired by.

"That's right, the Lipizzaners. Well, I'm proud to say that Doc passes on his temperament to every foal of his that drops on this property. He's a gem. Come meet our other boy, Fox."

I left the stall reluctantly and headed to the next one, this time a towering chestnut met us eagerly at the stall door, whickering under his breath. He had a thick white blaze and a bushy, red forelock that hung over his eyes. He was tall but had a thick chest like a bulldog, rippling with muscle; if he'd been a human he would have been a body builder, but he was just as friendly as Doc had been; actually, he was a little too friendly. He crowded close, reaching his nose out to nudge my pockets, clearly looking for treats.

"Sorry, Kade spoils him rotten. Good thing he's such a nice horse; he doesn't let all those carrots go to his head. Get back, you big lug. Out of our space."

I didn't feel quite as comfortable with Fox as I did with Doc, but I scratched his neck and admired his rippling, rust-coloured coat and tall white socks. He was a fancy-looking horse.

"There are fifteen stalls in this barn. The stallions have a permanent home here. We keep the geldings beside them, and any mares or fillies that come in go in those far stalls here. Not that it matters, these boys are as sweet as kittens even with the ladies around and they're the best of friends, too. They spend most of their time hanging out together side by side in their paddocks."

Another chestnut horse stood on the other side of Fox, wearing a blue cotton sheet to keep him clean. He glanced up briefly and then went back to his hay.

"Badger is a three-year-old. He's sold but stayed on for ninety days of training. We like to put a good foundation on them for their new owners if we can."

"Aww," I said, peering into the next stall after Badger's. There were two tiny, fuzzy horses inside, one chestnut and one black with a white star, eating together out of the same hay pile. "I've never seen a baby horse. What are their names?"

"A foal," my aunt corrected. "I honestly can't remember their names off-hand, they just came in from the pasture yesterday, but I can look it up for you. These two have been weaned already and gelded, and they're in for a refresher on ground-work and manners before they go to their new home next week. Not that training is very hard with these babies. They're already bred for easy temperaments and we imprint them at birth so they're super to handle right from the get-go."

"What do you mean, imprint?" I asked.

"Well, we handle them as soon as they're born. We touch them all over and handle their feet and practice light restraint. That sets their relationship with humans off on the right foot from the start. I can give you some books to read on it if you like. Or you can find some imprinting videos on the Google."

The door to the next stall stood open, but the trampled straw inside meant that someone probably lived there.

Another chestnut, this one darker, stood in the next stall over, looking fast asleep. His nose rested on the top of his door and he twitched now and then as if he were in the middle of a dream.

"Who's this one?" I whispered, laughing at his perfect obliviousness to the outside world.

"That's Red," Aunt Lillian said with a sigh. "He's got tons of personality, but none of the other traits our buyers are looking for."

She moved on abruptly and I stared after her in surprise. She sounded like she didn't like him very much, but from where I was standing he looked completely adorable. When he didn't wake up, I tiptoed past him.

The next few stalls stood empty and free of bedding.

"We'll fill them soon enough," my aunt said with a laugh, "the boys will be back today, and we'll bring in more. I just didn't want poor Bryce to have to clean five more stalls than he had to."

I peeked in the next occupied stall and saw a pretty buttermilk-coloured horse that was the spitting image of Doc, except that she had sweet brown eyes instead of blue ones.

"Aunt Lillian, what's that colour called? It's beautiful."

"Well, that's a buckskin, sweetie. This is Maisie and you probably guessed that she's one of Doc's daughters. She's a gem just like her dad."

"Is she sold, too?"

"Yep, Justin showed her this spring and summer, and we didn't even have to advertise before someone saw her in the ring and made an offer we couldn't refuse. They left her here for Justin to finish off the show season with her, though, to give her miles. It's a bit of a shame because we love having her around and she's a real favourite of his."

"Couldn't you have kept her?"

"Yes, I suppose we could, but then what happens next year when we fall in love with another young prospect? We run a business here, Astrid, and that business is selling horses. We do our best to breed them right and raise them right but, in the end, they have to go out in the world on their own. It's just part of life."

Next was a muscled blue-coloured mare with white flecks on her chest and sides, and white streaks in her mane.

"Kitty is a blue roan," Aunt Lillian answered my question before I could ask; she'd caught on by now that I basically knew nothing. "She was raised here, but we don't really have a job for her to do anymore; she's too sensitive for most guests to ride. I should have turned her out for the winter, but Casey's been keeping her going while we wait for her to sell. Now, these two are Tess and Cleo, who are just yearlings. They're going to France next month and we're getting them ready for the long trip."

"France?" I said in surprise, staring in at two more delicate cream-coloured clones of Doc who were sharing a stall just like the foals had been. Aunt Lillian was right, they were ALL adorable. How could you choose one over the other?

"There's a widening market for good stock there. Western

riding is increasing in popularity all over the world. The people who bought these two have been good clients for the last three years. They come every summer for a few weeks to ride and see if there are any young prospects that catch their eye."

I peered in the last stall to see a cute bay horse with a neatly trimmed mane and a shiny coat. She looked up and came to the door eagerly, looking for treats.

"That's Olive's horse, Salsa. They'll both head to California to live with Celeste in a few weeks. Bryce is taking it hard, of course, but Olive wants to go, and Celeste *is* her mother. She was supposed to leave earlier this summer before school started, but then Celeste's tour got extended and here we are."

We'd reached the end of the barn where there was a metal gate barring the way to the biggest indoor arena I'd ever seen in my life. It was way bigger than Claudia's and, instead of chandeliers, it had a series of skylights in the tall ceiling and windows in the walls that made the gigantic ring seem light and airy. Bleachers lined the walls on both sides; there was room for hundreds of people to sit.

"Wow, it's gigantic," I breathed.

"Sure is; we used to do lots of rodeo events here, so we needed a big space for working with cows. Your uncle loved those events, but I just can't seem to find the energy to run them without him. I'm not as social as he was; I prefer my peace and quiet."

At the far end of the arena, Bryce cantered a honey-coloured horse in circles on a loose rein. The horse snorted rhythmically with each stride, its nose stretched down and out, ears flickering backward at some unseen cue from its rider. Without warning it slid to a stop, rocking back on its haunches and spun in a high-speed version of a canter pirouette, its honey-coloured mane and tail swirling through the air like a cloud.

My aunt grinned and shook her head. "Isn't he something? That's one of our homebreds, Coyote, who's back in for further training. Bryce is not only our farm manager but our head trainer, too. Let's not disturb them now, Astrid, he's concentrating." We turned and slowly walked back down the aisle.

"Hay shed is on your left here, then the feed room, our office, and here's the tack room." She flung open the last door and I stood gaping at the huge room filled with stacks of saddles, bridles, and a million miscellaneous training tools, bits, and pieces of leather that I couldn't identify.

"Wow," I said again. "Aunt Lillian, how many horses do you have here?"

"Too many." Aunt Lillian laughed and then held her hands up slowly, moving her fingers up and down. I realized after a minute that she was counting. "Fifteen broodmares and two stallions; ten horses for ranch-work and guests, who are currently sitting around getting fat and lazy, some older sales horses, the remainder of this year's foal crop, we have some yearlings left, and a group of two- and three-year-olds that haven't sold yet. I guess that makes, well, somewhere around fifty-five or sixty."

"Sixty!" I said, turning to face her. "How do you take care of them all?"

"Well, the majority of them are turned out on pasture when they're not needed. We just take them a couple big round hay bales with the tractor and it feeds each pasture for a week. It's low maintenance except for all the fence fixing. We make do; you'll see."

"Oh, I'm sure," I said quickly, hoping I hadn't offended her. "I just can't imagine taking care of that many horses."

"Well, luckily, we have a real hard-working team here."

Yeah, but they must have to work non-stop to take care of all those animals, I thought, *and here I thought Claudia's barn was busy.*

I walked slowly back down the aisle, peering over the stall doors again at the shiny, well-muscled horses inside. They were different than Claudia's horses; shorter, with fine, shoulder-length manes and thick bull-dog chests. But, each horse was groomed until it shone, and they looked fit and muscled, without an inch of fat.

The sleeping chestnut, Red, was awake now and looking around blinking his eyes as if surprised to find himself in the barn.

Aunt Lillian looked away and moved quickly past him, but I stopped briefly to run my hand down his wide, white blaze. It was thicker than my hand and ran right down off the end of his nose, disappearing under his chin.

"Hi, there," I whispered, reaching up to arrange his forelock, "you're a nice boy, aren't you?"

He sighed happily and slowly reached his head down, pressing it into me and then just resting it there, as if asking for a hug.

"You're so sweet." I wrapped my good arm around his jaw and rested my head against his, breathing in his sweet scent.

"Come on, Astrid," Aunt Lillian called abruptly, sounding irritated.

I let go of him reluctantly, gave him a final scratch behind the ears, and hurried to catch up with her.

We headed back to the near-empty broodmare barn and walked quietly to Folly's stall. Folly still had her back to the door, but now her head hung low and her ears flopped to the side.

"Looks like we're ready," my aunt whispered. "You stay here. I'm going to put her halter on. We'll lead her out the front door and to the right. You go on ahead and open that gate and I'll meet you out there."

I went outside quickly, but I couldn't help looking back over my shoulder to make sure my aunt hadn't been trampled under Folly's angry hooves. Nope, they were coming; Folly had her ears pinned, but she lurched alongside my aunt in a fairly obedient way, only shaking her head grumpily as she neared the paddock.

"There you go, Madam." Aunt Lillian slipped off the mare's halter and stepped quickly back through the gate. Folly stood there for a moment, looking around in annoyance before she dropped her head and started lipping at the few blades of dried-up grass that dotted her paddock.

"She'll be hungry when the sedation wears off. Wait an hour or so and then you can throw a few flakes of hay over the fence for her. That's probably the best way to feed her for now until she has the chance to calm down. How on earth did you feed her at home?"

"She was fine," I said, sounding defensive. "At first only Liza fed her but, once she'd settled in, she acted completely different. Right now, she's hurt and she's probably missing Liza."

"Hmm, well, that might be true, but she still needs to act like a civilized horse if she's going to stay here. I can't have her hurting anyone. What if Olive wandered into her pen? Or a stranger? I wish I'd have known what she was like before she got here."

She laid a firm hand on my shoulder and turned me to face her. "Astrid, I'm just worried. I don't want anyone to get hurt and that includes you. We'll give her a good chance to heal here, just like I said I would, but I want you to promise me that you won't take any chances with this horse. You need to stay safe."

I nodded, leaning my forehead against the metal fence, trying to get a handle on my sadness. Why hadn't my dad just bought me a normal horse like Quarry? Things could have been so much different.

Why didn't you refuse to ride her? A nagging little voice in my head whispered. I watched as Folly limped around her paddock in slow motion and when I looked around again my aunt was gone.

Folly edged closer to me, head hanging and her ears flopping to the sides. I shifted down the fence until I was standing right in front of her. "Hey, Folly," I whispered. "You have to stop being so mean to everyone. Nobody's going to hurt you here. You need to get strong and healthy, so you can get back to Liza."

It might have been my imagination, but it seemed like Folly went very still when I said Liza's name and then she slowly lifted her head to look at me, her ears flickering forward, and she whickered sleepily under her breath.

"That's right," I said encouragingly. "I'm going to make things right for you, Folly. I will do everything I can to make sure you're okay from now on. We can be friends again, you'll see."

Folly's happy expression vanished, and her ears flattened. She dropped her head, shifting around until her back-end was pointed at me, her message clear.

"Fine." I sighed. "Have it your way."

I heard the high-pitched whizzing of a power tool as I headed back to the barn. Broken boards lay in the aisle and my aunt was already drilling two new ones up to replace the wood Folly had destroyed.

"Astrid, could you go take care of Donkey, please? Wash his cut with some warm water and soap, then puff some of that wound dust on it to help it dry up. It's in the feed room in the First Aid kit. I'm just going to finish here, clean these two stalls, and then head to the house to do some paperwork. You yell if you need anything, but I doubt Donkey will give you any trouble. Lunch is at noon, so I expect you can entertain yourself until then."

"Um, okay, thanks." I turned on my heel and moved quickly to the feed room, feeling like I'd been dismissed. I stood and surveyed the room, looking for something that resembled a First Aid kit. Finally, I saw it: a grimy metal crate that had once been painted white, with a red cross printed across the top. I gingerly opened the lid, relieved to see that it was clean and well organized inside. I rummaged around until I found some antibacterial soap, a bottle marked "wound dust" and a handful of clean, neatly folded towels.

I pulled an empty bucket off the stack near the sink and rinsed it clean before filling it with hot, soapy water. When it was half full, I tucked the wound dust bottle and the cloths under one arm, and lugged the sloshing bucket back down the aisle to Donkey.

He was picking at scraps on the far corner of his paddock, but as I approached he made this high-pitched huffing sound under his breath, like a rusty hinge swinging back and forth in the wind. He pricked his ears, peering eagerly through the metal rails at the bucket.

"Sorry, buddy, it's not grain. I'm going to clean up your cut."

His eyes opened wide in alarm at the sight of the sudsy water, and he snorted and backed away, his giant ears swirling anxiously in all directions.

"What's the matter boy, you don't want me to fix you up?" I started to open the gate and then remembered the bag of carrots back in the feed room that had come with Folly. "Hang on, I'll be right back."

As soon as I came back with a handful of carrots his whole attitude changed. He let me slip his halter on and carefully wash the wound. It turned out to be quite shallow once I'd cleared the blood away, and it disappeared completely once I'd puffed the wound dust onto his chest.

"There you go, you greedy boy." I laughed, patting him as he searched my pockets for more carrots. "You ate everything." I dumped the water and stood back considering him. He had dirt and bits of straw all over his rough-furred coat; the only clean part on him was the spot I'd just washed.

"You need a good grooming, Donkey. Would you like if I brushed you?"

He blinked his big, brown eyes at me and gave a sigh that I interpreted as a "yes."

I put the bucket and first aid stuff back where I'd found them and then scrounged around until I found a dusty grooming kit.

"Gross," I said, looking at the inch of dirt and hay particles layering the brushes in a solid, grey crust. I could only imagine how Marion would react if she saw the standards of cleanliness here; she'd probably go into anaphylactic shock just looking at all this dust.

I took the whole kit back to the sink, ran the hot water again and squirted soap all over them before giving them a good scrub. It was very satisfying to see the dirt swirl down the drain and everything come clean. I washed the grooming box itself last and then dried everything carefully with a towel.

Much better. I hauled the grooming tote back to where Donkey was patiently munching on his hay pile and set to work. It turned out that he loved grooming almost as much as he loved food. He leaned into each brush stroke, contorting his neck so I could get at the itchiest spots. It took me almost an hour to get him clean and basically, I'd just transferred all his dirt onto my own clothes. He looked good, though; his silver-brown coat gleamed.

"Wow, now that's a fine-looking animal," an amused voice said behind me.

I turned to find a real-life cowboy leaning over the fence watching with laughing eyes. I froze, taking in the muscles, the chiselled jaw, the electric blue eyes, the real cowboy hat and dusty boots. It was as if he'd sauntered off a photo shoot for one of those exotic commercials for perfume or cars or expensive watches. He was all sharp-cheek bones and deep-tanned skin, form-fitting jeans, and a melting smile. He was so pretty I could hardly breathe.

He raised a questioning eyebrow at me and I realized I'd been staring at him in the most ridiculous way. I looked back quickly to Donkey, reaching out to pet his neck just to have something to focus on.

"Sooo, you must be Astrid." There was a thumping sound as the guy vaulted over the fence effortlessly and hit the ground with his dusty boots. "We'd heard you'd come to stay with Lillian. Don't let her overwork you, though. She's a slave driver."

I looked up sharply, ready to defend my aunt, but he was grinning. And standing much too close to me.

"I'm Kade." He held out his hand as if expecting me to shake it.

"Astrid," I mumbled, before I remembered he'd already said he knew my name. I reluctantly held out my hand, trying not to flinch when his rough, calloused fingers practically swallowed mine. His grip tightened when I tried to pull away and I felt a moment of panic until he laughed and let go.

"I saw your mare. She'd be nice looking if she'd lose the attitude."

"Yeah," I said, finding my voice with difficulty. I looked down at Donkey, not meeting Kade's eyes. "Yeah, well, she's hurt right now, too."

"I saw that. She going to heal?"

I shrugged and cleared my throat nervously. "I'm not sure. The vet back home said to wait and see. She just came yesterday, so she's not settled in yet."

"You going to ride Donkey while you wait to find out?" He reached out and tugged one of Donkey's long ears slightly too hard. Donkey snorted and backed a few steps away, and I wished I could do the same.

I looked up to find him grinning down at me.

"I'm broken, too," I said, holding up my cast. "It'll to be a while before I ride again. If ever."

"What? Because of a little cast? Jeesh, we need to toughen you up. My brother and I have broken so many bones between us we've stopped counting. I did the rodeo one year with busted ribs and a neck brace. You only need one arm to ride anyway."

I looked at him closely to see if he was kidding, but his expression was serious.

"I'm not pulling your leg, Astrid; you ask Casey, she'll tell you all about it."

"Really? She didn't seem like she wanted to talk to me very much last night."

Kade's face darkened. He frowned and opened his mouth like he was going to say something but changed his mind at the last minute. Instead, he laughed and replaced his frown with an easy smile.

"Casey's all right. Some of the kids at school are giving her a hard time. You give her a chance and she'll come around."

I wasn't sure what to say so I gave Donkey one last pat and gathered my brushes back into their tote. "Well, I'd better get going. Aunt Lillian said I had to be back at noon for lunch."

"Sure, I was just headed that way. We usually all have lunch in the main house together on workdays so we can keep each other posted on ranch stuff. I'll drive you back."

"Oh, okay." I didn't want to drive anywhere with Kade; everything about him from his fake charming smile to his dangerously good looks put me on guard. But I didn't want to be rude to anyone on my first day at the ranch, either. I lost my voice again as we walked back through the barn so I could stash my brushes away and grab Folly a flake of hay from the big hay room.

She didn't even look up when I pushed it through the bars of her paddock. She didn't give any indication that she'd noticed me at all.

I sighed and then reluctantly followed Kade to the jacked-up, lime green pick-up truck he'd parked right in front of the barn.

"Wow, that truck is huge," I said, staring up at its gigantic tires.

"Yeah, she's a beaut, isn't she? She came with a three-inch lift, but I upgraded it to seven. She's chipped and straight-piped; a prime, smooth-running machine."

"Right," I said blankly. "All that sounds good. Really good."

Kade's truck smelled like a mixture of brand new leather and the overpowering cardboard air freshener thing that swung from his mirror. It was shaped like a painfully thin girl wearing only a skimpy red bikini and cowboy boots and it wiggled around suggestively every time the truck hit a bump.

Kade didn't stop talking about the love of his life, his truck, until we got back to the house. I made a lot of vague, encouraging noises and studied him when he wasn't looking. He was much older than me, in his twenties at least and, like I'd suspected when I first saw him, he was hands-down the best-looking guy I'd ever met. Even better than Thomas Ling.

He didn't sit still even once, tapping his hands on the steering wheel or turning to look at something in the woods at the side of the road, or rummaging in the center console between us. He had a restless energy about him that made me think of a wild animal pacing in a cage. I just wished he'd pay more attention to his actual driving.

The parking lot by the house was now full of trucks. Aunt

Lillian's old rusty bucket of a truck, Bryce's shiny black one, Kade's truck and another white one all lined up neatly side by side. Kade and Bryce's vehicles were somehow sparkling clean like they didn't spend all day driving on dusty, gravel roads, but the white truck matched Aunt Lillian's with its mud-spattered sides and dead bugs squished on the front end.

"Shall I escort you to lunch, my lady?" Kade jokingly held out his arm to me, pretending to be like a knight, all chivalrous, but there was something sort of proprietary in the way he moved in close to me, like he automatically expected me to do what he said, that scared me a little.

I backed away a few steps, blushing at how silly I was being. Why did he put me on edge like that?

He hasn't done anything wrong, he's just being nice. I told myself. *Stop being stupid.*

"I'm going to go wash up for lunch," I said quickly, trotting up the steps ahead of him. "I'll see you."

I pushed into the house without looking back and ran up the stairs to the safety of my room. As soon as I saw my face in the bathroom mirror, though, I burst out laughing. I not only had dust covering my face, and my hair, in a grey cloud, but it was also stuck to the bandage over my nose. I looked like an Egyptian mummy that had just broken out of a filthy tomb.

Yeah, I don't think he was flirting with you, I laughed at myself, relieved and a bit embarrassed, *he was just being polite. Weird, but polite.*

It was a good thing I had an appointment booked soon with the doctor. These bandages weren't going to hold up to ranch life for very long. I pulled out the extra roll of tape they'd given me at the hospital and carefully layered a few strips over the dusty bandage on my face. It looked better, not great, but better.

Voices floated up from below along with the sound of forks scraping on plates. I was late. I walked as quickly as I dared down the overly polished staircase and went to the kitchen, still feeling a bit like an outsider.

"There you are, Astrid. Load up your plate, I hope you like tacos."

I *did* like tacos, just like I liked almost every type of food on the planet. If it was edible and not made of tofu and sprouts I would probably like it.

There was no way I was going to be able to assemble a shell with just one hand, so I put all the fixings loose on my plate so I could eat it with a fork like salad. Like a delicious, meaty salad.

"Hey, Astrid, come sit your pretty self over here next to me," Kade said loudly, scooting the chair beside him back so I could sit down.

I halted in my tracks, heat rising up my neck into my face. I didn't want to be rude, but I didn't want to sit next to him, either.

"Kade," my aunt said casually, giving the taco beef mixture on the stove another stir, "you know Astrid is fifteen years old, right?"

Kade made a coughing, choking sound and I looked up in time to see him quickly shove the chair he'd pulled out for me back against the table. "Well now, Lillian, how was I supposed to know that?" he grumbled. "She looks older."

"Maybe you could have asked first. She's also my niece, in case you've forgotten, so that means Astrid is off limits to you;

save your never-ending charm for your string of girls in town and my poor working students."

Kade's face went red and he looked down at the table, muttering something under his breath.

Lillian's jaw tightened, but she ignored him. Instead, she turned and gave me a reassuring smile. "Don't pay him any attention, Astrid. Lately, he can't seem to help chatting up every girl within a twenty-mile radius, but he's mostly harmless. Mostly. If he gives you any trouble, just let me know. I'm wise to his ways."

Blushing and completely mortified, I made my way carefully to a chair as far from Kade as possible. I was just about to sit down when I realized another person had come into the room, and he was now sitting right beside me.

"Oh," I yelped, trying not to stare.

"Hi, Astrid, I'm Justin. And yes, we're twins. But, don't worry, we're not identical."

"No, not at all," Kade joked from across the table, perfectly recovered from his moment of embarrassment. "I'm better looking, for one, and smarter, and the ladies love me."

"Right." Justin snorted. "Yep, that's the only difference between us."

They quieted down when Bryce came in and everyone fell to eating.

I ate my lunch silently while the people around me kept up a steady stream of conversation about horses, cows, and never-ending repairs to fencing and structures. Apparently, when you had a thousand acres the work didn't stop for a single minute.

I kept my head down, trying to study the twins out of the corner of my eye without being too obvious. They were very much alike, but you wouldn't mistake them for one another. They had the same deeply tanned skin and blond, curly hair. It looked like everyone in the family except Casey took after their dad, Bryce, in colouring.

They both had sharp cheek-bones and strong jaw lines, but somehow Justin's face was softer, with less of an edge. Justin wore glasses, too, and his eyes were brown behind them rather than the striking hypnotic, ice blue that made Kade seem so exotic. I could see why lots of girls would fall all over Kade, but he was too pretty to be comfortable around. At least for me.

"You settling in okay, Astrid?" Bryce said kindly. "You figuring out the lay of the land?"

"Yes, I'm starting to. I met some of the horses today. They are so beautiful, especially Doc and Donkey."

There was a moment of silence and then everyone burst out laughing. Justin choked on his food and then hit me on the shoulder good naturedly. "Are you comparing my magnificent stallion to that scrubby donkey, Astrid?"

"Donkey's beautiful," I protested. How could anyone not think that his soft grey fur and huge eyes were lovely?

"He is now," Kade surprisingly came to my defense. "She's brushed him within an inch of his life. He looks like he's ready for a parade."

"I like grooming," I said, blushing again.

"Well, that's good to know." My aunt laughed. "We'll have to put you to work up in the training barn soon then."

"I really don't mind," I said quickly. "I like to help. And I like being with the horses. I'm thankful that you took me and Folly in."

"Of course," my aunt said, looking surprised. "I'm happy to have you here."

"Folly? Is that your horse's name?" Justin asked quietly, fixing me with an open, interested look.

"Yes, her real name is Faustina, but everyone just calls her Folly."

"And she's a real pain in the butt already," Kade broke in, grinning at his brother.

"She's still settling in," I said quickly, glancing at my aunt to see if she was still annoyed with Folly breaking the stall. "She was better at home. She's still in pain from her accident, too; she's been through a lot."

Kade snorted, but Justin nodded thoughtfully. "Some horses need time to settle into a new routine. What are your plans for her?"

I was heartily sick of everyone asking me this. Why did everything need to be planned out? Wasn't it enough that she just came here to heal and decompress from her accident?

"Um, I guess I just want her to heal from her injuries first. As soon as I know she's for sure sound then I'll send her back to Liza like I promised."

Justin frowned in confusion but before he could ask more the awful phone on the wall shrilled into action. Nobody else jumped but me; I guessed they were all used to it by now.

"Triple Hills," Aunt Lillian said and then her face creased into a frown. "Oh dear, yes, he's here. I'll get him. Bryce, it's Casey's school."

Bryce shook his head and pushed his chair back forcefully.

"Bryce here. Uh-huh," he said a bit too forcefully. "She did, huh? Yep, I'll talk to her. Thanks for calling, Mrs. Renning. I'll take it from here. No, no, I'll make sure she understands."

Bryce slammed the phone down on the hook and breathed in deeply through his nose. "Right," he said finally. "That was the school secretary calling to tell me that my *daughter* was in another fight. They want someone to pick her up right away."

"I'll get her," Justin said easily. "I have to pick up some things at the feed store anyway."

"I'll go with you," Kade said, pushing back his chair. "I've got some errands to run. Astrid, you should come with us. We can show you town."

"Oh, it's okay," I said quickly, thinking of how unhappy Casey would be if I showed up with her brothers. "Aunt Lillian had some chores she wanted me to help out with."

"Oh no, you go with the boys and let them show you around. I don't expect you to work all the time. And take your phone with you so you can check for messages; I know my working students took advantage of every opportunity."

"Fine," Bryce said, "but I expect you to bring your sister straight home; she's in a lot of trouble and I don't want you two encouraging her. She needs to smarten up."

Kade and Justin shot each other a look and it was easy to see that they didn't think much of what their dad said.

"She needs to learn how to deal with these kids at school like an adult without throwing punches." Bryce went on, talking more to himself than to the rest of us. She's too hot-headed. Just like you two were."

Kade grinned at his dad and pushed his cowboy hat further down on his head. "You got that right; we got in some great fights in school."

"Right, well, I don't want Casey spending her whole high school career in the principal's office. You two never cared about school, you knew you wanted to work with horses, and your mother and I supported you on that, but Casey says she wants something different and the path she's on right now is taking her right in the opposite direction of what she wants. Understand?"

"Okay, okay," they mumbled half-heartedly.

We scraped our plates and stacked our dishes in the dishwasher before Aunt Lillian shooed us out the door.

"I'll drive," Kade announced and Justin didn't argue. He started to move to the back door of the truck to offer me the front seat, but there was no way I wanted to sit beside Kade by myself. I ducked under his arm and climbed into the back seat before anyone could argue.

"That kid," Justin said, shooting his brother a look as he slid in beside him. "She's in school two weeks and she's already been sent home twice."

"Just like her brothers before her," Kade grinned but Justin frowned.

"It's not funny, dude. What if they expel her?"

"Then she'll go somewhere else or she'll stay home and work on the ranch. I don't know what mom's going to say, though."

"Oh, she'll say plenty, I'm sure. She's looking for any excuse to force Casey to go live with her."

"Can she do that?"

"Probably not, she's lucky she's getting Ollie for the year. She knows that. But she can make Dad's life a nightmare if Casey doesn't settle down."

They fell into a moody silence and I studied the landscape

passing by outside the window. I'd been half-asleep the first time I'd driven these roads and my impression had been one of desolation, but today it looked beautiful. The dried-up brown hills didn't seem quite so barren. There were also stands of towering green pine trees and when we came out of the hills I could see blue mountain ranges looming in the distance.

We were only about twenty minutes from civilization. We rolled down a big hill and a small town stretched out in front of us at the edge of the lake.

"That's Triple Hills," Kade said.

"Oh, like the ranch? Was it named after the town?"

"Nope, other way around. The ranch came first, it's over 150 years old and it was an outpost on the way to the first gold rush. People would stop to pick up food and supplies on their way up north, and the town built up around it over time. It was a big trading center back in the day."

"Wow," I said, impressed. "I didn't know that."

"Lillian has some books in the library at home if you want to read up on it," Justin said, "that is, if you like history."

"I do, actually," I said just as we rolled into the outskirts town.

"This place is probably small potatoes compared to what you're used to," Kade warned. "No movie theatre or shopping malls here; if you want any of that, you'll have to go to Williams Lake. It's the next town over."

"No, this is nice," I said, "the city I came from isn't very big, either, although we do have malls and movie theatres; I just didn't go to them much."

"Oh, we thought you were a big-city girl from Vancouver."

"Vancouver *Island*," I corrected. "The cities there are way smaller than Vancouver."

"Sorry, we can't do the full tour today," Justin said. "We'll just swing by the feed store, go pick up Casey, and then be on our way."

"Wait, no, we should get Casey first," Kade argued. "Dad's going to ground her bad when she gets home. The least we can do is take her out for lunch before she has to go face the music."

"Okay, you're taking the blame if dad freaks out, though."

"I always do." Kade slammed on the brakes and did a terrifying U-turn in the middle of the road. Luckily, there weren't any cars coming because I don't even think he checked if the road was clear. The tires screeched and suddenly we were facing in the opposite direction.

The drive to the school was only a few minutes. We pulled up in front of a medium-sized brick building with a playing field out back and asphalt basketball courts in the front. Casey must have been watching for us because as soon as we pulled into the parking lot she banged open the front door and ran down the steps toward the truck. She had an ice pack pressed to one eye and the rest of her face was blotchy with tears. An older man strode out behind her, marching down the stairs with a grim look on his face

"Oh, Casey," Kade muttered under his breath. He slid out of the truck and opened the back door so she could jump inside, slamming it safely behind her before turning to intercept the man who was probably the principal. Justin got out of his side of the truck, too, and the two boys stood side by side, making a barrier between the man and Casey.

"Kade, Justin," the man said in a not very friendly way. "I was expecting your father."

"Hey, Principal Hale," Justin said. "Dad's busy at the ranch right now, but he asked us to pick Casey up. We heard she ran into a bit of trouble."

"Just have your dad call me, boys. I'd like to speak with him. We need to come to some resolution or I'm afraid Casey will have to finish her education elsewhere. We have a zero tolerance for fighting at this school."

"Of course," Justin said smoothly, "are the other kids in trouble, too? Casey came home with a bloody nose last week and it looks like her eye today. I'm pretty sure she didn't do that to herself."

"The other girls will be disciplined, but there are several witnesses who say that in both cases it was Casey who instigated the fights."

"Yeah, I'll bet they did." Kade's hands tightened into fists.

"You guys, let's just go," Casey growled, knocking her fist on the window to get their attention. "It's not worth it." Then, unexpectedly she started to cry.

"Are you o...?" I started, but she hunched her shoulders and turned her face abruptly away.

I sat frozen in my seat, invisible, not knowing what to do. A faint thwunking made me sit up and look at the grassy field across the road from the school.

Oh, I thought, forgetting all about Casey. *This is the school I was supposed to go to. They have archery here.*

Three boys were lined up at the edge of the playing field facing a bank of hand-made foam targets that had been set up in front of a huge pile of sand and dirt to keep the arrows from launching off into the woods.

I watched them carefully, running my gaze expertly over the battered wooden recurve bows, the stance of the archers, the arc of the arrows as they flew. *They're not very experienced*, I thought, mentally correcting this one's stance and another's draw. *I wonder where their coach is?*

I winced as a tall, lanky boy shot arrow after arrow, missing his target every time, his arrows buried in a tight grouping into the wall of sand just to the left of his target. I knew it would just take one small adjustment to change everything for him.

I put my hand on the door latch, just about to hop out and give him a few pointers, when Kade yanked the driver's side door open and slid inside.

"You be sure to tell your dad to call me," the principal said loudly, turning away. His gaze shifted to the archers across the field and his expression grew even darker, if that was possible.

"Yes, sir," Kade called, his voice tight with anger, "we'll make sure he does."

Truck doors slammed and then Kade stomped his foot on the pedal and we shot out of the parking lot, spraying gravel in all directions. I turned around just in time to see the principal headed toward the archers, his face thunderous.

Nobody spoke, and the only noise was the rumble of the truck and Casey's muffled sobs.

"Your pick for lunch, Casey. What do you want to eat?" Kade said finally.

"N… nothing," Casey hiccupped. "I just want to go home."

"Naw, you don't want to go home right now, little sis. Not

while dad is still so worked up. We'll stay in town for a bit until he cools off."

"Grilled cheese then," Casey said ungratefully. "And why is *she* here?"

"Don't be rude," Justin said mildly. "Astrid lives at the ranch now, so you might as well get used to it and stop being mean. She's nice, aren't you, Astrid?"

He turned to grin at me and I smiled at him weakly. I wasn't that interested in being friends with Casey. She seemed kind of unstable and I'd had my full share of rudeness from my old, back-stabbing, ex-friend Miranda back home. I didn't need to make the same mistake again. Still, I wasn't about to be heartless when someone was sobbing beside me.

"I didn't like school very much, either." I said, saying the first thing that popped into my head, "Everyone else always seemed to be having fun except me."

"Yeah, but you went to rich-people school," Casey sniffed. "You didn't have to worry about people beating you up every single day."

I frowned at her, thinking back to my years at Sacred Heart. People laughed about my weight behind my back; I had my own special nick-name, Fat Camp, because my dad regularly sent me to a "health spa" to lose weight a few times a year. I'd never fit in, but nobody had ever threatened to *hit* me before. Still, I vaguely remembered some people getting shoved into their lockers and I knew one older girl had to leave school because she was teased so badly, although I couldn't remember about what. I'd been so focused on my archery career at that point, and my obsession with the unattainable Thomas Ling, that I'd hardly noticed anything else.

"I think people are pretty much the same everywhere," I said finally. "You just have to focus on what's important to you and ignore everything else."

"Yeah, that's easy for *you* to say," Casey spat. "You have everything handed to you on a silver platter. Not everyone is as stinking-rich as you."

"What?" I asked, stunned. My shock gave way to a steady stream of anger. *She knows nothing about you,* I told myself furiously. *She's just crazy.*

"I Googled you." Casey turned her blotchy face to look at me and sniffled. "When we heard you were coming, Olive and I did a search and found…."

"Casey, lay off," Kade growled, cutting her off. "You're being stupid. You should hear yourself."

Casey set her jaw defiantly and then abruptly deflated like a balloon, shoulders sagging. "I know," she said. "Astrid, I'm sorry, I don't know what's wrong with me lately. Just ignore me."

"Fine," I said, all too ready to get as far away from her as possible.

We pulled up in front of a diner, our truck one of ten similar, jacked-up trucks in the parking lot. I didn't think I'd seen a single, normal, small car since I'd arrived.

The painted sign on the door said Triple Hills Diner in sparkly letters. And underneath it, Free Wi-Fi.

Yes, I whipped out my phone and was delighted to see the flood of messages lighting up my text icon.

A bell over the door jingled as Justin opened the door and I looked up from my phone long enough to follow everyone inside. My stomach rumbled as the smell of frying food hit me.

It was impossible I'd be hungry after our big taco lunch, but there it was, the curse of my existence; I was always ready for more food.

It was a seat-yourself sort of place, so we filed to a booth in the back corner, right by the window. I made sure to slide quickly in beside Justin on the orange vinyl seat. I had no desire to sit near either Kade or Casey.

"Hey, *Kade,* you didn't tell me you were back in town." A pretty waitress wearing a faded yellow apron appeared beside us, her eyes fixed hungrily on Kade. She crossed her arms over her chest, an anxious smile plastered on her face.

"Oh, Lacey." Kade jerked in surprise and then quickly recovered, sending her his heart-melting smile. "Sorry, I just got back in town this morning. I was taking some yearlings from the ranch down to Vancouver and then I did a little road trip. I'm still catching up."

Her eyes lit up and she dropped her arms to her sides, nodding. "Yeah, that's what my sister said. She passed your truck on the highway this morning and called me right away. But you could have phoned me yourself from the road."

"Sorry, babe. You know how I am with this technology stuff."

"Yeah." She was smiling now, a faint blush staining her cheeks. "Well, maybe we can hang out again now that you're home. I...I'm free this weekend."

"Of course, anytime for you, sugar," Kade winked at her. "Any chance we can get my sister one of your famous grilled cheese sandwiches? She's had a rough day."

The waitress glanced at me and Casey for the first time, taking in my cast and bandages and Casey's rapidly blackening eye. "Well, what on earth happened to you two?"

"Horse," I said just at the same time Casey said, "fight."

"Well, horses and fights account for most of the injuries around these parts." Lacey laughed. "Plus, bulls, alcohol, and fast driving, I guess.

"Okay, one grilled cheese with fries and a chocolate milkshake like usual for the streetfighter and what about for the rest of you?"

Despite my guilt over eating two lunches in a row I got a small plate of fries and a strawberry milkshake. I hunched over my plate and gleefully opened my messages.

Hilary: *Hello? Astrid, what happened to you? Have you been kidnapped?*

Hilary: *Hey, we're freaking out here. Rob said he didn't hear from you at all. Forget this, I'm getting my mom to call Marion.*

Hilary: *My mom talked to Marion. Are you seriously going to have to go the whole winter without cell service? What planet have they sent you to?*

Hilary: *Seriously though, glad you're alive. Send us a message when you can. Quarry's good so don't worry about him. Liza's with Claudia in the hospital, she caught a cold. We can't wait for you to come back, though, miss you tons!*

Rob had sent a slanted picture of him, Artimax, and Ferdi, all grouped together in front of his barn.

Rob: *Where are you? Hilary said she heard from you once and then nothing. Do I need to beat up any cowboys for you?*

"Is that your boyfriend?" Justin asked, looking over my shoulder at the photo.

I felt myself flush beet-red. "Yes. Well, no. He's a friend." I stopped, then looked back down at the picture. *He likes me*, I thought, *and I like him; better than almost any other person. But I won't see him for nearly a year. He'll find someone new by then.*

"Those are nice looking horses," Justin said, smiling. "What does he do with them?"

"Dressage and eventing," I said, glad the topic had changed from my relationship status. "He's a great rider."

"On or off the horse?" Kade looked up from across the table, laughing at his own stupid joke, ignoring the disgusted looks from both his siblings.

"Just ignore him." Justin shook his head. "His mind is always in the gutter lately."

"Yeah, he's kind of gross," Casey added, coming out of her depression long enough to poke her brother. "He's always prowling around someone. I don't care, though, as long as he keeps stringing along the waitress there, we get a discount on food."

"Hey, keep your voice down," Kade hissed. "It's not like I promised her anything. She just keeps calling. Anyway, I'm buying your lunch; you could pretend to be nice and grateful."

"Thank you for lunch, Kade," Casey said in an overly-sweet, sing-song voice.

Before everyone was finished eating I managed to send long-winded texts to Hilary and Rob, and Claudia and even sent a quick one to Liza to let her know that Folly had made it safely.

As soon as we were done eating, Kade went up to the front to pay our bill and chat Lacey up while the rest of us piled back into the truck. Casey and I sat as far apart as possible in the backseat.

*****

Kade kept a running commentary while he drove, telling me about every building, landmark, and person we passed on the way back through town. Pretty much every business along the main street was called Triple Hills. There was the Triple Hills Bakery, Triple Hills Hardware, Triple Hills Grocery and, to add variety, TH Mechanic and Fuel. They even had a brightly coloured gift shop called The Trip that Kade swore sold drugs out of a back room if you knew the secret password.

"That's not true." Justin laughed, but Kade just nodded knowingly.

He and Justin seemed to know just about everyone; they both gave small waves to the driver of nearly every truck they met. Casey ignored us all, just sank lower in her seat and pretended to sleep.

The feed and tack store was housed in a huge, metal, domed building. As soon as we pulled in, Casey tugged a battered textbook out of her backpack. "Don't take forever," she said, hunching into the corner of her seat without looking up.

A set of wind chimes jingled as I filed in after Justin, Kade following uncomfortably close behind me. It was like he had no concept of personal space at all. I forgot all about him, though, as I breathed in the scent of leather and cleaner and feed all mixed together. It smelled like heaven I walked to the middle and turned to take everything in, zeroing in on the bookshelves near the back.

Earlier, I'd had an idea that maybe I could study horse psychology like I had horse massage. I'd become fairly good at massage from just reading a book and practicing on Claudia's horses; maybe there was something that would help me figure out Folly's volatile mood swings.

"Hey," a stocky, muscled girl with a wide, smiling face and spikey, purple hair popped her head out from behind a display of metal bits she'd been organizing. She had a ring in her nose and a tattoo of a running horse on one arm. "Can I help you find anything?" Her gaze shifted abruptly over my head and her eyes lit up like she'd just been handed a winning lottery ticket. "Kade!" She practically screamed, "you're home!"

She brushed past me, crossing the room in one bound to wrap herself around him like a tight sweater.

"Abbie," Kade said weakly, hugging her tightly before prying her off him. "Hey, I thought you'd gone up North to work. We had that going away party for you and everything."

"Guess I changed my mind," she said, grinning up at him. "There are a few things in this town worth sticking around for. I left you like a hundred messages."

"Yeah, something must be up with my phone. I just got back in town today. I'm still catching up."

"Well, you'd better catch up quick, cowboy. I don't like being kept waiting." She stepped in close to him again and I moved quickly to the bookshelf before I could hear or see anything embarrassing. Aunt Lillian was right; Kade clearly got around.

I ran my fingers along the titles on the shelf and found a few on horse training that looked like they might be helpful. I'd read lots of horse books over the summer with Claudia. She'd always insisted on her students being as educated as possible when it came to horses. But Claudia's horses had been gentle and well-trained; there'd been nothing in her books about how to work with a horse that hated you.

"Find anything helpful?" Justin said, appearing at my side.

"I'm not sure," I said honestly. "I found a few books on horse training, but I don't know where to start."

"These are good books," he said, looking down at the stack I'd set aside. "But most of these deal with riding issues; from what Lillian told me, you need to start with basic groundwork first with your mare. Here, try these two. No system is perfect, but they'll give you a place to start. I have some at home you'll probably like, too."

"Thanks," I said, my heart sinking as I realized Aunt Lillian must have told everyone about Folly's episode that morning. "I'm sort of working my way through this blindly. I think I remember most of the things Liza did when she started handling her but, you know, I'm also not Liza. She seemed like she could handle anything Folly threw at her. She..." I paused, looking over my shoulder to make nobody was listening, "she was never terrified of her."

I stopped short, waiting for Justin's reaction. I didn't know why I'd suddenly confessed to him that I was scared when I'd done my best to keep it from Aunt Lillian.

"Everyone's afraid sometimes, Astrid. Horses are big, powerful animals. Sometimes you're going to get hurt, even with a nice horse. When you add a horse like Folly into the mix, well, your odds of getting injured go up. You need to find a way to work with her and still stay safe."

"I'm not sure how I'm going to do that. Even going in the paddock with her feels dangerous."

"Then go with your gut feeling and stay outside the paddock at the beginning."

"But, how am I supposed to—"

"Hey, are you two coming?" Kade called from the front of the shop, a hint of desperation in his voice. "Dad's going to wonder where we are."

Justin laughed. "I guess we should rescue him."

I took the long way to the cash register, quickly looking over all the tack and products on display. One thing I'd learned about myself during my time at Claudia's; I could spend hours in tack stores just looking at everything. I hoped that I'd have a chance to come back here again.

I came away with three books, two bags of crunchy horse treats and, at the last minute I remembered to buy two bags of beet pulp for Folly and a bag of what Justin called "low-maintenance feed." I toyed with the idea of buying her some nicer, softer hay since she didn't seem to like the coarse stuff she was eating, but thought that might somehow insult Aunt Lillian. Folly would just have to get used to roughing it for now.

Abbie barely looked at me the entire time she rang up my order; she only had eyes for Kade. He leaned against edge of the counter nearest her, pretending to flip through some catalogues while he was not-so-secretly eyeing up her cleavage. If he wanted to escape Abbie so badly then he was sure sending her some mixed messages.

"I'll meet you guys in the truck," I said quickly, edging toward the door.

I slid back into the truck beside Casey, not caring that she didn't even glance up at me. I opened one of the training books, flipping through to the section on biting and rearing. Hopefully there was something in there that could help me.

After a couple minutes, I looked up to find Casey staring at me thoughtfully. One of her eyelids was already swollen and she was probably going to have quite the black eye once the bruising started, one to match the fading bruises over her nose and other eye.

"Yes?" I said, pointedly, waiting for her to say something sarcastic.

"Why did you come here?" she asked. It didn't sound like she was being rude, she sounded genuinely curious. "I mean, why would you leave your home and your friends and come all the way out *here* in the middle of nowhere?"

"It's complicated," I said, turning back to my book. I wasn't about to reveal too much to Casey. I didn't trust her. "My family's going through some stuff and it was easier for me to come live with my aunt. Plus, I thought it would be good for Folly."

"Oh," was all she said and then fell silent again.

Kade and Justin arrived back at the truck and Kade backed into the big barn so they could fill the entire truck-bed with bags of grain.

"Bye, Kade!" Abbie called, waving as we squealed out of the parking lot. "Call me!"

"Seriously?" Casey muttered. "Another one? Why can't you speed-date girls who live out of town? We have to shop at that store all the time. I think I liked you better when you were dragging around love sick over Flori—"

"Shut it, Casey," Kade growled, glaring at her in the rear-view mirror.

She glared back at him a moment and then dropped her gaze back to the book. "Sorry, Kade," she said in a small voice. "I didn't mean that."

The ride home after that was silent. Both Casey and I studied our books, and Justin and Kade seemed lost in their own thoughts.

They dropped me and Justin off at Aunt Lillian's house before heading back to their own since Justin needed to pick up his own truck.

"Later, Astrid," Kade called, revving his engine. "I'll drop your stuff off in the feed room." Casey said nothing, just stared out the window without even looking at me. She was probably thinking about the long lecture she was about to get from her dad. I'd been in that spot many times, so I felt a pang of sympathy for her.

Jake trotted down off the porch steps and woofed at the truck as they pulled away, his hackles up and his tail wagging stiffly.

"Good boy," I whispered, reaching down to stroke his wiry coat with my good hand.

"See you, Astrid," Justin called, getting into his own truck. He paused with one foot on the running board. "Look, it's none of my business, but do you want some help with your mare?"

I froze, trying to think of the right words to say to him. *I'm scared of her, but I don't know you and I don't want to see her get hurt again and I don't know if you'll try to muscle her around or beat her and I don't know if I can protect her.*

"Yes," I said slowly, "I do want help but...." I bit my lip.

Justin watched me thoughtfully and, when I didn't say anything more, he slid the rest of the way into his truck. "Tell you what, how about if I just come down and meet her with you tomorrow night when I'm back from school. There should still be enough daylight to assess her. I won't even go in with her unless you say it's okay. I can give you some ideas and you can choose whether to follow them or not."

"Oh," I said, exhaling the breath I hadn't realized I'd been holding. "Yeah, that would be great, thanks."

"See you then."

I watched his truck pull away and then walked slowly back to the house.

I was glad to finally make it back to my room. My body ached from tension and from my super-grooming session with Donkey that morning. I needed pain killers and a nap more than anything.

I spent the rest of the day passed out in a medication-induced stupor and only woke just in time to feed Folly. There was no sign of Aunt Lillian when I went downstairs and, after waiting around for a while hoping she'd show up to give me a ride, I pulled on my boots and headed on foot down the short cut to the barn.

It wasn't the same suffocating heat as yesterday, but it was still hot, and by the time I was a quarter way to the barn I was damp and puffing with exertion. Up ahead I heard running water and soon I came to a small bridge that I didn't even remember driving over the day before. I guess I'd been too busy trying not to fall out of Lillian's rust-bucket of a truck and die to notice my surroundings.

I stopped on the bridge to catch my breath, leaning carefully over the side rail, watching the half-dried stream struggle through the rocks below. There was only about a foot of water now, but the sides of the stream bed were carved deep, so I guessed it was a wilder river in spring time. A bird called somewhere off in the forest, a sharp startled cry that shook me out of my reverie. Folly would be waiting for her dinner.

I moved down the trail faster now, stopping only at the last rise before the barn to admire the way that the sinking sun lit the whole log barn so it looked like it was glowing from within. I could see Folly moving restlessly in her paddock, her copper coat almost pink-tinged. Even though she was lame, hadn't been brushed in days, and her untidy mane stuck up in all directions, I was struck by her beauty all over again.

I always forgot how stunning she was; it was what had made Cole buy her in the first place, even though she was awful. It was what had made Liza fall in love with her, and maybe even what had made my Dad buy her. There was something almost otherworldly about her, as if she'd descended from a line of beautiful and powerful rulers and had only landed in my undeserving lap by accident. Come to think of it, that's probably *exactly* what had happened. If she was as well-bred as everyone said, I bet her ancestors *were* owned by royalty.

My next step snapped a dried-up branch in half with a loud crack and Folly swivelled her head around to study me as I came down the hill toward her. Ears forward, ears back, ears forward, ears back; unable to make her mind up whether I was a friend or an enemy.

Yeah, I feel the same way about you, too. I sighed as she finally shook her head at me and hobbled off to the farthest end of her paddock.

I passed right by her without stopping and went into the barn to get her dinner. Hay first; Claudia always insisted that the horses needed hay in their bellies before they got their grain. I grabbed two flakes from the hay room, frowning at the rough texture. Folly was used to the soft, electric green flakes from home; even I could see that these looked much less appetizing.

"Here you go, girl," I said as I got back to the paddock. I squished the hay through the pipe-rail fence one flake at a time. "You eat this up and I'll go get your grain."

She gave me the equivalent of a horse stink-eye and ambled over to push at the hay disinterestedly. *No, not appetizing at all.*

To my surprise, Kade had not only dropped my bags of beet pulp and feed off in the feed room; he'd also soaked a small bucket full for Folly's dinner.

Wow, he's not such a bad guy, after all, I thought, *as long as you don't want to date him.*

I mixed Folly's medication, supplements, and pellets in with her food and dumped it in a low feed tub. I awkwardly carried it out to her by holding the edge with my good hand and balancing the bottom of the tub on top of my cast. I was counting the days for my arm to heal; everything took ten times as long to do as it would normally, and I was seriously done with being injured.

Folly was waiting for me when I got back, facing me with a sullen expression. She didn't exactly attack when I shoved the feed tub cautiously under the fence. Instead, she slammed her body flat up against the rails and raised a back hoof threateningly as if letting me know that the flimsy fence was the only thing stopping her from kicking.

"Yeah, you're welcome," I said with a sigh, "glad I spend all this time worrying about your happiness when all you do is act grouchy. Goodnight then."

She didn't watch me leave. I went back to the barn to soak the next morning's breakfast and then walked slowly, wearily up the trail.

When I let myself back in the house there was no smell of fried food and buttery mashed potatoes, and no chattering voices like there'd been last night. Tonight, the house was strangely dark and silent; only the light in the kitchen was on.

"Aunt Lillian?" I said, peering in at where she sat at the long table, her chin resting on her hands. She stared morosely down at a stack of papers in front of her.

"I hope you don't mind eating light tonight, Astrid," Aunt Lillian said, looking up distractedly. "I finally got motivated to catch up on some of this accounting and I don't dare stop now."

"Anything I can help with?" I asked timidly. My dad had always been extra-cranky when he had to pay bills, so I was used to tip-toeing around, especially when tax season hit.

"No, dear, I think I've made a dent in it anyway. I was so silly to let Trent take care of the business end of things all these years, now that he's gone it's frankly overwhelming. After he passed away, it was Florian who talked, or bullied, me into getting all this stuff done and now she's gone, too. I know the workings of this ranch inside and out, but some of this paperwork still makes my head ache. I left you a platter of finger foods on the counter."

"Sure," I said, trying not to feel disappointed at the lack of a real dinner. After all, I couldn't expect her to cater to me every night.

I took a plate out of the cupboard and filled it from the tray of meat, cheese, pickles and fruit she'd left out and sat down quietly at the table. She barely looked up when I sat down, and I found myself trying to chew as quietly as possible without crunching so I wouldn't disturb her.

"Aunt Lillian," I said finally, "is it okay if I take my food out on the porch? I want to try the swing."

"Of course, dear, whatever you like," she glanced up, as if surprised to find me still sitting there, smiled vaguely and then looked back down at the papers in front of her.

Jake struggled up from his dog bed as soon as he saw that I had a plate of food and followed me outside, claws clacking on the wooden floor.

Even though the evening was well upon us, it was still hot, even in a tee shirt. I carefully sat down cross-legged on the big porch swing, setting my plate beside me and leaning into the gentle swaying motion.

It was so quiet out here in the country. Even though our condo back home was on the top floor of our building, we could still sometimes hear the traffic from below, plus sirens and airplanes. Out here there was just nothing but the light wind in the trees and the sound of Jake rustling on the porch. And with no city lights to get in the way, the sky was ten times darker than the sky at home.

I ate my meager dinner in silence, struggling with the feelings of loneliness that welled up inside me.

Don't be such a baby, I told myself sternly, *this is no big deal. People leave home and start new lives all the time. Think of it as an adventure.*

Jake lay at my feet, gazing up at my plate and following the path of my hand each time I lifted a piece of food to my mouth. He whined low under his breath and I tossed him a piece of cheese, which he snapped up eagerly, licking his chops and looking for more.

Aunt Lillian was gone when I went back inside, and the tray of food had disappeared. I put my plate in the dishwasher and climbed wearily to my room. Even though I'd only been here a couple days it felt like it had been a lifetime.

It was early, but there seemed to be nothing left for me to do but shower and get in bed. At least maybe I could find a book from the shelves in the nook to read myself to sleep. I had the horse books I'd just bought, but right then I was craving fiction.

The shower felt amazing, even if I had to half freeze myself by keeping my cast out of the heavenly stream of water. I'd wrapped it in plastic, but I still couldn't risk the cast getting wet. One of the nurses at the hospital had told me horror stories of people who'd went around wearing damp casts and had gotten fungus growing like mushrooms beneath it. I had enough going on in my life without fungus.

I towelled off and threw on a pair of yoga pants and a sweatshirt before padding quietly down the hall to the reading area at the end. Aunt Lillian had shown me earlier how the fireplace could be turned on just by flicking a switch.

The flames danced away happily, cheering me slightly, and I scanned the bookshelves for something interesting. Many of the books were on plants and animals, but there were some fiction books, although most of those seemed to be old westerns with guns and stagecoaches on the covers. Still, they might be interesting if they had horses in them.

I took my time, delaying the moment when I'd have to go back to my lonely room. Finally, I grabbed a few, shut off the fireplace and headed back to bed.

Chapter Four

I woke up ten minutes before my alarm went off, feeling more hopeful than I had the evening before. The temperature had dropped during the night and I shivered as I dressed in the chilly morning air.

I tiptoed down the stairs. The house was quiet, only the ticking of the big grandfather clock in the hallway breaking the silence. Even Jake was missing from his dog bed.

I went to the kitchen and grabbed two apples out of the basket on the counter; one for me and one for Folly. Sometime in the night while I'd slept, I'd come to a decision about Folly; she was my responsibility and I was going to do whatever it took to fix the damage I'd done. Even if that meant asking for help.

Folly, on the other hand, had not had a good night. I found her standing sullenly in one corner of her paddock, her back turned to her unfinished pile of hay, head down, and trembling in the morning cold.

"Oh, Folly, you probably needed your blanket on last night, didn't you? And you hardly ate your hay."

She turned to look at me half-heartedly when I spoke,

flattened her ears and swung her head in an irritated circle.

I frowned at her uneaten hay pile. That wasn't good; she'd clearly picked through it for the good bits and left the rest.

I climbed carefully onto the fence rails and leaned over, studying her. "There's not much grass in here for you, is there? You're probably bored."

Folly shifted her hind legs and hung her head lower, ears drooping, ignoring me. She looked miserable.

"Would you like an apple?" I slipped the apple out of my pocket and held it out, waiting hopefully for her to look over, but there was no response. "Are you sure you don't want an apple?" I bit into it, crunching as loudly as I could.

She swivelled her head in my direction, pricking her ears with interest and then flattening them again as if embarrassed to be caught being a nice horse.

"It's super delicious," I said invitingly. "Probably the best apple I've ever tasted." I took another small bite.

This time she nickered under her breath, the first positive thing she'd given me in a long time, and took a few tentative steps in my direction before stopping. She tossed her head up and down a few times, ears moving uncertainly in all directions.

"Good girl," I praised, "here you go."

I raised my arm high over my head to toss the rest of the apple toward her and in one second she transformed from a sulky horse into a fire-breathing dragon. Ears flattened, eyes blazing with malice, she shot toward me so fast I hardly had time to react. She hit the fence with full force, knocking me backward so hard that I landed on the ground with a thud. She squealed a high, unnatural scream and whipped around, kicking the fence. Hard.

The metal bars clanged and shuddered with the impact, but at least the fence held up.

She squealed again in frustration, holding up a back leg as if it hurt and limping over to her fallen apple. She sniffed it with a bear-like grunt and then crunched it angrily between her big, dangerous teeth, staring at me the whole time she ate.

"Ow." I sat up slowly, taking my time to make sure nothing else was broken. I ached all over, but I could move all my limbs. I stood up and brushed the dirt and grass off myself carefully, glancing around to make sure I didn't have any witnesses. I stared at Folly with tears stinging my eyes. Why couldn't she see that I was trying as hard as I could to be her friend?

Sniffling, I limped back to the barn to mix up her breakfast.

There was no friendly Donkey to greet me this time; since Folly clearly hated him, he'd once again been turned out to pasture to keep the baby horses company. It felt strange walking into an empty barn, passing rows of vacant stalls. The place had a hushed air of expectation, as if something momentous was about to happen.

Folly must have heard me mixing her grain because when I emerged from the barn she'd moved to her gate and was leaning over it, flipping her head up and down impatiently. Her ears swivelled back and forth in that nervous manner she had; forward and inviting and then snapping back against her head; flat and hostile. Her mood swings were truly terrifying.

I saw with dismay that sometime in the night she'd dragged her rubber feed tub far into the middle of her paddock, and there was no way I was going to be able to reach it without being killed. With a sigh, I turned to trudge back to the barn for another feed tub, but I only got a few feet when the combination of clanging metal and a panicked neigh made me whirl around.

She wasn't hurt; she stood in the corner of her paddock closest to me, eyes fixed anxiously on her bucket.

"I'll be back girl," I said to reassure her. "I just need to get you a new—"

She squealed again and flailed out with one front foot, sticking her entire hoof abruptly through the fence, hooking her pastern over the rail. She hesitated and then slowly began to lean back, the tendons in her front leg straining against the pressure, the metal panels bending ever so slightly in her direction as she pulled the fence toward her....

"Folly, stop!" My heart thudded in panic. She was going to hurt herself or break the fence, and I wouldn't be able to do anything to stop it. I shook the bucket in my hand, hoping to distract her, and instantly she moved forward, taking the pressure off her leg and nodding her head up and down encouragingly.

I took another hesitant step toward her and she moved her foot slightly so that only the bottom of her hoof rested on the edge of the fence.

Another step toward her and she nickered under her breath and then put her foot down completely.

"You are such a big faker," I said grumpily. "Fine, here, have it your way." I pushed the whole bucket under the fence like she'd wanted me to and was rewarded by her not attacking me. She stuck her face into her breakfast like a normal horse, slurping and snuffling at the wet beet pulp, working her lips through the mash to sift out pieces of grain and carrot first.

Tentatively, I reached out to carefully run the tips of my

fingers through her silky mane. She flinched when I touched her and stamped a front foot, but she didn't stop eating and she didn't rip my arm out of its socket.

"There's a good girl," I said softly. "See, we can be friends."

Suddenly, she threw her head up. I snatched my hand back, but she wasn't looking at me this time. She was looking over my shoulder with watchful eyes.

I turned to see Casey riding by on the blue speckled mare, Kitty, that I'd met the day before.

"Sorry," Casey said, nodding at me. "Didn't mean to startle her. Just passing by." She gave her mare a little kick so it jumped into a trot to hurry past us.

"That's okay," I muttered. I hoped Casey hadn't been lurking around watching when Folly had attacked me. Surely, if she saw, she'd blab it to my aunt.

When Folly was done eating and had gone back to root unhappily through her hay, I fished the empty bucket out from under the fence and went back to the barn to soak her dinner beet pulp. Then I went to the hay room to survey Aunt Lillian's supply. The stack I'd taken flakes from for Folly and Donkey was made up of the stalky, pale green hay that Folly didn't like. But, behind it, off to one side was a whole wall of untapped, dark-green leafy goodness. It even smelled delicious.

I'm sure Aunt Lillian wouldn't mind if I took just one bale of that stuff, I thought, gazing up the straight wall of hay. There was no way to climb the stack to get one of the easily accessible bales on top, but there, in the corner just a few rows up, was a bale that hadn't been completely buried in the stack. It stuck out a good two feet and I could see the strings. If I could just wiggle it free carefully then I wouldn't disturb the rest of the neatly stacked hay.

I shifted it back and forth as gently I could, pulling first on one string and then the other with my good hand, easing it slowly toward me inch by inch until it gradually slid free and dropped to the ground.

There, that wasn't too hard, I thought, inching the bale backward by one string, *I'll just slide this—*

My thoughts were interrupted by a soft, whooshing sound. The ground around me trembled and I just had time to take a few running steps toward the door before the side of the stack collapsed and spilled toward me in a waterfall of tumbling hay bales. The first bale hit me in the chest, sending me flying backward into the wall. I cried out in fear just as the rest of the stack came flowing toward me.

"Oh my gosh, Astrid, are you okay?"

I opened my eyes to see Casey's anxious face staring down at me.

"I'm not sure," I said weakly, wincing as Casey began throwing hay bales off me left and right. "I hit my head."

"Stay still," she commanded, "don't try to move until I get you unburied. What on earth happened?"

I stretched gingerly as soon as I was free, relieved to find that nothing else was broken. I just had more bruises layered on top of the ones I already had. How was it that I was in a perpetual state of injury?

"You sure attract some bad luck," Casey said, echoing my thoughts. She reached down and helped me to my feet. "What on earth would cause that stack to fall, anyway?"

"I was trying to get Folly some of the nice hay," I confessed tearfully, "she doesn't like the stuff she's eating."

"That's Lillian's alfalfa mix for the broodmares. Why didn't you use the ladder?" Casey asked, raising an eyebrow and motioning to a metal ladder that I hadn't seen, propped up against the wall next to what was left of the ruined stack.

"I…I guess I didn't see it. Aunt Lillian's going to kill me for making such a mess. She'll probably send us home."

Casey's face softened. "No, she won't. She's been talking about you visiting for weeks."

"Really?"

"Really." She got a calculating gleam in her eye. "But, you *know*, she might change her mind when she sees all this mess. It's going to take at least an hour to have this all re-stacked, and it's not like you can even help, what with your arm hurt like that."

"Yeah." I sighed. "I know. I'm useless right now."

"Well," she said, her Cheshire-cat smile widening, "maybe we can arrange it so she doesn't have to find out. *Maybe* I could do you a favour and get my brothers to re-stack this for you before Lillian sees it."

"Thanks, that would be great," I said cautiously, not trusting this sudden level of helpfulness.

"So," she said, changing the subject abruptly, "you're not starting school for a few weeks, hey?"

"Um, no, I'm going to wait until I can function better. Right now, I still need to nap like twice a day. That's hard to do when I'm in school."

She laughed and then dropped her gaze to the ground, kicking her boot into a loose mound of hay.

"I heard you were going to the doctor today, mind if I come along?"

"Oh," I said, surprised she'd known about it at all. Lillian had probably called over there to ask one of them to drive me to town. "I don't mind. Don't you have school today, though?"

"Three-day suspension for fighting," she said with a grimace. "Dad went through the roof. I'm stuck cleaning the whole barn by myself as punishment, but I don't care, I would do it all over again if I had to. Luckily, Dad had to go to Kamloops to get the trailer fixed and pick up stuff for Ollie's trip to California. He won't be home until late tonight. Kade is supposed to be keeping an eye on me, but you know how that goes. Anyway, I'll see you at lunch, I've got chores to finish."

And with that she was gone, leaving me to wonder what on earth had just happened.

I went up a couple of notches in Folly's books when I brought her the new hay. Her eyes lit up as soon as she saw me coming with a couple flakes of electric green clamped under my arm and she did a horsey jig of happiness and hobbled over to her old hay pile, swirling her head in circles as if telling me right where to put the good stuff.

"All right, all right," I said, pushing the hay through the fence quickly to avoid her eagerly snapping teeth, "glad there's something you approve of, anyway."

I looked at my watch. It was not even nine o'clock and I was already bruised and exhausted.

I trudged back up the rutted "short-cut" to the house, puffing up the hills that had seemed so easy earlier that morning.

This is how I'm going to work off all the food Aunt Lillian keeps piling on me, I thought, gasping for breath. *This is how everyone stays so thin.*

The smell of bacon frying met me at the front door, and my stomach grumbled eagerly. The apple I'd eaten first thing that morning had long since disappeared.

"Oh, good, just in time for breakfast. How's Folly this morning?" Aunt Lillian stood at the kitchen stove holding a spatula; Jake parked at her feet, looking longingly up at the bacon grease ready to drip off the end.

"Um, she's good," I said, not offering any more details.

After my eventful morning, breakfast tasted better than ever, and I had no trouble shovelling in a whole plate of food. We were just finishing up when Kade pushed open the front door without knocking.

"Ready to go, Astrid?" He sniffed the air appreciatively and came into the kitchen without being invited.

"I just have to get changed and grab my stuff," I said, putting my plate in the dishwasher and heading upstairs.

"Okay," he called after me. "Take your time; I'll just help Lillian with these leftovers."

I wish it wasn't Kade driving me to town, I thought nervously. I knew everyone said he was harmless, but he still made me uncomfortable. He was a bit like Folly; beautiful, but unpredictable and potentially dangerous.

I was even more uncomfortable when I found Casey hunched down in the backseat of the truck, peering furtively out the window.

"You two took *forever,*" she said in a stage-whisper. "Quick, get in, I don't want Lillian to see me and tell Dad."

"Why are you coming if you're not allowed?" I asked, frowning. I didn't want to be dragged into her mess. I looked over at Kade, but he had a grin on his face as he started the truck. I guessed he didn't care very much about breaking any rules, either.

"Oh, it's fine," Casey said, pulling herself upright as soon as we reached the end of the driveway. "He didn't specifically *say* I couldn't go to town today. Only that I had to get all my chores done, which I did. We re-stacked all that hay you knocked over, too, just so you know. And, even though he says your horse is spoiled rotten, Kade here brought you a truckload of Timothy from the training barn. It's not as potent as the alfalfa, but she should like it."

"You did? Thank you so much," I said in genuine delight, smiling. "I owe you one. Both of you."

"That's what I was hoping you'd say," Casey said, and then she turned to stare out the window with a satisfied smile on her face that made me nervous. I had the feeling that owing Casey a favour was not a great place to be.

*****

The doctor's office was in a small, grey-sided wooden house with a small sign stuck in the lawn that just said 'Physician'. The lobby was small but nice with a wall-sized tank stocked with tropical fish and a giant shelf full of books to read.

I hardly had time to look around before a stooped grey-haired man came out to shake my hand.

"You must be Astrid, come on in and we'll see what we can do for you."

It felt so nice to have the bandages off that I hardly winced when he cleaned my face up with some damp gauze and then deftly clipped the sutures out of my cheek. It hurt a bit, but it was over before I even had time to complain.

"Looking good," he said, tilting my chin up so he could study my face critically. He ran his fingers lightly down the bridge of my nose without hurting it and then turned away abruptly.

"I've spoken to your surgeon back home. The plan is to keep your splint on for another month or so. Honestly, the bones are probably stable enough now to go un-splinted, so I'll leave the decision up to you; they're usually pretty strong after two weeks, but it does take another six weeks to heal completely. You're staying up at Triple Hills, right?"

"Yes," I said, assuming he meant the ranch and not the hundred other places named Triple Hills around here.

"Well, if you're doing any farm work, or are riding horses, or even if you're a light sleeper who does a lot of tossing and turning at night, then it's my suggestion that you wear the splint. It wouldn't take much to re-break that nose again."

"Okay," I said, thinking of the many ways I'd been injured since just that morning and the fact that Folly tried to kill me on a regular basis. "That's fine. I don't mind having a splint."

"Okee-dokey," he said with a smile, "coming right up."

It didn't take him long to fix me up and soon, I walked out of the office with a brand new blue splint over my nose, a bottle of medicated cleaner for my incisions, and strict instructions not to get dirty. As if *that* were possible.

"Oh, that's much better," Casey said as I got back to the truck, "come on, let's go to lunch to celebrate."

We ate at the Triple Hills diner for the second time that week but, thankfully, Kade's favourite waitress wasn't there. Kade wasn't there, either, but Casey said he'd planned on showing up once he'd finished some errands.

My new nose splint gave me so much more freedom than the bandages that I felt like a whole new person. I saw a few people glancing my way curiously, but I just ignored them.

For the first half hour, we just ate our food in complete silence, both focused on our phones. I downloaded dozens of emails and sent everyone I knew quick texts to let them know I hadn't completely disappeared.

"So," Casey said, nervously pushing at the ice in her drink so it made little clinking sounds against the glass.

"Yes?" I looked up, annoyed at being interrupted.

"Well, I was wondering…" She dropped her voice to barely a whisper, looking over her shoulder first to make sure nobody was paying attention to us. "I mean, I had an idea. It's probably stupid…."

"O-kay," I said, taking a drink of chocolate milkshake through the straw and setting my phone down with a sigh.

"I want Redmond," she said and then clapped a hand over her mouth, looking shocked that she'd said the words out loud. But her embarrassment was quickly replaced by a look of intense ferocity. She pushed her glasses up her nose, put her hands flat on the table, and stared at me with determination.

"What do you mean? You want to go to my school?"

"Look, I know you didn't mean to take my spot. I know it wasn't your choice. But, the fact is, it should have been *me* at Redmond, not you. That should have been *my* scholarship. And if you're not even going there for two weeks then you should let me take your place."

"*What?*" I said, staring at her in shock.

She stopped abruptly, chewing at one of her cuticles. "I applied for that scholarship a long time ago. I was so close to getting in, my grades last year were amazing, and I know I totally belong there. I aced the interview and they seemed to love me, but then I didn't get in and they wouldn't even tell me why. Then *you* just showed up and got the spot like *that* when you don't even want to go there at all."

"Oh, Casey," I said. "I had no idea. That *is* unfair. And you're right. I don't want to go at all. Your school has the archery and that's all I care about. Sure, I get good grades, but it's not like I have this burning passion to go to university or anything. I just want to concentrate on archery right now; I can always go back and get a business degree later."

We were both quiet for a moment, contemplating our fates.

"Astrid," Casey said slowly. "I know you don't owe me anything since I've been such a cow to you, although I did practically save your life by unburying you from those hay bales. But couldn't we just try it, just this once? It would only be for two weeks."

She stared at me wide-eyed and anxious, looking about half her age.

"I'm so sorry, Casey," I said, sighing, "but my dad would literally, and I do mean literally, kill me if I did anything like that. He's not nice like your dad, he's scary; I could never risk it."

She looked down at the table, tears welling in her eyes and

spilling down her cheeks. "Please, Astrid," she said. "I can't stand one more day there."

"Why, though?"

She sniffled loudly and shook her head. "Everyone is just awful. I'm the only one that even cares about making something of myself. And then I get beaten up for it. Haven't you ever wanted something so badly that's just out of your reach?"

"Yes," I said softly, not even having to hesitate to think about all the things currently right out my reach.

"Well, I want Redmond. I belong there."

She looked down, hands shaking, and my heart went out to her. She truly looked awful.

"I'm so sorry, Casey, but there's nothing I can do. I wish there was."

"Fine," she said miserably, pushing her food away, "forget I said anything."

She pulled her phone out and started tapping away furiously, not saying another word until Kade came to pick us up.

*****

Aunt Lillian was thrilled when she saw my new nose brace. "That's more like the little girl I remember," she said, pulling me in for a hug. "You'll be right as rain in no time."

I thought of telling her about my conversation with Casey, but hesitated at the last minute. It wasn't any of my business anyway.

Late that afternoon, after I woke up from my nap, I busied myself organizing the feed room in the broodmare barn. It kept me from being too impatient waiting for Justin to get home from school. I was anxious to see what he had to say about Folly.

First, I scrubbed all the brushes and brush boxes with soap and boiling water until they were free of grime, and set them out in the sunshine to dry. I didn't even have my own brushes for Folly, but Aunt Lillian had said I could use whatever I liked, so I picked out some that were in reasonably good condition and put together my own brush box with everything I needed. At some point, I would hopefully be able to brush my own horse without her trying to kill me.

I banged all the blankets clean of dust with a broom, swept the walls of spider webs and washed the grime off the first aid box. Then I cleaned all the halters and hung them carefully back up so they dangled in neat rows instead of all jumbled together. I swept the single window, and dragged all the Rubbermaid into neat rows at one end of the room. I swept the floor and stepped back to survey my work with satisfaction. *There, that's more like home.*

"Wow," Justin said, coming up behind me, "it looks like new-money in here, Astrid; we'll have to get you working on the tack room in the training barn next. Kade just throws his stuff everywhere. I, of course, am perfect." He laughed and winked at me. "You ready to introduce me to your mare?"

"Yes," I said, gulping nervously. *I have to trust him*, I told myself, *he's not going to hurt her.*

We walked in silence to Folly's paddock.

"Wait, don't lean on the fence," I warned him as he drew closer, "sometimes she bites."

"Okay." He didn't argue, and he didn't look at me like I was crazy or at her like she was a monster. He just stood a few feet back from the fence and watched her.

"Hey, Folly," I said to her. "I brought a friend for you to meet. He's not going to hurt you."

She looked up from her hay pile and snorted, watching us with distrust, ears flicking nervously back and forth.

"How do you feed her?" Justin asked quietly.

"I push it through the fence."

"Can you handle her at all at this point?"

"No," I admitted, "she'll attack me."

He nodded and stepped carefully up to the fence, leaning his arms on the top. I held my breath, waiting for an explosion, but Folly ignored us both.

"What are your goals for her?"

"To heal her up and get her back to Liza?" I said tentatively, but he shook his head.

"No, I mean your short-term goals. What do you want to be able to do with her right now?"

"Brush her," I said and sighed. "Put her blankets on, and treat her like a normal horse. Not have to watch over my shoulder to see if she's going to attack me. I'm supposed to start hand-walking her in a few weeks and I want to throw up just thinking about it. Right now, I can't even get near her."

"Sounds reasonable," Justin said. "What sort of things can you offer *her*?"

"I don't...." I stared at him blankly, thinking of all the times I'd tried to be nice to Folly and she'd rejected me. "Nothing, I guess. She hates everything."

"Keep thinking," he said casually, not taking his eyes off Folly, "there must be something."

"Well, she likes food, a lot," I said slowly. "Is that what you mean? I can offer her food, and I can hang out with her and brush her if she'd let me, and I know a bit about horse massage. I think it would help her muscles if she'd let me work on her. And, well, I guess I can offer her safety. I won't let anyone hurt her again."

"Okay." Justin looked satisfied with my answer. "You have some things to offer her then. We just have to give her some better tools for negotiating."

I sputtered with laughter. "She has *zero* negotiating skills. She would be the worst business-person ever. She would be more like a dictator having a tantrum."

"Right, she tries to get what she wants through intimidation and fear. Some horses become like that when they don't think they have any other way of communicating, and some of them are just born bossy. It's your job to show them a different way. Is she smart?"

"Very," I said, "way too smart."

"I bet. So, first, the method I'm going to suggest is going to take a lot of time and patience on your part. A lot of it. Just let me know now if that's not going to work for you."

"No, I have lots of time," I said quickly. "I'll do whatever it takes."

"Secondly, because she's learned to use her strength against humans, I want you to keep *your* sessions on the outside of the pen right now. Don't go in with her until I'm a hundred percent confident she can handle it, okay?"

"Okay," I said reluctantly. "But how can I brush her and put her blankets on and off if I can't go in there?"

"You'll just have to be patient a little longer. I'll clean her paddock once a day if you help me with my horses in the training barn. She'll be fine without a blanket for a few weeks yet. Okay?"

"Sure," I said, all images of me bonding with Folly after one session fading away.

"First of all, I'm going to clean her paddock so I can see how she reacts. I'll take a lunge whip in with me. That's not to hurt her with; it's just to keep me safe if she tries anything. Are you all right with that?"

"I think so," I said. But, honestly, nothing Justin had said had given me any reason to think he'd want to hurt Folly. I had to trust him.

Justin went to the broodmare barn and came back pushing a wheelbarrow with a manure fork and a lunge whip balanced in it. He pushed it right up to the gate and stopped.

Folly's head swung up and she laid her ears back, her lips pulled back in a snarl.

"Okay, so even outside the gate she's anticipating trouble. Her adrenaline goes up the second she has to interact with humans. Why is that?"

He looked over at me, but I just shrugged and shook my head, looking quickly down at the ground to avoid his gaze. Folly had been aggressive since long before I met her. It wasn't my fault she distrusted humans.

Isn't it? A small, cold voice in my head said, *she was starting to trust people before you and Cole took her over. She trusted you and you betrayed her.*

My breath caught as I thought of that last ride on Folly; the day of the accident. She'd been seconds away from being put down and that had mostly been my fault. She had no reason at all to trust humans at this point. Tears welled in my eyes and I took a deep shuddering breath and brought myself back to the present where Justin was still talking away.

"We want her to feel safe in her paddock, but we need to make sure she respects people's boundaries, too," he said, carefully unlatching the gate.

"Wait," I started to say but it was too late. Folly had sidled closer while he'd been talking and the second the gate opened, she lunged.

He wasn't looking directly at her, but he must have seen her coming from the corner of his eye because the moment she dove, he grabbed the whip and cracked her *hard* across the neck and chest before she could get within five feet of him. She stopped with a shocked look on her face and quickly backed up about a dozen steps.

"Good girl," he said calmly, as if nothing at all alarming had happened, "that's a good mare."

I stood there wide-eyed and shaking, wondering how on earth he could be so unmoved by all that terrifying power bearing down on him.

He glanced over at me. "She backed up a few steps, Astrid, so I'm just going to stand here and give her time to process. She needs to know that I'll never come after her and hurt her, I'm just establishing my personal space."

"Okay," I said weakly, still trying to come to terms with the fact that he'd hit her. *She attacked him, she deserved it,* I told myself. And yet, wasn't she just defending herself? Humans *had* hurt her in the past. *I'd* hurt her in the past, so how was she supposed to know who she could trust and who she couldn't.

Justin inhaled loudly and slowly let the breath out through his mouth. "A tense horse holds their breath," he said to me, "you can help them relax sometimes by regulating your own breath."

"That's what Claudia said about riding." I turned to him in surprise. "She always told me to center myself and concentrate on my breathing first, that I had to be aware of my own body before I could ask a horse to do anything."

"Yep, works the same way on the ground, go ahead and give it a whirl."

Trying not to be embarrassed, I inhaled and exhaled loudly like Justin was doing and to my surprise, Folly snorted and let out a deep breath of her own, dropping her head down and turning away slightly to lip at some fallen hay.

"Good job," he said quietly, pushing the wheelbarrow past the gate, and carefully latching it behind him without ever letting Folly out of his sight.

With a little squeal, she wheeled and kicked her hind foot in his general direction, but she was much too far away to get anywhere close to hitting him. She swirled her head around and hobbled to the other side of the pen.

"Good girl," he said again. "See, Astrid, she made a good choice there. She's allowed to have her opinions, she's allowed to pin her ears and squeal and be a mare, she's just not allowed to do it in my personal space."

Folly flattened her ears at him a few times as he quietly cleaned her paddock, but eventually she moved to the far corner by her shelter and pretended to sleep.

"See, she's smart," Justin said, once he'd finished and was

safely back on my side of the fence. "She's just the type of horse that sees everything in black and white. She needs to know the rules upfront, and once she does she'll more than likely follow them. It's the not knowing what to expect from people that drives her crazy. Now, let's work on her feeding routine. Go grab her some of that nice hay while I dump this wheelbarrow."

I did as I was told, still in shock that Folly hadn't killed him or even so much as attacked him after that first instance. It was such a big step that I nearly felt like crying with relief.

I came back with a leafy flake of timothy and went to stand with Justin who was watching Folly from about fifteen feet outside her paddock.

"Okay, new rule: she doesn't get fed unless she's polite."

"Oh, great," I said, "how do you plan to get her to do that?"

"Easy, you let her make the right choices. So, let's start walking toward her with her hay. See, ears pricked, and she looks polite and interested, so that means we keep moving. Okay, now stop." Justin laid a hand on my arm as soon as her ears flattened, and she got that ferocious-tiger look on her face. "So, you can tell by her expression that you've reached the edge of her comfort zone. That's where you start to run into issues. That angry face she's making is her warring with herself. She wants the food, but doesn't want the human that goes with it. So we stop, just like we did, and if her ears stay pinned for more than a few seconds then we take a step back."

We took a step back together and I nearly burst out laughing at the look of shock on Folly's face. Her ears shot forward and she bobbed her head, looking longingly at the hay tucked under my arm.

"Good, ears pricked means we can walk forward." Her ears wavered and then flattened, sweet Folly warring with evil Folly. "Stop. Wait. Okay, take a step back."

We repeated the same thing over and over again, two steps forward, one step back, always working our way toward her. It took forever but, in the end, I was standing next to a polite Folly who grudgingly let me push her hay through the rails without snarling at me.

"Perfect, the first couple of times seem to take forever." Justin grinned at me. "But, if you do that every time you feed her, it's going to get better and better every day. That bad behaviour will fade away and one day you won't even remember what she was like before."

"Really? It seems so, I don't know...."

"Boring, repetitive? You'll have to trust me, Astrid, if you put the work into this then she's going to reward you twenty times over. Sure, you could yell at her every time you feed her or just ignore it and risk getting bitten, but this way she's learning new behaviours herself, not just reacting to you."

"Huh?" I said.

Justin sighed. "I'm probably not the best teacher. How about I help you do feed later tonight, we'll do her grain, too, so I can see how she handles that and I'll give you some books to study so you can see if this type of training is for you."

"Oh, I'm for any training where I don't get attacked and she doesn't hate me so much," I said. "I'm probably just a slow learner."

Justin laughed. "Give yourself some credit. It takes time to learn new skills, for both you and Folly. Now, care to give me a hand with my horses?"

"Yes," I said excitedly. I'd missed working with horses like crazy. I'd always felt peaceful and fulfilled at Claudia's barn, at least until Cole had come along and ruined it.

*****

It was a good thing they had the indoor arena because, even though the sun was starting to fade, Justin had five horses to work with. My job was just to take their blankets off, brush them, put their exercise boots on, and have them waiting for him to tack up. There was no way I could even begin to lift the bulky, western saddles; even with two good arms, it would have taken all my strength to move them.

When he was done riding, he'd pull off their saddles and I'd throw a cooler over whatever horse he'd finished with and walk them at one end of the ring until they were ready to be brushed and put away.

Watching Justin ride was real interesting; it was almost like watching Liza ride. He melded seamlessly with each horse so that his aids were invisible. He rode Doc and Mina, the chestnut Badger, another buckskin named Josie, and then a young blue roan named Lexi.

All of them were easy to handle and had impeccable manners. They politely moved sideways the second I asked and followed beside me like well-behaved dogs on a leash.

In the ring, they seemed happy and willing, too. Western riding was a bit different than the dressage I was used to, but the principals of collection, suppling, and relaxation seemed roughly the same. Justin rode one handed most of the time and kept more of a loop in his reins than I was used to; almost all his aids came directly from his seat and core.

There was more of an emphasis on canter work, or lope work as he called it, and not as much time spent at the trot as at Claudia's barn. The lateral work used a lot more neck bend than I was used to, and what I'd mistaken for pirouettes were actually spins and rollbacks, which required completely different footwork than the dressage version.

"This is my last horse," Justin said as he swung up on Lexi. "You can head up to the house for dinner if you like or, if you wanted to, you could brush that chestnut down there. He's been feeling a little neglected."

"Do you mean Red?" My stomach did a flip-flop of excitement.

"That's the one. He could use a good brushing. Bring him into the ring when you're done, if you like."

I grabbed a brush box and went eagerly to his stall. He nickered in surprise when I slid his stall door open and came right over to see me, sniffing the brushes and then touching me lightly on the cheek with his soft nose. He whuffled his breath into my hair and then turned back to his hay.

I brushed him thoroughly, starting with the curry to loosen the fur and dirt on his coat and then finishing with a silky, soft goat-hair brush that made his copper coat shine. I found a bottle of show-sheen in the tack room and sprayed his mane and tail, separating out each hair until everything lay smooth and flat.

I looked up when I heard Lexi's hooves clopping up the aisle. I hadn't realized so much time had passed.

"Lead him on into the ring," Justin said, "just walk him around and I'll be there in a few minutes once this girl is put away."

I slipped Red's halter on and slowly led him to the ring. He followed me obediently enough, but he dragged his feet and went as slow as possible, his ears sagging to the side the closer we got to the ring, and his eyes closing as if he were about to fall asleep.

He walked around the ring like a zombie, nothing at all like the eager, animated horse I'd spent the last half hour brushing.

"What's wrong, boy?" I asked him, stopping and just petting his neck. He closed his eyes tighter and his head sank slowly down until it was inches off the ground.

"We're not sure, exactly," Justin said, coming into the ring. "He was your Uncle Trent's horse originally. He just went downhill after your uncle passed away. We've had him turned out for over a year; he's sound, he's fed good food, but he's so sour in the ring that nobody will buy him. He's never mean; he just looks lazy and depressed. Just take his halter off and we'll let him play a little. He perks up when he starts moving."

"Poor guy," I said, slipping his halter over his head.

Justin came up beside me, holding the lunge whip. "Here, I'll show you the basics of how I free-lunge him and then you can practice with him whenever you like. He's incredibly safe so he's a good one to play with and he needs the exercise."

I stood back while Justin clucked and shook the whip at Red's hip until the horse obediently ambled out to the rail and started to trot half-heartedly around the ring. "I'm just going to show you how, using the angles of your body, you can change his direction, speed, and rhythm."

I watched Justin closely as he put Red through his paces. The big horse picked up speed, looking happier with each passing moment. Justin hardly had to do anything to get him to step up into a canter or change directions; it was like he was communicating with him telepathically.

"Here, you try," he said, handing me the lunge whip.

"Okay," I said, chewing nervously at the inside of my cheek. I'd tried to pay attention, but I didn't feel at all confident that I could duplicate what Justin had done.

Red had stopped dead the instant Justin's focus was off him and now he stood in the corner of the ring, watching me with mild interest as I approached.

"Um, walk, please," I said tentatively, pointing the tip of the whip at his haunch.

To my surprise, he moved into a slow shuffle across the ring.

"It worked," I said, smiling triumphantly at Justin.

"Of course it worked." He laughed. "Try for a trot."

"Uh, trot?" I said. "Off you go, Red, get-up, ter-rot. Please?" But he steadily kept plodding around the ring.

"You need more animation, Astrid," Justin called. "I don't think he believes you. You're inviting him to play with you so start trotting."

Invite him to play? I thought. *What does that mean?* Suddenly, I remembered what the horses on pasture looked like when the wind blew across the fields and they'd all be charged at once with the same electrifying urge to run. Their heads would shoot up and they'd power off together as one unit, moving and turning in harmony like a flock of birds. Keeping that memory in my head I began trotting toward Red, waving the whip up and down and not caring how silly I looked. "Trot, Red."

The horse opened his eyes wide as if I'd suggested something shocking and stepped away from me, snorting and breaking into an energetic trot as if he'd tapped into a hidden well of power. He transformed into a completely different horse.

"Great job," Justin said, "keep it up."

We trotted three times around the big ring and by that time, I was puffing with exhaustion. I was doing way more work than Red was.

"Ask him to change directions, just come across the ring here and block him with your body, then point the whip at his head and shoulder."

Red faltered, not sure what I was asking, but then he swerved and took off in a trot the other direction.

"Well done. A few more circuits and then ask him to halt."

"How?" I asked.

"Just make it inviting to stop," he said simply, which I thought was the vaguest direction he could possibly give.

I brought my energy down and moved into an easy walk and, after a few seconds, Red copied me and did the same thing.

"Good boy," I called, "easy boy, you can stop now. Just whoa, Red."

I halted and, to my delight, he stopped, too, twitching his inside ear toward me.

"Come on, Red," I called, walking away from him toward Justin, "let's go in, buddy."

He didn't follow me right away, just stood watching me quizzically, but when I picked up his halter he bobbed his head and marched over to where we stood.

"Wow, you're such a good boy, Red," I told him, petting him all over.

"You're good with him, Astrid. I think you'll make a nice

team. He can be your project, if you like."

"Really? Yeah, I'd like that. As long as Aunt Lillian doesn't mind. I don't want to accidentally ruin him or anything."

"Oh, I don't think you have to worry about that."

Even though it wasn't perfect, it had been an exciting experience. It reminded me of my first lesson with Claudia. From the outside, nothing much had happened and yet, it felt exhilarating, like a door to a whole new world had opened up in front of me. For the first time since losing Quarry, I felt that tranquil happiness that came with working with a horse as a partner.

"Thank you," I whispered quietly to Red when I had him all tucked into his stall for the night. He rested his nose gently on my arm and blinked his eyes sleepily a few times. "Goodnight."

Chapter Five

Justin said he'd drive me back up to the house; it was already dark outside and I hoped Aunt Lillian wasn't mad that I was out here so late. We'd never talked about when I should be home for dinner and it wasn't like I could text her to let her know.

We fed all the horses their dinner and then went to do Folly last.

Tossing the horses their hay was much easier here than at Claudia's; we didn't have any hay nets to tie up and no water buckets to fill or dump since these guys all had huge tubs outside in their paddocks.

Folly stood waiting impatiently for us when we arrived to feed her dinner. But her eagerness made the session go faster; I guessed she was more motivated when she was hungry. It took us half the time to get her to stand nicely for her hay. Then we went back for her grain.

"Feeding grain is where she can get scary," I warned. "She's greedy."

"No problem, we'll just work with what we have," Justin said, not looking worried at all. "We don't change our program, we just get more patient."

I needed more than patience to make it through the tantrum that followed. Folly started out perfectly, and it wasn't until we were about five feet away that she flattened her ears for the first time. And then when we stepped back, she completely lost her mind. She squealed, she bucked, she flung herself against the fence. She bared her teeth and snorted and crashed around like a wild animal.

"She's going to hurt herself," I groaned, chewing anxiously on my thumb nail. "She's going to damage her tendons or break a leg. Maybe we should do this another night when she's feeling better."

"Hang in there," Justin said tranquilly, "she's almost done. She just has a lot to say. Trust me."

Finally, Folly stopped for breath and, for just a second, her ears flicked forward questioningly.

"There," he whispered, "step forward."

We made it another three steps before she let out another angry squeal and swirled her head. She gave us a deadly stare.

"Just wait for her," Justin said.

Instead of flattening her ears again, Folly snorted, dropped her head and yawned, her eyes rolling back in her head, and then she shook her whole body and watched us approach, her eyes soft.

"Good mare," Justin said quietly, gently pushing her bucket under the fence. Folly stuck her nose in it, but she didn't seem as angry as she usually did when she ate, not like she was guarding her food. She looked, well, almost happy.

"That's perfect, now let's give her some space."

"Wow," I breathed, "that was amazing. She totally transformed into a different horse."

Justin smiled at me, but didn't say much more until we'd driven back to Aunt Lillian's. "Here," he said, handing me a thick book as I slid out of the truck. "You should read this. It will tell you everything you need to know. Let me know when you're done because I have about twenty more where that came from."

"Operant Conditioning and Reward-Based Training? Um, why does this book have a man in a wetsuit on the cover and why is he petting a walrus? This doesn't seem to have much to do with horses."

Justin burst out laughing. "It's just another term for force-free training, Astrid. And the concepts were originally developed by handlers of marine and zoo animals, large creatures you can't move around with force. Horses have a lot in common with them."

I looked down at the walrus's smiling face skeptically. "Okay, if you say so. I'll read it."

"Good, now I have to leave early for school tomorrow, but if you can be at the barn by six then I can help you with breakfast."

"Thanks," I said gratefully. "I'll be there."

Aunt Lillian wasn't mad at all about dinner. "I figured you'd be out late once you started working with those horses," she said laughing. "That's usually what happens around here."

She'd cooked a roast and some crispy baked potatoes and steamed vegetables. She even had the delicious melt-in-your-mouth biscuits again.

When she asked me about Folly, I was enthusiastic for the first time.

"She's great," I said happily. "I think she's finally settling in. And Justin let me work with that chestnut, Red."

"Oh?" Aunt Lillian said, her lips tightening.

"Is…is that okay?" *Please don't tell me to stop working with him*, I thought, crossing my fingers.

"I guess so," she said and shook her head before laughing low under her breath. "But we have better, fancier horses here if you want to work with someone else."

"No," I said quickly. "I like him best. Please."

She looked over at me in surprise, eyebrows raised. "Well, he's safe enough, anyway. Yep, you work with him as much as you like."

"Thanks," I said, exhaling the breath I didn't know I'd been holding. "I appreciate it."

Chapter Six

I woke up and stretched luxuriously, humming a tune under my breath as I got ready in the chilly morning air.

I had a great day planned: I was going to do the training sessions with Folly, after breakfast I'd take my laptop to the barn, figure out the dial-up thing and send some emails, and then work on reading the book Justin had loaned me. I'd gotten part-way through it the night before, but it was dense reading and I didn't have my computer to look up the terms I didn't know. I'd made a list of them to research today. How on earth had people learned anything before the internet?

It was actually cold when I crept downstairs. I took a few apples from the bowl in the kitchen, grabbed a headlamp off the shelf by the door, and pulled on my boots. I wished I had a jacket, but I had to make do with my one long-sleeved shirt and a thin hoodie.

The sound of clicking claws let me know that Jake was headed my way. "Do you want to come for a walk, buddy?" I asked, grateful for the company. It was awfully dark out for a walk in the woods all by myself.

The darkness wasn't scary with Jake trotting along beside me like a sentinel. We reached the top of the hill above Folly's paddock just as the first blue streaks of light spread across the sky.

"Morning, Folly," I said, moving past her, heading toward the barn. I was used to her either ignoring me or snarling when she saw me, but today, to my surprise, she followed quietly along the fence-line and stood at the gate, watching while I walked away.

Huh, I thought, *something's changed.*

I turned on the outdoor floodlights so I could see her standing in her paddock and went to the feed room to mix her breakfast.

"All ready, Astrid?" Justin stood in the doorway smiling and I gaped at him, hardly recognizing him without his regular jeans, boots, and hat.

"Wow, you look…good," I said, then blushed furiously. I'd meant it as a compliment, but it came out sounding silly.

"Not too citified?" he joked. "Come on, I'm here for moral support, but you get to do the dirty work. I can't get covered in dust and horse slobber before class."

I laughed, set Folly's bucket down in the barn aisle, and went to get her hay.

"Don't be disappointed if she's back to square one," Justin said. "This takes endless patience and you have to work at their speed, not ours, okay?"

"No problem," I said, clamping a flake of hay under my arm and picking up her bucket. I was getting to be an expert at juggling things with one arm. At about fifteen feet away I set her bucket down and, at Justin's nod, started walking toward her with the hay. Ears forward, ears back, ears forward, ears back, squeal, buck, ears forward; and repeat. We only had to go through that twice before she got her hay, and it didn't take nearly as long for her grain as it had yesterday. Within ten minutes, Folly was just a normal horse eating breakfast happily in her paddock. Well, almost normal.

"Okay, this is kind of amazing," I said as I walked Justin to his truck. "I think it's working."

"It always does." He grinned and sent me a smile. "Horses are like a puzzle; you patiently work on them piece by piece until it all comes together. You'll be friends with her in no time."

Friends, I thought, *maybe like Quarry and I were friends.* I'd never thought of Folly like that, but now I had a tiny glimmer of what that might look like in the future. *Maybe.*

I was singing when I got back to the house. The long walk had made me hungry, and the smell of eggs and hash browns met me at the front door, pulling me toward the kitchen.

"Eat up, Astrid," Aunt Lillian said as I washed the dirt off my hands at the kitchen sink. I eyed up her skillet with open glee. She placed a heaping plate of food down at my place at the table. "We have a busy day ahead of us."

"Oh, sure, I was just going to get some reading done and check my emails—"

"Plenty of time for that later," my aunt interrupted. "With Justin at school all day we're more short-handed than ever and I need you to pitch in. Bryce has his hands full getting ready for their big trip to California so Kade's doing all his chores. That means we're on our own today. We're going to check on the broodmares and take hay to horses and cows out on pasture.

There's not enough for them to eat out there right now so we have to supplement with hay. Do you know how to drive?"

"What? No. I'm not old enough."

"Oh, well, that doesn't matter out here. Driving around on the ranch is the best way to learn; you have 1000 acres of wide-open spaces to practice on. Casey can drive already, and I dare say Olive will learn before too long. I guess country kids mature faster than city kids."

I raised my eyebrows at her, but didn't say anything. Casey didn't exactly strike me as a model of maturity.

"Besides, I don't like the idea of you walking down that path by yourself for much longer. It's fine now, but soon it will be dark in the mornings and at night. You'd be a prime target for cougars and bears."

"Bears?" I looked up.

"Oh, these hills are full of predators: bears, cougars, you know. You should probably take Jake with you when you're wandering around by yourself."

Great, I thought. *I've been wandering around by myself for days. I could have been eaten at any moment; what other dangers had Aunt Lillian neglected to tell me about?* I looked skeptically over at Jake who was staring longingly up at my aunt, a string of drool hanging from his muzzle. Despite his size, I had the feeling he wasn't going to be a heck of a lot of help against any predators.

After breakfast we piled into the truck and drove down to the gigantic hay barn that stood off by itself on the far side of the training barn. Aunt Lillian threw open the huge double doors, revealing stacks of giant round bales of hay. They were huge, each one standing higher than my head.

"Drop the tail gate, Astrid. I'm going to load a couple of these guys."

She disappeared into the barn while I struggled with my passenger side door, and then struggled for even longer to get the stupid, rusted tail gate latch to open. Why was everything on this ranch ten times more difficult than they were at home?

By the time I'd done that, Aunt Lillian was lurching toward me on an old blue tractor, carrying a round bale impaled on some sort of deadly-looking tractor-spike high in the air.

"Stand back," she yelled and then neatly dumped a bale into the truck bed before going back for the next one. I stood way back and watched in awe as she easily maneuvered the tractor around. The old truck sagged under the weight, its tires bulging in an ominous looking way.

"All right, get in, you're driving."

"Oh, but I can't," I said, before I could stop myself. "I'm injured."

I was rewarded with a disapproving frown. "Astrid, hop in," she said firmly.

"Fine," I said before she could launch into a lecture about city kids not having any life skills. I slid into the driver's seat and slammed my door harder than was necessary.

"Good, now you go as slow as you like, Astrid. We're not in a hurry so take your time. Gas is there, brake is there, and steering is there. Keys are in the ignition. You'll figure it out."

It took me about five minutes to figure out how to even start the thing. Our cars at home just had a little button you pushed to start them. This thing had keys stuck in the steering wheel and you had to turn it hard all the way to the front and hold it there while it considered whether it wanted to start or not. All the while, Aunt Lillian stared out the passenger side window as if she didn't know I was struggling.

Finally, after some coughing and wheezing, the truck roared to life, but when I gingerly stepped on the gas pedal it made a revving sound without moving forward. I tried a few more times and then turned to look at my aunt in exasperation.

"Oh," she said, "sorry, I should have told you how to put it in gear, I guess. Foot on the brake and then move this lever until the D is lit up. D is for drive," she added helpfully.

"Great, thanks." My voice came out more sarcastically than I'd meant. I saw now where Casey had developed her attitude.

I wrestled the lever and then, ever so slowly eased off the brake and was rewarded by the truck lurching forward a few feet. Despite being annoyed with my aunt, I couldn't help but grin at her. She smiled back and gave me a gentle slap on the shoulder.

"And just like that, you are a driver." She laughed.

We lurched across the pasture at a snail's speed with Aunt Lillian only telling me which direction to head in. She got out whenever we reached a gate and waved me on through and shut it behind us. The sun was shining, the air was warm but not boiling, and I was enjoying myself.

"Okay, we'll get the cow pasture over with quickly and then move on to the horses. Just park up on that hill there. That's right. P is for park."

I restrained myself from an eye roll; I wasn't a complete idiot.

"Now, stand hard on the brake for a minute, it's liable to roll backwards if you don't; that emergency brake rusted out last winter. I'm just going to get the rock from the backseat."

I held my foot on the brake and turned to see her out of the truck and fishing around on the floor behind the passenger seat.

"Ah, here it is," she said triumphantly, holding up a large white rock in both hands. "Let me just set it behind the back tire and then we can push that bale out."

I had no idea what she was talking about, but since she was now crouching down behind the back tire, I stomped on the brake for all I was worth so I didn't run her over.

"All right, good girl, just pop out here and give me a hand."

I carefully eased off the brake, yelping when the truck gave a small lurch backward before, presumably, hitting the rock, and then clambered outside. Aunt Lillian was already up inside the bed of the truck and had squeezed herself in between the two giant bales of hay.

"Okay, hop up in here and we'll push this guy out. We want to get this done quickly before *they* come."

"Before who comes?" I asked, staring up at her incredulously. How on earth was I was supposed to get up there?

"The cows, of course. Climb the *tire*," she said impatiently, as if it were completely obvious. "Come on, we haven't got all day."

I obediently put my feet up on the tire and then somehow, mostly by grunting and sweating, heaved myself into the bed of the truck.

"Put your shoulder into it," my aunt commanded, pushing her body weight against the giant bale. "They're on to us."

I glanced up and saw, on the horizon, a herd of fat, brown and white cows moving slowly toward us at a leisurely pace. They didn't *look* very intimidating.

"Let's go," she snapped. "I want to get out of here before they get any closer."

Her energy was contagious, and we heaved at the bale, using shoulders, feet, and knees until finally, impossibly, it toppled off the edge of the truck.

The cows were closer now, a smaller one picked up a trot and some of the other's followed along.

"Astrid, get in the truck," my aunt said, giving me a little push. "We need to get out of here."

The lead cows picked up speed and Aunt Lillian leapt to the ground and scrabbled for her rock. I moved as fast as I could and had the truck in drive and ready to go by the time she was back inside.

"Hit the gas, Astrid," she said, dropping the giant rock onto the floor at her feet. I wasn't exactly ready to start speeding at this stage in my driving career; I was using one hand plus the tips of my fingers of the casted arm to steer. But a few minutes of careful maneuvering over the bumpy path and we'd left the cow pasture far behind.

"Phew, I'm glad that part's over with," my aunt said, flopping back in her seat. "Next stop, broodmares."

I was too busy clutching the wheel in a death-grip to keep the truck moving in a straight line to ask questions, but part of my mind wondered why she'd started acting so strange. Why had the cows scared her so much?

Down by the lake where the grass wasn't completely dead stood a herd of the fattest, gentlest horses I'd ever met. We parked down close to the water and, once we'd heaved the second hay bale off, I went from horse to horse, stroking their soft noses and straightening out their long, tangled manes.

"They've been running wild all spring and summer," my aunt said affectionately, scratching a tall, sharp-boned, chestnut behind the ears. "The babies were weaned a few months ago. They'll stay out here happily until the temperature drops and the snow sets in, then we'll have to bring them inside. I'm sure we'll have our hands full taking care of them all this year."

"They're beautiful," I said, "and they look so happy."

"They should be, they have cushy lives here. Hey now, Beezy, are you going to have a filly or a colt this year?" She leaned down and kissed the chestnut right on the forehead, a move that surprised me. "Astrid, I'm glad you like them. The breeding side of the operation has always been my special project. Trent liked the training and showing, but I just liked these sweet ladies and the little ones."

"Aunt Lillian, which horse is yours? I mean, I know they're all yours, but which one do you ride the most?"

"Actually," she said, running her hand down Beezy's leg to examine a small cut just below her knee, "I don't ride anymore."

"You don't?" I stared at her in surprise.

"Nope. After your uncle died, I lost interest, I guess. Not in the horses themselves," she added quickly, "just in riding. It was something we always did together. This ranch was our dream, and without him the dream lost most of its lustre."

"Oh," I said, turning to pet a black mare who was gently searching my pocket for treats. "I'm sorry."

"So am I. But that's all in the past now; time to move forward."

We had to go back and get hay from the big barn and repeat

the process three more times before everyone had been fed. Besides the cows and the broodmares, there were foals and young horses separated into various age groups, and older ranch horses loafing together on a hillside.

"We don't start the young ones until there's an interested buyer or we have room in the sales barn for new projects," my aunt explained. "We have too many to keep up with right now. Bryce and the boys can only do so much, and this time of year is always slow for sales. Most of our business happens in the spring."

Despite being mainly unhandled, all the young horses were friendly and interested in seeing what we'd brought for them. The little weanlings with their fuzzy coats and sticking up forelocks and manes were my favourite. They pushed around us, jostling to get close while Donkey looked on, supervising his tiny herd like a proud parent. They were all adorable: mostly chestnuts and buckskins with some palominos, blacks, and a bay thrown in. I couldn't imagine how a potential buyer could stand in the middle of this herd and choose just one of them. I'd end up taking them all home.

By the time we had finished, I was limp with exhaustion, sweaty, and extremely itchy from the bits of hay that stuck to my arms and my neck. Some had even managed to work inside my clothes next to my sweaty skin. Starting school was suddenly looking better and better.

*****

Justin had told me that Folly would learn fastest if I did a series of short sessions with her throughout the day. I'd decided to feed her a bunch of small meals instead of dumping all her hay at once. I was exhausted after our busy morning, but I made sure to make that long walk to the barn twice more so that Justin would see how much better she'd gotten just in a day.

She was a fast learner, and by the last feeding she stood politely until I got right to the fence and pushed her hay through. Only then did she snatch it out of my hands like a tiger. It was a work in progress.

"You're doing a great job," Justin said, when he got home from school and started working on her paddock, "this is the beginning of having a conversation with her. You're laying down the groundwork for a relationship."

I didn't understand everything he said, but I listened as well as I could, and I tried to copy the way he was around Folly, his confident body language and his aura of perfect calm. He never got upset, never seemed afraid or lost his temper with her, even when she made awful faces at him from the other side of her paddock.

I wonder what Liza would think of him, I thought. *I bet she'd like him; they're so much alike.*

Folly hadn't charged the gate when he'd opened it this time, although she'd definitely thought about it. She'd glided up and sidled smoothly past him like a shark, eyes bright with devilish anticipation. But as soon as he clucked gently under his breath, she'd squealed in irritation and hobbled away to eat her hay. After that, she'd only looked up from time to time to keep track of his location, but she hadn't bothered him at all.

"That's so much better," I said when he'd brought the wheel-barrow out, "when do you think we can start doing ground-work with her?"

"Baby steps," he said, "we do an infinite number of baby-steps. We move at her pace. She'll tell us when she's ready."

After that, we fell back into yesterday's easy routine of me grooming and him riding, and then I brushed Red and gave him another slow-motion work out. By the end of that session, I was again puffing and red in the face; Red knew how to make me work.

*****

Since Bryce was away until late, Aunt Lillian had invited the rest of the family over again for a late dinner, and I helped her make a giant lasagna with about twelve layers of meat and cheese in it.

Then, while she whipped up another insanely delicious pie— this one with strawberries and rhubarb—I made salad and garlic bread, something I actually knew how to make without needing any direction.

Just before everyone arrived, the phone shrilled its awful scream from the wall right beside my head, making me jump.

"Oh, please get that, Astrid," my aunt said, "my hands are still covered in flour."

"Hello, uh, Triple Hills?" I said, speaking into the receiver gingerly.

"Astrid, is that you? It's Marion. I hope I'm not interrupting anything."

"Oh, hi," I said, unexpectedly happy to hear her voice, "no, we're just having dinner."

"Hello, sweetheart, I don't have much time, but I just wanted to tell you the good news. Your father and I talked over your request and we've decided that you can choose the school that you like. You can go to the local school if that's what you want."

"Seriously?" I said, dancing up and down in excitement. "You'd really do that? Thank you so much!"

"You're welcome. We do want you to be happy, darling, and if this is what makes your year away from home better then we're willing to go along with it."

"Wow, I can hardly believe it, thank you."

"It's your choice, darling, but are you absolutely sure you want to go to this school? You've thought it through?"

"Yes," I said quickly, "I have."

She sighed. "Well, then that's what we'll do. Are you feeling well enough to start on Monday? They'd prefer you to start as early as possible."

"I think so," I said. "I was going to wait, but if it means that I can start archery then I'll go whenever you like."

Marion's soft laugh echoed down the line. "Well, as long as you feel up to it. I'll call the school tomorrow. We're off to a meeting now, Astrid. I'll call you after the weekend to check in."

"Aunt Lillian," I said, after I'd hung up, "I get to go to the school with the archery. I'm so excited."

"Well, that is wonderful. Sounds like everything is working out fine for you then."

I practically hummed my way through dinner, caught up in the delirious excitement of everything falling into place for me. This whole year was going to be full of horses, archery, and amazing food. What could wrong now?

I pulled Casey aside right after dinner to tell her the good news. She'd been quiet and withdrawn all night; she'd hardly eaten at all.

"That's great news," she said dully, as soon as I told her. "I'm happy for you, although why you'd want to go to a stupid school like Triple Hills is beyond me."

"Casey," I said firmly, "this means that maybe you can go to Redmond. They have the space, so I bet you'd get in now."

Her eyes lit up for a second and then dimmed. She shrugged. "I don't know, they didn't let me in last time. And my dad will probably say no."

"Come on," I said, giving her shoulder a little shake, "you have to at least try. This might be your chance. I thought you'd be excited."

"Yeah," she said, looking more animated, "I guess you're right. I'll ask him. Thanks, Astrid."

She gave me a quick hug.

Chapter Seven

The next morning, I got up early again and headed down to the barn to meet Justin. Part of me felt bad about making him get up so early before school, but the other part of me just wanted to spend as much time as I could working with him. I felt like I learned something new every minute I spent with him.

Today, Folly seemed even more mellow. She nickered softly under her breath when Jake and I came down the hill, and followed me eagerly down the fence line as I headed to the barn to get her breakfast.

Justin thought she looked better, too.

"She's doing great," he said. "Now we're going to ask her one more thing. Before you push the hay through the fence, you're going to wait until she turns her head slightly away from you. She won't like it at first, but she'll understand what you want fairly quickly. It's a sign of respect when one horse yields to another. It can be very subtle so just watch for it. I'll tell you when to push the hay through the fence."

"Okay," I said uncertainly. I wondered why we were pushing a new behaviour on Folly when she was acting so good. Wasn't that only going to upset her and wreck everything?

She kept her ears pricked right until I stood about a foot from the fence and then she stuck her nose through the bars and tried to grab the hay from my hands.

"Back up one small step," Justin said quietly, and I moved back obediently even though my instinct was to feed her the hay she obviously wanted so badly.

Folly stuck her head out further, pinning her ears and squealing in irritation. She couldn't reach me, but the anger and frustration in her eyes was scary. It took everything I had not to chuck her the hay and run.

"Just wait for it," Justin said, and like clockwork, she stopped pushing on the fence and stood back, staring at me quizzically. "Wait for it."

Folly bobbed her nose up and down a few times and then tipped her head slightly back toward her shoulder. "There. Give her the hay."

I breathed a sigh of relief and threw her hay in. She didn't look upset at all; in fact, she looked pleased with herself.

"I…I don't understand what just happened," I said. "Why did we do that?"

"She's not allowed to mug you for food, Astrid. When she reaches forward and grabs the hay from you like that, you're basically telling her that it's okay to aggressively invade your space any time she likes. When she tips her head away or yields, then she's giving you permission to enter *her* space. It sort of turns the tables on her and puts you on equal footing in the relationship. Does that make sense?"

"It does," I said thoughtfully. "Everything is so subtle,

though, how do you even know all of this stuff?"

"I was born into it," he said. "You've seen my dad ride, and my mom's a big-name trainer in the states; she tours all over teaching symposiums with her hotshot new boyfriend. She's much better with animals than she is with humans." He laughed self-consciously. "I've got to run, see you tonight."

"Thanks again!" I called after him. I wondered what he'd meant by that comment about his mom. I knew she was some trainer in California, but everyone had been pretty vague about her. Out of all of Bryce's kids, only Olive seemed to like her.

I raked the hay out of the barn aisle and soaked beet pulp for Folly's dinner. I looked at my watch, but it was still so early. I wasn't sure if Aunt Lillian would even be up yet.

"Come on, Jake," I called, "let's go see if we can help out at the other barn."

To my surprise, a big metal pipe-rail corral like Folly's had been set up in front of the training barn. Two dozen red and white cows stood in there, all eating hay at the far end.

I paused to watch them, leaning on the fence and resting my head against the metal bars.

"Don't get too close to them," a voice said right by my ear. "They'll get you."

I jumped then rubbed my elbow where I'd banged it sharply against the fence. "Ow. Do you always creep up on people like that?"

"Sorry." Kade laughed. "Just playing with you."

"Are they really dangerous? They look harmless."

"Naw, they're okay. I mean, any big animal can squish you…." He stopped abruptly, colour rising into his cheeks.

"That was a stupid thing to say, sorry, Astrid."

"Um, it's okay?" I said, not understanding his embarrassment. We stood in an increasingly uncomfortable silence until I thought of something to say.

"Casey's going to reapply to Redmond now that I'm not going," I said. "I hope she gets in."

"I guess so, it seems like a lot of effort to me, but she seems to want it badly."

"Couldn't your dad just send her there if she wants to go so much? She seems miserable at her school now."

He frowned and shook his head. "It's expensive, Astrid, and Casey's only fourteen. Dad thinks she should stick it out at her own school, which is perfectly fine by the way, and then she can transfer over when she's older and knows what she wants. He just doesn't want to pay out all that money and then have her change her mind. Casey's stubborn, though; she probably won't."

I felt a gentle bump against my hand and looked up to see one of the cows standing next to the fence, looking at me expectantly with dark, shining eyes.

I reached out tentatively to touch its fluffy coat and was surprised at how soft it felt. It leaned into my touch, and I reached up to scratch it behind the ears.

"Oh, it's so friendly," I said, "and soft. It's beautiful."

"They're good looking animals, that's for sure. Lillian has a great breeding program. The carcass quality is top notch."

"Carcass…ew…you mean like their body parts?"

"Uh, yeah, that's kind of why we have cows, Astrid. For eating."

"Oh, but this one's so nice," I said, stroking the cow's wide, fat blaze. "How can you eat the ones that have this much personality?"

"I'm sure they *all* have personalities," Kade said with a laugh. "He's probably one of the ones we had to bottle feed last year. It makes them super friendly. Don't get too attached, though, he and his friends here are leaving tomorrow. They'll get fattened up and be steaks and hamburgers next."

"Oh!" I drew my hand back. "That's awful."

"Why? He'll taste great. And he had a good life here. Wouldn't you rather eat something that ran around on pasture instead of locked up on a factory farm somewhere?"

"I'd rather not eat them at all."

"Well, then you'll have to become a vegetarian, I guess. You were tucking into that bacon pretty good the other day, though, so let me know how that works for you."

The cow reached out and bumped me with his cold, wet nose, and I gave in and went back to scratching him.

"Aunt Lillian was afraid of them yesterday," I said, "when we were bringing them their hay. Why doesn't she like them?"

Kade froze, his face dark with emotion. "You aunt has her reasons," he said gruffly. "But, if you keep your distance from them, you won't get hurt. I've got to go, I have work to do."

"Wait, do you need help? I could groom—"

"Nope!" he called over his shoulder. "I got it covered."

With that, he turned abruptly and stalked toward the barn, leaving me behind.

Well, that was strange. I thought, watching Kade walk away. *Very strange.*

Chapter Eight

Since nobody seemed to need my help with the horses, I finally got to spend a day reading and catching up on emails.

Aunt Lillian had told me she would be holed up in the office in the big barn most of the day, so I gathered up my books and my laptop, and tagged along with her.

I stopped to say hello to Red and feed him an apple before I followed my aunt to the office.

There were two cushy green leather chairs in the office and we each pulled up one on opposite sides of the big wooden desk. I set up my laptop and keyed in the password for the dial-up internet that my aunt had given me, and waited impatiently for it to connect; which took about a thousand years.

"I wish I knew more about computers," my aunt said from her seat across from me, "Bryce was kind enough to set up our website, but he's too busy to update it all the time."

"What do you need updated?" I tapped my fingers impatiently as my laptop laboured away to make a connection with the outside world.

"Oh, we're way behind on the sale photos. The pictures we

have are almost a year out of date and only about half the herd is listed. I wish I'd gotten caught up on it this summer like I'd intended."

I looked up with interest and then stood up to come around and look at the website.

"Wow, that looks so good," I said, peering over her shoulder. The photographs must have been taken in greener times because the whole ranch was transformed into a lush vista of pastures. "Is that what the ranch looks like in the spring?"

Aunt Lillian laughed and nodded. "Sure does, this heat-wave has certainly done a number on our scenery. But it's not those photos that I care about. It's the horses.

"All these need to be marked as sold," she said, pointing to a screen full of horses I didn't recognize, "and then the current stock needs to be added. We should have every horse on here, even the broodmares, just for reference. I'd hoped to do it this summer when they were looking their best, but I guess it will have to wait until next year now."

"Oh, well, could I do it for you?" I asked curiously. I had a bit of time left until school officially started for me and I had some free time on my hands.

"I don't see why not," Aunt Lillian said thoughtfully. "Yes, that would be very helpful, thanks, Astrid. I'll lend you my camera and if you can start by taking photos of all the horses then I can get Bryce to show you how to upload them to the website when he gets back from California. I'm not sure how he does it and I don't want to bother him now."

"Sure," I said, "I can start any time."

We spent the rest of the day quietly. I wrote huge gigantic

emails to Hilary, Rob, Marion, Claudia, and even to my old archery coach, Earl, which were practically novels, telling them all about my time here and filling them with descriptions that I just couldn't fit into my scattered texts.

Once I was done with that, I sat quietly and read my training books, writing down anything useful on a pad of paper. I slowly copied a diagram of a horse standing with concentric circles drawn around it, like layers of an onion.

Justin had told me that I not only needed to understand how my position on the ground impacted each horse I was working with, but also how each horse had a different-sized space bubble, or awareness zone, that I had to take into account.

With a horse like Red, you could walk almost right up to him before he reacted, but a horse like Folly had a comfort zone that was like twenty, or more, feet away from her, and a true wild horse might have a zone that was miles and miles wide.

I didn't entirely understand what he was talking about, but I did know that Folly could get very angry at me when I wasn't even anywhere near her. I hoped we could figure it out.

Chapter Nine

Saturday morning, I leapt out of bed, and then yelped as my feet touched the cold wood floor. I grabbed a pair of wool socks out of my top drawer and hastily slipped them over my frozen feet then tiptoed to the window and was surprised to find a thin layer of frost covering the ground.

Folly was shivering when I reached her paddock and I decided today was the day I would learn how to put her blankets on. I couldn't let her go through a whole winter like this.

I fed her breakfast and then climbed up on the fence to watch her eat. Justin had said he was going to sleep in this morning, but that he'd help me work with her after lunch. I had no idea what he had planned.

I reached out tentatively and ran my fingers through Folly's lengthening mane. She shivered at my touch and for a second I froze, holding my breath and waiting for an attack that never came. Gradually, I let my breath out and moved my fingers gently over her withers again. This time she shifted closer and it almost felt like she leaned into my touch. A clump of hair loosened under my scratching fingernails and fell off.

"Oh, Folly, you're filthy," I said softly. "And you're losing your summer coat. You're a little late to be shedding; hopefully you grow a nice, thick winter one to replace it."

I carefully slipped off the fence, not making any sudden moves that would put her on her guard.

She was still in the same place when I came back with a box of brushes and I pulled out the small rubber curry comb and cautiously climbed the fence again.

She didn't even look up when I started gingerly working the brush in circles over her withers, but now she definitely leaned into my hand. Bits of dirt and hair fell to the ground with every stroke and I shifted down the fence so I could work on her topline and reach down to do the shoulder closest to me. I lost myself in the grooming routine and only looked up to check her face from time to time to make sure she was still content to not kill me. She was happy; she chewed her hay with her eyes half-closed, and now and then heaved a sigh of contentment.

I carefully switched from the round curry to a straight one so I could sweep all the loosened dirt and hair off her in short, smooth strokes. The little teeth of the brush must have felt good because she leaned into the brushing even harder and twitched her upper lip when I hit an especially itchy spot.

I brushed everywhere in reach and then moved on to a softer body brush, bringing the shine back into her now-dusty coat. Then I carefully ran the mane comb through her disorderly hair until it lay flat against her neck. When I was done I stepped back and surveyed her with satisfaction. At least one side of her was clean anyway. I would just avoid looking at the other side.

"Hey, nice job." Justin stood a few feet behind me, surveying

Folly with a pleased look. "She sure cleans up nice."

"Thanks, she loved it," I said. "She used to like being brushed, especially when Liza did it."

"Sounds like she trusted Liza."

"Oh, she did. She loved her."

"Well, how about if I see how she feels about the halter and you could try brushing the other side?"

"Really? Do you think she's ready?"

"Only one way to find out," he said with a grin.

He already had her halter and a lead rope slung over his shoulder, and he slowly went to the gate and eased it open.

"Hey, Folly," he said as she swung her head around to look at him. She stared at him mildly, still relaxed from her grooming session. Her ears flickered uncertainly, but she didn't look angry; she was more interested in what he was doing.

He walked slowly toward her, only stopping when her head came up and she got that wary, defensive look on her face.

"So, you can see that she's showing me I've reached the edge of her comfort zone," he said to me. "This is the distance that she feels comfortable with humans in her space. You always want to respect, or at least acknowledge, that distance."

"But, that's like twenty feet away from her," I said. "How am I supposed to get closer to her if she doesn't want people in her space?"

"It's not an impenetrable force field, Astrid." He laughed. "You can cross over into her personal space. You just have to acknowledge that it's uncomfortable for her. Just like if someone walked straight up to you and stood two inches away from your face to talk to you. If a stranger did that, you'd feel threatened and you'd probably get either scared or angry."

"Yeah, like Kade," I said without thinking. "He always stands too close."

Justin shot me a strange look. "He's not one for recognizing boundaries," he said slowly. "But he does listen if you tell him to back off."

He went on when I didn't respond. "But if it was someone you liked that got too close, then you wouldn't feel threatened, or not as much anyway."

"So, I change my relationship with Folly and she won't be so defensive when I move into her space?"

"Exactly, it will help, anyway. When I'm walking toward her, I pay attention to her body language. When she looks uncomfortable, I pause and maybe even back up a step. There, watch her expression."

When he backed up toward the gate, her defensive posture immediately relaxed, and she swung her head back toward him, looking surprised and interested. When he walked forward again, he was able to take a few more steps into her bubble before she tensed up again. Again, he paused and waited for her to relax, when she didn't, he backed up another step and, like magic, she dropped her head and nibbled at some hay.

"See, when you take the time to even acknowledge their comfort zones, they feel like they're being heard and respected. Lots of people just march right up to a horse and strap a halter on its head without caring what that must feel like to the horse. A well-trained horse can handle being treated like that, even though they might not like it. But for wild horses, or sensitive horses like Folly, it drives them crazy."

When he got right up next to Folly, she backed up a few steps, snorting like she didn't know how to handle the situation. She didn't attack, though, and she didn't pin her ears at him.

He smiled slowly and pulled a horse cookie out of his pocket and offered it to her. She reached her neck way out and cautiously lipped it off his hand, watching him closely while she crunched it between her teeth.

To my surprise, Justin didn't reach out and put her halter on. Instead, he backed away and went to the other side of her paddock. Folly looked surprised and took a few tentative steps after him, before turning back to her hay.

"She did great," he said, coming over to stand beside me. "She's a smart mare, Astrid."

"Yeah," I said, trying not to be disappointed, "but you didn't put her halter on or anything. I thought we were going to brush her."

He crinkled his nose and shook his head. "That's your timeline, Astrid, not hers. A good horse trainer has to work with each horse as they are on each day. You can't impose your ideas on them; you need to work on making them want to partner up with you. Once you've done that the rest is easy. Didn't you see how hard she was trying there at the end? She's actually scared under all that bravado. We'll try again this afternoon. Now, come on. I have a chore I need help with."

We left Folly working on a flake of hay and walked in companionable silence past the broodmare barn and over to the training barn. The sound of tranquil chewing met us on all sides; they were all still eating their breakfast, too.

I scratched Doc gently behind the ears and then moved over

to stand in front of Red's stall, peering inside at where he was napping in the far corner with one hind leg propped up.

"Hey, big guy," I said softly, leaning over the door.

He blinked at me sleepily, so I slid the door open and moved inside to stroke his soft neck.

"He's so sweet," I said, running my hand over his shoulder. "Why is Aunt Lillian trying to sell him?"

"Well, he's a bit of a puzzle," Justin said. "Red was your uncle's horse and your aunt can't make up her mind what to do with him. On the one hand, he is the laziest ranch horse you have ever seen in your life. All the horses here are hard-working except this guy. He hates cows and cow-work, he's slow as molasses, he gets tired on long trail rides, and he falls asleep whenever things get too boring, or too exciting, for him. What he would probably like is to have someone who just wants to fuss over him and do light trail riding, and take him around in circles in the ring once in a while."

"Aww, poor guy," I said, watching his lower lip begin to quiver when I reached an itchy spot under his mane. "Too bad I'm broken; I'd love to ride him if he's safe."

"Oh, he's safe. The only danger is that he'll fall asleep. Here, why don't you get him cleaned up and I'll grab his tack."

"Sure, I can brush him for you. I'd love to see him under saddle."

Red was already spotless. I ran a soft brush over his fuzzy coat to wipe off the dust and picked the straw out of his mane and tail. He closed his eyes in bliss while I worked and soon, his head began to sink toward the floor, followed by the sound of gentle snoring.

Justin appeared carrying a big western saddle, a thick pad and a bridle over one arm. I opened the stall door to let him in, and he laid the pad on Red's back and then effortlessly tossed up the saddle.

"This is a trail saddle, so it has double rigging; that means two cinches, one for the front and one for the back. It looks complicated the first time, but it's easy once you get the hang of it. Watch carefully so you can do it yourself later."

Do it myself? I can't even lift these saddles let alone figure out all the straps.

I tried to pay attention while he looped a long piece of leather in some complicated pattern to attach the girth to the saddle and then buckled up the back cinch, but I was lost after the first few seconds. A dressage saddle was much less complicated. At least the bridle was almost the same; only the nose-band was missing. There was still a snaffle like I'd used on Quarry; Red opened his mouth automatically for the bit without even cracking his eyes open.

"Yep, laziest horse ever," Justin said. "Now hang out here for a second while I get Doc."

I worked on straightening Red's forelock from under the leather brow-band, so it didn't occur to me to ask why Justin was saddling two horses until he was standing in front of me again.

"Come on," he said, "follow me outside."

I opened the stall door and Red shuffled after me out of the barn and into the morning sunshine.

"Here, use the mounting block," Justin said, swinging effortlessly into his own saddle from the ground. "That will be easier on you."

"Are you kidding?" I skidded to a stop. "I can't ride like this; I have a broken arm and a nose splint. The doctor will kill me; my dad will kill me."

Justin looked around and raised an eyebrow at me. "I don't see anyone else here, Astrid. Just us and two steady trail horses ready to go. Red's very well trained, so you shouldn't need your reins at all if you can cue him with your seat. He'll probably just follow Doc."

"Fine," I grumbled, partly annoyed that he'd tricked me into this. But, stronger than my irritation, was the unexpected bubble of happy excitement welling up inside. I hadn't realized until just that minute how much I'd missed riding.

I led Red over to the mounting block and walked up the steps slowly, feeling overwhelmed.

Don't be silly, I told myself sternly, *you've ridden a hundred times. Remember how it was with Quarry? You were never afraid of him. Red is kind and gentle, just like Quarry. He's not Folly; he won't try and kill you.*

Still, it took everything I had to make myself put my foot in the wide leather stirrup and carefully swing onto his back. For a second, I froze there, clutching the saddle horn with one hand. I didn't know what its purpose was, but it looked like it had been stuck there as an anchor for terrified people like myself.

"You okay over there, Astrid?" Justin sat easily on Doc, reins draped loose over the horse's neck, watching me with a quizzical look on his face.

"Yep," I said, taking a deep breath, letting go of the horn long enough to lean down to give Red a shaky pat on the neck. "Just getting used to being up here again. Are you...are you sure he won't do anything scary?"

"Positive. He's as good as gold."

"Okay then." I sat up and gathered my reins lightly in my good hand. "Let's go."

"All right, cowgirl," Justin joked, pointing Doc in the direction of the far mountains. "We won't go too far for your first ride; we don't want that creature to pass out from exertion. Did I mention how lazy he is?"

Red pricked his ears in half-interest and then obediently turned to follow Doc up the trail past the barn. The bulky saddle felt weird in contrast to the dressage saddles I'd used before, but it wasn't uncomfortable. Gradually I fell into the gentle rhythm of Red's easy walk and found myself sinking into the saddle, my attention turned to pick out his footfalls. It wasn't hard once I got the hang of it.

Although he was more animated out here than in the ring, his pace was way slower than Folly's or Quarry's, so his footfalls weren't quite so defined. They blended in a nice rocking motion that swayed me gently from side to side and soon, I was able to relax and actually look up and enjoy the scenery.

The morning frost had long melted away and the sun was warm on my bare head. Justin had tricked me into this ride so smoothly that I hadn't even thought to put a helmet on. But even though I felt a stab of guilt, I was also enjoying myself too much to turn back.

"You *are* a good boy, Red," I said, reaching out to straighten his mane. He flicked one ear lazily back at me, but didn't change his ambling pace.

The trail climbed steadily, following the ridgeline that looked down over the bowl-like pastures with the lake at the bottom.

Horses and cows dotted the hillsides, and I could see Donkey, a grey speck far below, guarding his little herd of foals.

I turned in the saddle to look back toward the ranch buildings and could just make out Folly, now lying down in her paddock, stretched out in the sun. I'd never seen her relaxed enough to do that before.

Justin rode ahead of me silently, lost in his own thoughts, but somehow, I didn't mind the lack of conversation. I too was caught up with sounds of the fall afternoon and the feel of Red plowing steadily along the trail.

The ground changed from a trampled dirt trail to a rocky foot path between piles of ever increasing boulders. The grass disappeared and was replaced by moss and tenacious, stalky plants that clung to the hillside in an effort to survive.

I drew in a deep breath; the air felt clearer up here somehow, and the breeze ruffling my hair was crisp. Even Red felt the change, his head came up and he had a mild spring to his step.

"Look," Justin said, as we came to the top of a rocky plateau.

I turned to where he pointed, my eyes widening.

We were on top of a bluff and in front of us, on the other side of the ridge from the ranch, was a view that stretched on and on for miles. I could see the town huddled against the shores of the big lake, roads snaking out from it in all directions. Beyond it, acres of woods and rolling fields stretched out in front of us like a kid's board game.

"It's beautiful," I whispered. "Like a painting."

"This is one of my favourite spots," Justin said. "I like to come up here when I need to put things into perspective. When I start feeling as if my problems are big, I ride up here and realize how small my part in the world is; I'm just a drop in the bucket."

I nodded, staring at the vast landscape. It was weird how this was just one tiny bit of the country I lived in, which was only one tiny bit of the world, which was only a tiny bit of the universe, and so on and so on. He was right, it did make me feel small, but not in a bad way. I felt centered and calmer than I had in a long time. It reminded me of the feeling after practicing yoga back home.

We sat there for a long time and then both horses seemed to decide all at once they'd had enough. They looked at each other, turned at the same time and began the slow trek down the hillside before we could ask.

"Sure, Doc, whatever you say." Justin laughed. "I guess it's time to go."

The ride down was just as wonderful, but by then my muscles were starting to protest and I shifted around in the saddle, trying to find a comfortable spot. I would be sore that night for sure.

"You were such a good boy, Red," I said petting his neck over and over once we'd reached the bottom. "Thanks for taking care of me."

I kicked my feet out of the stirrups and leaned forward to swing down from the saddle and promptly stabbed myself in the ribs with the horn.

"Ow, what is this thing here for anyway?" I shimmied awkwardly to the side and somehow managed to slide ungracefully to the ground.

Justin just laughed; he'd already turned to lead Doc away, so he didn't see the glare I shot him.

Chapter Ten

Later that day, I got my wish about being able to handle Folly myself.

Justin worked with her again just as evening settled in, and this time she was much more accommodating. After following him around the paddock politely for a while Folly walked right up to Justin and rested her nose softly on his arm. He'd praised her and given her a handful of grain and then had worked on slowly petting her neck and shoulders, watching her closely to see if she'd have any big reactions to being touched. But she hadn't attacked him or even so much as pinned her ears.

After that he'd had me get her halter and lead rope so he could see how she reacted to them. He'd worked with her again loose around the paddock, checking to see if she wanted to work with him before calmly slipping on her halter. Then he'd led her up to her shelter and tied her loosely to the ring and brushed her gently all over. She'd closed her eyes while he curried her neck and shoulders, and the itchy spot behind her withers, but she threw up a hind foot in warning when he came near her hind legs.

I thought he'd get mad at her, but he didn't.

"It's okay, I get it," he said, moving back to her shoulder without making a fuss. He'd brushed her a few more minutes and then called to me. "Go grab her blanket, Astrid, we'll put it on."

When I came back with the blanket he motioned me to come inside. "Just put it in the shelter there and come on over for a second."

I hung the blanket up and then moved cautiously to his side, suddenly nervous to be on the same side of fence as Folly.

"Here," Justin said, handing me a soft body brush, "start at her neck and work your way back, just like you would any horse."

Folly flicked her ears back, but didn't react when I laid the brush on her neck. I worked my way across one side of her body and, when Justin gave me the nod, I moved carefully to the other side and then I brushed her mane.

This is finally happening, I thought, my eyes welling up with tears. *I'm actually brushing her; no sedatives, no tricks, no fighting; just me and her being normal together.*

I stepped back when I was finished, surveying her with pride. Justin picked the blanket up and, when she didn't acknowledge it as anything scary or threatening, he slid it over her back. She didn't flinch; if anything, she heaved a contented sigh of happiness.

That night, long after dinner, when Aunt Lillian and I were quietly reading in the living room and eating cookies, we were startled by a sharp banging on the front door. Jake woke up abruptly from his nap, barking and looking around in alarm.

"What on earth?" Aunt Lillian strode the front door and threw it open only to have a hysterical Casey fall inside.

"I hate him," she sobbed. "I hate him and I'm not going back to that house until he's gone."

"Oh sweetheart." Aunt Lillian wrapped her in a tight hug. "Come on inside, you don't even have a coat. What on earth is going on?"

"He won't let me go," she sobbed. "They said I could get in on a partial scholarship and he said noooooo."

Her words trailed away into more crying as Aunt Lillian led her to the couch and made her sit down.

"Astrid, put the kettle on," Aunt Lillian said. "Casey, you need to calm down and tell me what's going on."

I moved slowly to the kitchen counter, filled the kettle and set it on the stove's burner, all the while trying to eavesdrop on what Casey was saying.

"The secretary from Redmond called. They said that they could admit me, but only on a partial scholarship. I have my own money to pay for part of it, but dad said it was still too expensive and that I couldn't go. Lillian, it's the only thing I've ever wanted, and he couldn't care less. I'm not going back there until he's gone."

"Oh, honey, your dad loves you so much. You know he can't afford much right now. The divorce took a toll on him. You wait until next year and I bet you can go."

"But I *can't* wait until next year," Casey said desperately. "You don't understand. I won't survive there."

"Well, you're right, I don't understand. If there's something going on, then you need to tell me or your dad. Does this have anything to do with the fights you've been getting into?"

"No," Casey said quickly. "I just want to go to Redmond. I'm wasting my potential at Triple Hills. I can feel my future slipping away day by day."

Aunt Lillian sighed and rolled her eyes. "That is nonsense. You are going to go to university and do whatever you like with your life; nothing will stop you. You have a family that loves you and a beautiful place to live."

"Fine," Casey said sullenly, "whatever. Nobody cares that I'm miserable anyway. Can I sleep here tonight, though? I don't want to go home."

"Of course, I'll call your dad and let him know where you are. He must be worried sick."

Casey stayed huddled on the couch eating cookies and sipping tea until it was bedtime, and then she went up to the guest room beside mine without saying another word.

Chapter Eleven

Sunday morning dawned into another beautiful, frosty day, and I decided that fall was my favourite time of year. There weren't any bugs, the awful heatwave had grudgingly gone away, and the sun still shone brightly every single day.

Casey stayed in her borrowed room and refused to come down and take part in the impromptu going away breakfast Aunt Lillian threw for Olive, or to come and talk to her dad.

After breakfast, Olive bounced excitedly up the stairs to say goodbye to her sister, and when she came down she had tears in her eyes.

"I'm going to miss Casey," she said tearfully. "I wish she was coming with me, Dad. I think she's sad."

He ruffled her hair. "She needs to stay here and keep an eye on things. Your brothers would get into way too much trouble without her watching over them."

We all went down to the barn to help load Salsa and send them off on their big adventure.

"Right, well, I'm headed back to the house; come back when you're ready for lunch, Astrid," Aunt Lillian said.

Kade and Justin both tacked up their first horses to ride, and I started grooming Doc so Justin could ride him next. After a few minutes, Casey came slinking into the barn looking pale with dark circles under both eyes.

"Hi," I said, "are you feeling better?"

"No," she whispered in a broken voice, "my life is awful."

I didn't bother answering that; just ignored her and kept brushing Doc.

She didn't offer to help me groom and tack up Justin's horses, even though it would have made our progress that much faster. And she didn't help Kade, either. She just sat on the tack trunk across from Kitty's stall and stared moodily down at the ground.

When Kade came back in from the ring, he shot her an irritated look. "Would you stop looking so depressed, Casey. You acted like you could hardly stand Dad and Ollie when they were around. What's the problem now?"

"I don't know," she said, hugging her knees to her chest. "Everything's messed up."

"Well, pull yourself together, woman. Come on, saddle up Kitty. We're out of here. You, too, Astrid. I know you've been working with that ridiculous beast, so no excuses."

"He's not ridiculous," I protested just as Justin led Badger back in from the ring. "Is he, Justin? He's a wonderful horse, right?"

"Worst ranch horse ever," he said, winking at me to show he was just kidding. "Come on, Kade's right. You kids get those horses saddled. Time for a trail ride. Winter's coming soon, and we won't be able to do this much longer."

"I suppose so." Casey pulled herself wearily to her feet as if trail riding was the worst chore ever handed to her, and I quickly moved to Red's stall to get him brushed.

I noticed from the corner of my eye that Casey didn't have any trouble tacking up her own mare; even though she was shorter than me and rail-thin, she swung the heavy saddle up on Kitty's back like it was nothing.

We took the same trail as yesterday. Red plodded along while Doc bounced up the trail, head bobbing as he looked excitedly at the world around him.

Justin kept the reins loose and patted him from time to time, but Doc didn't put a foot wrong. He was excited, but still well under control.

Kitty marched along like the seasoned trail horse she was, looking mildly interested at the scenery, but not overly excited.

Kade rode the big stallion, Fox, ahead of us all, the horse's stride much bigger than Red's or Kitty's so soon, we were left behind, ambling along side by side.

"Hey, are you really okay?" I asked.

She shrugged. "I guess so." She opened her mouth as if to say more, but then shut it abruptly and kicked Kitty ahead into a trot, leaving me behind.

I didn't mind; I was relieved to see her go. The ride was much more relaxing when it was just Red and me sauntering along together.

Chapter Twelve

My alarm went off at 5:30 and I sat up in bed, fully awake. Today was the day I started school. For some reason, school in a new place seemed infinitely more exciting than my old school back home. I was actually looking forward to it.

I dressed in my barn clothes and headed down to see Folly under the light of my headlamp, not scared at all of the chilly darkness.

I didn't need Justin to help me feed in the mornings anymore. Folly knew her routine, and as long as I paid attention and was consistent, then she played by the rules. I didn't want to be late for school, but I couldn't go a whole day without seeing Red, either. I trotted over to the training barn and snuck inside to give him his apple.

He chewed it slowly, half-closing his eyes and crunching each piece thoughtfully.

"Have a good day without me, Red," I said, throwing my arms around his neck. "I'll see you tonight."

Then I headed back to the house as fast as I could.

I was washed, dressed, and ready way too early, so excited that I couldn't even eat my breakfast.

A truck pulled up outside, honking its horn.

"Oh, there's Kade. Have a good day, darling. I hope I gave you enough money for lunch. Call me if you need anything. Don't be nervous. Make lots of friends!"

"Okay!" I called, leaving my aunt hovering nervously in the doorway, wringing her hands like she was sending me off to war rather than a day at school.

"Hey," I said, climbing way up into the front seat since Casey was already in the back, her face pale and strained. Honestly, she looked ill.

"All ready?" Kade asked, stepping hard on the gas so that the tires sprayed gravel out the back, the truck lurching and fish-tailing up the driveway.

"*Must* you be such a show-off, Kade?" Casey grumbled from the back seat.

"Yep, born and bred. You'll take care of Astrid on her first day, right, Casey? Show her where to go and stuff?"

"Yep," Casey said unenthusiastically, staring morosely out the window.

But when we reached school she jumped out and ran inside without even looking back, leaving me behind.

"Well, that's nice." Kade shook his head at her retreating back. "You want me to walk you inside?"

"No, I'm fine." I was actually glad Casey wasn't with me; I didn't need her bringing down my good mood.

"Just go straight in the front doors. Office is down the hall on the left, about halfway down. Maybe don't say that you know me. I've spent many hours in there for bad behavior and they might get the wrong idea about you." He laughed and slapped me on the back. "Don't worry, you'll do great."

"Thanks," I said, sliding down out of the truck and slamming the door. I turned to look for the archery targets I'd seen last week, but they were gone.

Probably put away for winter, I thought, *there'll be a place to practice inside instead.*

There were a few people standing around, staring at me curiously, and I made sure to smile as I went up the front steps and pushed open the front door. Hopefully, I'd be able to make friends here. Aunt Lillian had said probably half the people at this school rode horses, so odds were that I'd be able to make friends with a few of them at least.

I made my way down the hall, weaving around people until I reached the office and pushed inside.

"Hello? Oh, you must be Astrid." An older secretary sat at a wooden desk in the middle of the room, her grey hair pulled back into a tight bun.

"Hi," I said, "sorry, I'm late."

"You're right on time, dear. I'm Mrs. Renning. Now, let's see, here's your timetable, and a map, and a list of the school rules. We had to fit you in whatever classes we could, I'm afraid. We obviously took gym class off your schedule; I guess sports are out for you this year."

She winked at me, making me laugh.

"Yes," I said, "except archery. I'm excited to join the—"

The door banged open and a tall, gangly boy stumbled in, his arms and legs too long for his body. He had glasses and a slightly crooked nose, and dark hair that stuck out from under a wool hat. Wide brown, intelligent eyes regarded me with a mixture of interest and alarm.

"Ah, here's Lincoln," the secretary said, "he'll take you on your tour this morning and drop you off at your next class."

"Oh," I said, happily, recognizing him as the boy I'd seen shooting at targets when we'd picked up Casey that first day. "I'm Astrid."

"Hi," he said shyly, his cheeks flushing.

"Well, go on then." Mrs. Renning made a shooing motion at us. "Enjoy your day and come back if you need anything."

Lincoln didn't say anything as he led me down the hall, he looked terrified, as if I were about to mug him and take his lunch money.

"This is the first floor," he said in a barely audible tone, "here is the cafeteria." He opened the door so I could see inside, and then let it fall immediately shut again. I wasn't quite sure how he'd been chosen as my tour guide; he could hardly say two words to me.

The school was easy to navigate, and I probably hadn't needed a tour at all since it was about a quarter the size of my old school back home. It was basically a large square set on two floors with the middle part open to a courtyard with a domed, glass room. I stopped at a bank of windows to admire the large, open square which was dotted with trees, stone benches, and shrubs. In one corner, there was even a small greenhouse and a flower and vegetable garden.

"They sell flowers, vegetables, and fruit at the local farmers market to raise money for the school," Lincoln said, clearing his throat nervously, "The Ag kids have a bunch of different projects running."

"Ag?"

"You know, the Agricultural program, for people who like plants and farming and stuff. They even grow food for the school lunch program."

He turned abruptly and headed back down the hall leaving me to hurry after him. *At least he managed to string a whole sentence together this time.*

By the end of the tour I was pretty certain that I wasn't going to hate it here. Everything was nice but old. The blue on the lockers that faced the court-yard had sun-faded to a pale aqua, the laminate tiles on the floor were cracking, but other than that the place looked decent. The few kids we passed in the hall stared at me with interest, but they didn't look mean at all; Casey had made everyone out to be monsters.

"So, Lincoln," I said, stopping in my tracks so he had turn around and face me, "where do you practice archery? I saw the targets outside have been taken down."

"Oh," he said, looking startled, "yeah, they made us take them down when the club disbanded. Principal Hale said it was too dangerous for us to practice now that our coach is gone."

"Wait, what?" I said, looking at him in horror. "What do you mean disbanded? That's the whole reason I came to this school."

"Oh," he said, eyes widening, "that sucks. Yeah, um, our old History teacher was our coach, but he left at the end of last year. And, his own kids made up half the team, so when they moved away we were kind of stuck.

"A few of us tried to start it back up this year but, well, nobody was interested. Principal Hale said that without a coach or more team members that we can't have a place to practice here."

"That's awful," I said, sick to my stomach. Not just for myself, but for them, too. That was so unfair.

"Yeah, I was looking forward to getting more competitive this year. Our team went to the Northern Flight School Competition last year and we had an invitation to go again this Spring. But, without a real team, we can't go."

"Oh, I've heard of that competition. There's prize money, too, right?"

"Lots of it. But we need a solid team of five people, plus a coach and some back-up shooters just in case. Right now, there are only three people signed up for archery and, well, none of us are very good."

I stood there in the middle of the hall, my mind whirling with possibilities.

"Show me where you used to practice," I said firmly.

"Um, okay," Lincoln said doubtfully, his forehead wrinkling with confusion. "We have to go through the gym."

He led the way down the hall to a set of large double doors. Right away, the sound of shouting and rubber soles squeaking on polished concrete met my ears. It looked like some sort of badminton tournament was going on. At least the cast on my arm kept me safely away from any high impact sports.

"Come upstairs," he said, sounding slightly more confident, "it wasn't much, but it was better than nothing."

Upstairs a small alcove ran along one side of the gym and was split into different rooms. On one side was a tiny workout room where a couple of guys sat around chatting on some weight benches. They both gave me a once-over look, up and down, and then turned away.

"Yeah, ignore them," Lincoln whispered, "if we don't get our archery space back then they have a plan to enlarge the work out room. I mean, how much more muscle can you build? Anyway, here it is."

He gestured to a room set off to one side. It was small, but the far end had some good targets set up and it would still be a safe place to shoot.

"I still come up here sometimes," he confessed, "but we're not allowed to bring our bows to school anymore."

"It's great," I lied. I turned around in a full circle, measuring the distance with my eyes. "So this must be, what, sixteen meters long?"

"Yeah." He blushed, "not quite regulation, but it gets the job done."

He looked at me worriedly, biting his lip, waiting for me to speak.

"It would be fine to start in," I said slowly, "but you'll need something better if you want to be competitive. How many people do we need to make up a team? I mean, for the school to give you your space back?"

"I don't know." Lincoln shrugged dispiritedly. "Probably like eight to ten."

"Okay," I said slowly, "that doesn't seem impossible."

Lincoln shrugged. "Well, like I said, there wasn't much interest. Look, I'm supposed to drop you off at Math now and then you have to go to Geography. But, if you like, I'll meet you afterward and you can eat with us at the cafeteria."

"Okay," I said quickly, taking any opportunity to avoid walking into a cafeteria full of strangers by myself.

Entering my first class as a newcomer was about as awkward as I'd envisioned, but the teacher seemed nice enough and a few people smiled at me quickly before looking away. Soon enough, I was too busy paying attention to the class work to have much time to worry about what people thought of me.

Like I'd expected, my classes were fairly easy. Being nearly a month late wouldn't hurt me too much and not having to scramble to catch up would give me more time with the horses and to sort this archery mess out.

Lincoln was waiting for me after Geography and I followed him down the hall to the cafeteria.

"The food's decent here," he said, smiling at me shyly. "They have a culinary prep program, so there's always something interesting on the menu."

We grabbed our lunch, which in my case was ravioli with three different cheese layers on top, and headed to a table where two boys were already sitting.

"This is Astrid, guys," Lincoln said, "she's new here. Astrid, this is Malcolm and Gage."

"Hey," they both said, looking away quickly.

"These guys were part of the archery club, before it disbanded."

"Oh," I said, looking at them with renewed interest. "So, what do you think we can do to get your club back up and running?"

They stared at me blankly as if I'd sprouted a second head and went on eating without saying another word. The conversation was clearly over.

Okay, I thought, *maybe they're a little slow, or shy, or just plain weird. Either way, I don't see them being much help.*

My afternoon classes went smoothly, and I was able to find my way around without getting too lost. I looked for Casey, but I didn't see her even once, not until I was headed for Kade's truck.

"Hey," she said, brushing past me.

"Hello to you, too," I said, climbing into the front seat.

As a surprise, Kade had bought us treats from the bakery to celebrate my first day of school, and he and I gorged on pastries while Casey sat glumly in the backseat, refusing to talk to us or share any food.

Aunt Lillian was delighted to see me when I got home.

"I made fresh cookies," she said, "sit down and I want to hear all about your first day. Did you make any friends?"

"Sort of," I said and then told her the bad news about the archery club. "I can't believe I switched schools just in time for them to shut the club down. That's just the kind of luck I have, I guess."

"Nonsense," Aunt Lillian said sternly, "luck is the outcome of hard work. You march in there tomorrow and demand a place to practice. Oh, and before I forget, I have something for you." She reached into her pocket and pulled out a set of keys. "The truck is yours while you're here, Astrid. I don't want you walking around in the dark at all hours. It's not safe. Mind you, don't drive it anywhere but on the ranch until you get your license, of course."

"Oh, Aunt Lillian, thank you," I said. "But what are you going to drive?"

"Well, I have Trent's old truck in the garage. I've been

meaning to haul it out for over a year, and I just couldn't bring myself to do it until now. So, you've given me the push I needed. Now, go on and work with those horses, and I'll see you at dinner."

I changed into my barn clothes and boots, and drove slowly and carefully down to the barn in my new truck. I didn't hate it nearly so much now that it was my own to drive. And as soon as the weekend hit I was going to vacuum every last inch of dog hair out of it.

I was exhausted from my first day of school, but I worked with Folly and brushed Justin's horses, and did some groundwork with Red even though I was half-asleep on my feet.

I drove back home, ate dinner, and then practically fell into bed, my whole body aching from the tension of the day.

Chapter Thirteen

The next day, I woke up determined to change my fortune.

As soon as I reached school, I said goodbye to Kade and Casey and marched straight to the office, not feeling at all nervous until I was inside staring at the kindly secretary with my words frozen in my mouth.

"Excuse me," I said, clearing my throat a few times before she could hear me, "how do I sent up an appointment with the principal?"

"Well now." She looked at me with surprised amusement. "Not many students ask to spend time with him."

"Please, it's important."

"In that case, I can absolutely set up a meeting for you; what is it regarding?"

"Archery," I said firmly. "I'm here to ask to have the archery club set up again."

"Oh, you don't need a meeting to do that. Just get ten signatures to prove you're a real club with real members, and we can assign you a meeting spot."

"Okay, and we can have our practice range back? The one upstairs in the gym?"

"Well, you get the ten signatures and we'll see what we can do."

"Thank you," I said breathlessly, practically racing out the door, "that's what I'll do then."

I sat impatiently through my morning classes and caught up with Lincoln in the cafeteria to tell him the good news.

"Don't you think we've tried that, Astrid?" He asked glumly. "Nobody's interested."

"Well, what if we motivate them? What if we lure them in with the prize money from the NFS Competition? Isn't it like five thousand a person or something?"

"Yep, it's five thousand for each team member plus equipment for the school. But, what's the point if we have no hope of winning anyway?"

"The *point* is to get your practice spot back and to be a real club again. The competition isn't until spring. We have months to practice and I'm a good coach. I've competed all over Western Canada and I helped with the younger kids all the time back home. Don't you want this?"

"I do," Lincoln said slowly, "but I'm a realist, too."

"No, you're a pessimist," I snapped, feeling an unfamiliar anger burn inside my chest. "I'm trying to help and you're just lying there, doing nothing."

I stopped, surprised at how mean I'd sounded. I hardly ever got angry or made a fuss over things, at least, not out loud. But it was frustrating how he'd just given up and wasn't even trying to make things better.

"Don't you even want to try?"

He stared at me and then his mouth curled in a small smile.

"Okay, okay," he said, "What is your plan then?"

"I'm not quite sure yet, but I'll think of something."

*****

That night, after chores and a brief stab at homework, I fired up Aunt Lillian's ancient computer and designed a fairly decent poster and a sign-up sheet.

Once my aunt had gone to bed, I printed off sixty copies and stuck them into my backpack.

Then I sat down to work on my speech.

Chapter Fourteen

The next morning, Kade let me practice my recruitment speech on him during our morning drive. Casey ignored us both, and when we arrived at school, she pushed her door open and hopped out before the truck even rolled to a stop.

"Bye," she said, not looking at either of us, "have a good day."

She walked off at a brisk pace, shoulders hunched, and wool hat pulled down low over her head.

"Is she showing you around at all, Astrid?" Kade asked, narrowing his eyes as he watched his sister walk away.

"Um, I actually don't see her very much. Not at all, really. I think we have different lunch periods, so we might just miss each other."

"Huh," he said, "well, she's been acting weird. I mean weirder than normal. Can you keep an eye out for her?"

"I can try," I said, promising nothing. I could imagine how thrilled Casey would be if I started monitoring her activities. Besides, I didn't have time to worry about Casey. I had a campaign to run.

I spent my free study period before lunch sticking up posters on every available space I could find. It wasn't that big of a school, so sixty posters went a long way. I was sure I could get at least ten people to show up for the meeting tomorrow, if not more. Surely, the money would draw them in.

Lincoln met me for lunch, and again we sat with Malcolm and Gage, who had loosened up enough to make complete sentences in my presence. They all admired my posters and agreed that my speech should go over well with everyone.

We were just finishing lunch when there was a sharp tap on my shoulder.

Lincoln's face paled as if he'd seen a monster and everyone within a three-table radius fell silent. I turned slowly to see a heavy-set girl standing behind me, a grim expression on her face. Her dark hair was cut unevenly just below her ears like someone had hacked at it with a pair of scissors. Her mouth was set in a hard line, and there was a faded bruise under one eye.

Her gaze flew to my own yellowish bruises and then down to my splint and her nose wrinkled as if she smelled something bad. Two girls stood nervously behind her, looking embarrassed to be there.

"I saw you this morning," she said ominously, crossing her arms over her chest. "You got out of that fancy truck with that lying, weasel Casey, didn't you?"

"Um, yes?" I squeaked. "I live at Triple Hills with my aunt. Casey's family has a house there."

"I know where she lives. So that means I can find her even if she's too scared to show her face around here anymore. You tell her I haven't forgotten. I'll be waiting to finish what she started when she gets back."

"Gets back?" I asked, confused. "What do you mean?"

"Don't play games with me," she said, leaning down so her hot, salami breath wafted over my cheek. "You're new here so you'd better learn right now who runs this school. Do you know what happens when people come on my turf?"

"Come on, Mara," Lincoln said, his voice barely a whisper, "we don't want any trouble."

"Shut it," she said, not taking her eyes off me. "What's the answer, loser?"

"Um, bad things?" I gulped, wondering how on earth I was going to get out of this.

"They get their face rearranged by me."

"Oh, well…" I laughed nervously. "My face has already been rearranged. I don't want to fight you. I've been hurt enough this year and I've made some mistakes. But I'm trying to change. I just want to focus on horses, archery, and to win that money."

Her gaze wavered. "What money? What are you talking about?"

"Here," I said, handing her the poster we'd been looking at. "There's a cash prize of twenty-five thousand dollars. I mean, you have to split the money between everyone on the team, but you still come home with five thousand of your own."

"Really?" she said, her eyes glittering. "And what are the chances of a team from here actually winning something like this?"

"Depends." I shrugged. "We might win if we can get the right people together. Why don't you come to our meeting tomorrow and give it a try? Right, Lincoln?"

"Yes," he squeaked, looking horrified. "Astrid here used to

shoot professionally, she knows what she's talking about."

I nodded, overlooking that 'professionally' bit. It sounded more impressive then 'practiced obsessively all the time because she didn't have anything else in her life'.

"Fine," she said, "maybe I will. But you watch yourself around this school. Don't forget who's in charge."

She turned on her heel and stomped away, her two friends trailing reluctantly behind her.

"Lincoln," I hissed as soon as they were out of earshot. "What on earth just happened?"

"Sorry about that, that's just Mara. She doesn't usually bother anyone. She acts tougher than she is."

I doubted that. I had the impression that she could have easily beaten me up.

"Fantastic." I looked down at the battered cafeteria table and shook my head. "What does she have against Casey anyway?"

"I don't know. They used to be friends, I guess."

"*Really?* I can't even imagine that."

"I think they had a fight over a horse or something, just before summer started. They've been fighting ever since. Casey says nasty things about Mara and Mara beats her up. That seems to be how it goes."

Huh, I thought, *so that's the reason Casey is so obsessed with getting into Redmond. I'd be scared, too, if that girl hated me. So why hasn't she told anyone what's going on?*

It took the rest of the lunch hour for my heartbeat to go back to normal.

The rest of the day went fine, but I was jumpy and nervous, expecting Mara to change her mind about killing me and haul me out back behind the dumpsters and beat me to a pulp. But, despite my paranoia, I didn't see her or her henchmen again, even passing in the hall. And I didn't see Casey, either, which was strange; surely in a school this size I'd see her at least once. *Unless she's avoiding you on purpose, of course.*

Kade's truck was parked outside when I reached the front steps, and I climbed inside gratefully. Casey was already slumped in the backseat with her eyes closed, wrapped in her coat, scarf and hat, even though it wasn't cold out.

"Hey," Kade said, "how was your day?"

"Good," I said, "at least until this girl the size of a UFC prize fighter threatened to beat me up."

"Oh no," Casey said, opening her eyes abruptly, "you met Mara."

"Yep, sure did. A little warning would have been nice, Casey. She could have killed me."

Casey looked down at the floor saying nothing.

"Mara?" Kade interrupted. "Like, your friend Mara? I didn't know she was still around. I thought she'd moved away. We never see her anymore, and she used to be at the ranch all the time."

"Yeah, Kade, we haven't been friends since last year," Casey said, rolling her eyes. "Thanks for noticing."

"You guys were inseparable, though. What happened?"

Casey's pale cheeks flamed a brilliant red. "None of your business. She's stupid now, that's all. She hangs out with her dumb friends, and smokes and beats people up and wastes her life. I have better things to do."

"Didn't she want to buy Dinah off you at one point? I

thought you'd worked out a deal with her. She sure loved that horse."

Casey looked out the window, a red blush staining her cheeks. "No, it didn't work out."

"She didn't want her?"

Casey twisted her face up into a scowl. "I don't want to talk about it, Kade."

"Huh?" he said. "I don't get it. I know you sold Dinah when I was away. So, if you didn't sell her to Mara then where did she go?"

"Okay, fine, not that it's anyone's business. I got a better offer from someone else. It was still a good home," she added defensively. "And I needed the money to get into Redmond. Mara had already made a payment on her, so she was totally angry. But I *gave* her the money back, so I don't see why she's still so upset. It's completely irrational."

"Wow, that's harsh, Casey," Kade said. "You can't back out of a deal like that once you've made it."

"I *said* I gave the money back, didn't I? It was just a horse, we have like a million others she could have bought; she didn't have to freak out over it. And she told everyone at school, too; she turned everyone against me."

Kade whistled under his breath. "That explains why Mara doesn't hang around at the ranch anymore."

"Oh, who cares? It's not like I need her anyway. She doesn't even try in school. Her answers in class are laughable, and she's completely rude whenever I point out her mistakes."

"Uh-huh," Kade said dryly, "I can imagine."

"What's that supposed to mean? Can I help it if I study hard and know more than other people? Mom says you're not supposed to hide your light; you're supposed to shine brightly, so I can't help it if other people are jealous of my light. I'm done with this school, Kade; I belong somewhere better."

"First of all, since when do you go around quoting Mom, of all people? And secondly, that school is perfectly fine. If you act like a stuck-up brat then you're going to get beaten up sometimes, Casey. Most people don't like being made to look stupid."

"Fine, I'll get beaten up then," Casey said with a shrug. "And I'll be laughing at them all from my mansion when I'm a billionaire and they are still waiting tables at the diner."

Wow, I shook my head and tuned her out for the rest of the ride home, thinking over everything I'd learned. So, Mara the thug was soft enough to be devastated when her favourite horse was sold from under her? That put her in a new perspective. And it didn't make me like Casey much more, either.

When we got to the house, I said goodbye to Kade and climbed wearily up the front steps, dropping my backpack in the hall beside my shoes. Jake met me at the kitchen with a happy woof and a wagging tail, and escorted me to the table where I collapsed with a sigh.

"You're home just in time, Astrid. I have banana bread coming out of the oven in three minutes. I'll put the kettle on."

Instantly, my spirits rose a few notches. I didn't know how I'd missed the delicious smells filling the kitchen, but now my mouth watered in anticipation.

Aunt Lillian set a chipped, ceramic bowl of butter on the table and a jar of jam, and turned to hover over the oven, her head tilted to the side like she was concentrating hard.

"Ah," she said as the timer dinged, "there it is. Let's just eat while it's hot, okay?"

"Sure," I said, eyeing up the loaf as she set it down at the table. "Why wait?"

My entire incident with scary Mara vanished when I took the first bite of lava-hot banana bread dripping with butter. My fingers were scorched and I'd burned my tongue on a molten chocolate chip but it was hands-down the most delicious thing I'd ever tasted. Maybe after I'd medaled at the Olympics, I could go learn to be a baker or chocolatier. Since I loved food so much, it would be nice to be able to keep myself supplied with delicious snacks whenever I wanted them. And there'd be nobody to stop me from eating food I loved once I'd grown up.

There was no sign of Justin when I went to work with Folly, so I gave her dinner and brushed her by myself, grateful that I could do even these small chores with her. She hadn't shown any signs of outward aggression in days and she looked so much happier than when she'd arrived here. Now the thought of having to hand walk her didn't seem quite so terrifying.

I left my truck parked next to Folly's paddock and ambled down to the training barn, surprised to see that Justin's truck wasn't there, either. Maybe he'd been held late for class or stuck in traffic on the way home.

"Hey, Astrid," a voice said so close behind me I nearly jumped out of my skin.

"Don't *do* that," I gasped, clutching my throat to hold back a scream. "You nearly killed me."

"Sorry," Kade grinned, looking not apologetic in the least, "I thought you heard me coming."

"Well, I didn't. What are you doing here?"

"I didn't have time to ride Fox today since I was busy ferrying you two brats around, so I'm riding him now."

"Oh." I picked up the box of brushes. "But it only takes about a half-hour out of your day to drive us around. What were you doing the rest of the time?"

"None of your business, little girl," he said, raising his eyebrows suggestively. "Let's just say the ladies need me."

"Ew," I said, sounding a lot like Casey. "Okay, enough said, I don't want to know."

I slipped past him and went directly to the safety of Red's stall, shutting the sliding stall door firmly behind me. Even though I'd grown to like him over our commutes to and from school, there was always something unsettling about being alone with Kade. It wasn't like I thought he'd hurt me or anything, but there was just something wild and reckless about him; he felt, unpredictable. He wasn't exactly someone you could trust.

I forgot all about him as I worked on Red's coat. His winter fur was thicker, fluffier, than Folly's, but his mane and tail were the same silky softness as hers, like strands of fine thread instead of the normal thick horse hair. I'd commandeered some of the nicer hair products I'd found lying around and had been using them on Red every day. By now his coat was practically glowing.

Hooves clopped on the aisle as Kade led Fox past me to the ring.

"Hey, you want to saddle up Red and I'll give you a lesson?" Kade asked. "You're here anyway, you may as well ride."

"Oh, that's okay," I said quickly, "it's been a long day. I'm happy just brushing him."

Kade's face darkened. "You mean you don't want a lesson from *me*," he said sharply. "You're all too happy to have Justin teach you lessons."

I jerked back, surprised at the harsh note in his voice. "What? No, I mean, Justin's just helping me with Folly, that's all. And we went on a few trail rides together and we're doing some ground work…. Lessons," my voice trailed off.

"Sure, whatever, you think that guy's won as many championships as I have? You think he's brave enough to ride bulls or work with some of the crazy horses I've worked with?"

"I…I don't know," I stammered, backing into Red for support. "I never thought about it."

"You know, you girls are always so quick to judge a man. I could not have tried any harder with Florian. I tried to be everything she wanted, and she just up and left. You're all the same."

"Florian?" I asked in confusion. "The cook?"

His eyes welled with tears. "I honestly don't know why I bother. Well, it's your loss then." Kade jerked on Fox's reins and stomped off toward the ring.

What the hell was that? I stood stock-still, my heart hammering in my chest. What had I done to make Kade so angry?

Fox's hoofs thudded from inside the arena, obviously already moving fast without time for a warm-up, and I relaxed a little. As long as I could hear them moving then I was safe. I leaned forward and buried my nose in Red's mane, inhaling his rich horsey sent. It was like a drug for me, an instant calmer that somehow made everything all right. Someone should figure out a way to bottle this scent.

"Everything okay in here, Astrid?" Justin stood in front of the stall, looking inquisitively inside. "Sorry I'm late."

"Oh." I pushed away from Red, embarrassed to be caught in such a private moment. "Sure, I'm fine. Kade's in there riding Fox."

"Okay." He frowned thoughtfully.

"He seemed kind of mad," I said, when he stayed silent. "He wanted to give me a lesson and he wasn't very happy when I said no."

"He had a bit of a blow-up on the phone with our dad," Justin said slowly. "Dad's worried that he's going off the rails and he told him he should be more like me. It didn't go over too well with Kade." He paused and then laughed. "I'm lucky to have such a wild brother; next to him I look like a saint."

"He said something weird about Florian. He sounded very angry and, he was almost crying."

"Oh. That's not good."

"Okay, what's the deal with Florian? I know there's a mystery, but nobody will tell me what it's about."

"No big mystery. Florian was a working student here for a long time. She was Kade's girlfriend."

"What? I thought Florian was an old, grandmotherly-type cook."

"No." Justin laughed. "She was the same age as us. She came here when she was about twenty and left this year. She came to Canada on a whim, she wanted to break free from her crazy family back in Spain. It was supposed to just be for a summer, but she never left. She was great; she was just the type of person that everyone comes to depend on. Your aunt loved her; she thought of her as a daughter. And Kade worshipped the ground she walked on."

"Really?" I said skeptically.

"Yep, he wasn't always like he is now. When she left, he went a little nuts. He took off to find her, and when he came back he wouldn't say what had happened. He wouldn't speak about her again."

"Oh, that's so sad. Why did she leave?"

"Nobody knows. She just packed and left in the night. She left a note for Lillian and a note for Kade, and went back to her family in Spain. Kade was devastated. He really loved her."

"That's awful," I said, wondering if that's when Kade had become such a lover of all ladies.

"Come on, grab this pony's halter and we'll do a quick session in the ring. I'll get Doc."

I slipped Red's halter on and took the time to straighten his forelock so it lay neatly down the center of his blaze before I led him into the aisle.

"Oh, I see," Kade said sarcastically as soon as we entered the arena. His cheeks were flushed with exertion. Even Fox was puffing, his chest and neck marked with sweat; they looked like they'd galloped the entire ride. "That's how it is."

"Lay off, big brother," Justin said, grinning, "we're just playing around with the horses here. I'm sure when Astrid's ready to go professional she'll turn to you."

"Huh," Kade said, but he looked less annoyed. He jumped off Fox and started pulling him in the direction of the stalls.

"He looks a bit hot still," Justin said casually. "You don't want to walk him first?"

"Naw, he's fine. He's fit; he'll cool out fast."

"Sure." Justin shrugged. "But Lillian will be out to check on them tonight and you know she'll notice. She's warned you before. Is that what you want, Kade? To be fired."

Kade's jaw clenched and he shook his head. "Honestly, I don't know. Maybe. I don't know what I want anymore."

Justin nodded slowly. "I get it, Kade, I do. Cool him out, brother."

It looked like Kade would ignore him, but at the last minute he turned and released the latigo on his saddle, one side of the cinch dropping to the ground with a jingle. He yanked the saddle off Fox, who, startled at this rough treatment, leaned backward, eyes wide.

"Come on, Fox," Kade growled, "don't be an idiot." He tossed his saddle over the in-gate and led the horse back across the ring.

Doc was only wearing his halter and lead rope, too, and he looked around with interest at this interruption to his routine. Red followed slowly behind me, hay trailing from his lips in his signature style, eyes half-closed.

"We're you this lazy for Uncle Trent?" I joked, hugging him around his neck.

"Nope," Kade said, overhearing me as he led Fox past, "he was a pistol of a horse for Trent. He was the handiest horse with cows."

"Seriously, what happened?"

"It was the accident. Your uncle was trampled to death on a cattle drive at a neighbour's ranch. He had a heart attack and just fell off, and got banged up pretty badly. Red's never been the same since."

"*What?*" I stopped dead and spun around. "Are you serious?"

"Unfortunately, yeah. It happened right in front of everyone, but it was so fast that it was too late to help. Your aunt blames herself, of course. He'd complained about chest pains earlier, but they didn't think it was anything serious."

Kade was walking alongside us now. "He was a great man," he said, patting Fox on the stallion's neck. "And he loved this ranch and these horses, and the cows, too. That's why it's so frustrating seeing it all go to waste."

Justin raised an eyebrow but didn't say anything.

"When your uncle fell, it scared the cows, and Red was knocked over, too, but he got up and pushed through that herd of cattle, and stood over Trent's body until help came. He's probably the reason your uncle lasted another few hours so he could say goodbye to Lillian."

"That is so sad," I said, running my fingers through Red's mane. "He's a hero and Aunt Lillian doesn't even like him."

"She likes him; she just finds it hard to be around him. After your uncle died, Red went into a depression that lasted a long time. He would barely eat, and the vet didn't know what was wrong. He pulled out of it eventually, but he was never quite the same after that."

"Oh, poor Red," I said, stroking the horse's neck softly, "that's heartbreaking."

"It was," Justin said. "It was a long, sad time on the ranch, and I think it affected every one of us. I don't think anyone's over it yet. Mom moved to California right after that, she divorced Dad, and then Florian left—"

"All right," Kade said sharply, clapping his hands together. "That's enough of that. Time to mount up, Astrid, hop on that pony."

"What are you talking about? He doesn't have any tack on."

"Oh yeah, right." Justin grinned. "Guess it's impossible then." He arched his eyebrows and swung lightly onto Doc's back from the ground without any effort at all.

"Definitely impossible," Kade added, swinging onto Fox with the same ease of motion as his brother.

They sat on their horses as if they were born there, grinning at me in challenge.

"Come on, Astrid, swing up."

"Very funny," I said, "torment the girl with the broken arm, why don't you?"

"Oh, come on, we're not making fun of you. The mounting block is right there." Kade waved his arm toward a plastic block in the corner by the door. "Live a little, Astrid. You know Red's as steady as they come."

"Fine, but if I get hurt...." I turned on my heel and marched toward the mounting block.

Red stood like a rock for me to mount, not moving a single muscle. I couldn't even tell if he was breathing. I tied his lead rope to the other side of his halter so I had reins, and slipped them over his head. Then, without giving myself time to think, I slid onto his broad back in one motion.

"You okay, Red?" I leaned down carefully and patted his neck. He flicked an ear back in question, but otherwise remained motionless. "All right, let's just walk."

I brushed my calves against his sides and, after a slight hesitation, he moved forward in the slowest of walks, more like a dragging shuffle.

Both Kade and Justin burst into laughter. "See, we told you. There's no way that horse will hurt you. That would be way too much effort on his part."

I breathed a sigh of relief, slowly relaxing into the swaying gait.

"What about the cows?" I asked, moving across the arena toward them. "You said he doesn't like them; does he panic and bolt whenever he sees them?"

"No." Kade laughed again. "He goes to sleep."

"What? You're teasing me again."

"Nope." Justin shook his head. "It's true. He has some sort of cow narcolepsy. Whenever he's near them he goes to sleep and refuses to move. You can hit him, you can spur him, you can swear or yell, but until you get off and lead him away he's not moving."

"Seriously?"

"Seriously. It's not the best trait for a ranch horse to have."

"Poor Red," I said again, tightening my grip on his mane. "Don't worry, I won't make you go near any scary cows."

Kade and Justin exchanged a look I couldn't decipher, but I was too busy concentrating on staying centered to think much about it. It was my first time riding in any arena since my horrible time with Folly, and I had some mixed feelings about it. And I was already regretting not wearing a helmet. It had seemed natural to ride without it out on the trail, but in here I felt fragile, like an egg that could be all too easily cracked.

I brushed my legs gently against Red's sides, trying to get a feel for him, and to my surprise he arched his neck, marching into a much more forward walk.

Whoa, I thought, caught off balance for second. *Where did that come from?*

But the next moment, he sagged again and went back to his regular shuffle.

"Hey, Astrid." My daydreaming was interrupted by the sound of cantering hooves. I pulled Red to a stop in the middle of the ring and turned to find Kade and Justin cantering along, side by side, so close their knees almost touched. Doc and Fox moved steadily forward, not breaking stride or swerving at all. Their legs moved in unison and when they turned down the short side of the arena, Fox looked like a faint, perfect outline of the smaller Doc.

Suddenly, Kade slid backwards onto Fox's rump and, in a move so slight I barely saw how he did it, he was sitting on Doc's back behind Justin and then, just as quick, Justin had transferred over to Fox.

"Whoa, how did you do that?" I asked in amazement, but their only answer was laughter.

They made the switch again and Kade moved Fox into a tight circle without even touching the reins hanging on the big stallion's neck. Without faltering he swung down off Fox's broad back and hit the ground for just a second before bouncing once and vaulting back upward to be seated again. Fox never broke stride or so much as hesitated. Kade scooted backward again until he was sitting over the horse's hips and then he rolled forward, palms flat out and pushed himself upward until he was doing a handstand. It only lasted a few seconds before he carefully lowered himself into a sitting position again. He pulled Fox to a stop and sat there grinning and catching his breath.

"Phew, haven't done that in a while. Glad to see I haven't lost my touch."

"I don't know, that handstand looked a little shaky." Justin laughed, trotting over to where I stood with Red. "See, Astrid, you don't need any special equipment or two working arms to communicate with horses. You just need to show up and be present with them."

"Well, you'd need the arms for the handstand." Kade grinned. "Unless you can do it onehanded?"

"Um, no," I said. "I'm not that coordinated. The only thing I'm good at is archery."

"Oh, well, you'll have to take up horseback archery then."

"What?" I said loudly, not sure I'd heard him right. Startled, Red woke up with a snort and took a few steps forward before drifting back to a halt. "Wait, what are you talking about?"

"Horseback archery," Kade repeated, "there are clubs and competitions all over the world. I assumed you'd know about it."

"No." I shook my head. "I didn't." I sat still, my mind whirling in a million directions suddenly caught up in a whole new galaxy of possibilities. It was like the moment I shot my first bow, the first time I watched Claudia ride Quarry, the time I saw Rob floating so fearlessly out over the lake on the rope swing. It felt like a huge fissure opened between what I knew before and what I knew after. Almost like stepping out of one life and into another. I shook my head to clear it and looked up at them with a dreamy smile.

"All right, your turn," Kade said, oblivious to my thoughts, "see if you can get that lazy creature to trot."

They were both looking at me expectantly, so I held tightly

to my lead-rope-reins and gently tapped Red's sides with both my calves. There was no response at all; he didn't even break into a walk. I tried again with slightly more pressure and, with an audible sigh, he moved forward sluggishly, practically tripping on his own feet as he ambled toward the rail.

"I think you're going to have to let go your death grip on that rope." Justin laughed. "You can't expect him to move forward like that. You can trust him, I promise."

"Oh," I said, looking down at my whitened knuckles. "I didn't know I was doing that. Good thing there wasn't a bit in his mouth." I let out almost all the rope, just holding on to the very end, and then I squeezed him very precisely with both my legs at the same time thinking forward thoughts. He moved forward a little faster but still seemed dull and listless.

"Less leg, more seat," Justin said, "you're forgetting about using your abs."

Oh, right, I'd almost forgotten. I'd barely ever squeezed Quarry with my legs, except to softly guide him somewhere. But riding Folly in her drugged state had meant that I'd had to become pretty aggressive with both my legs and hands as she'd become less and less responsive.

"I'm sorry, Red," I said, "I think I've almost forgotten everything Claudia told me."

I took a deep breath and closed my eyes, concentrating on relaxing first and finding the rhythm of Red's footfalls. They were hard to find since he was practically dragging his hind legs, but gradually I began to move with his steps.

Slowly, Claudia's instructions came back. Center myself first, let my legs drape around him softly, draw myself upward, ribcage open and arms hanging softly at my sides.

As soon as I adjusted my position I felt a small change in Red's steps. His back rose up slightly beneath me and his hind legs propelled us forward with more energy. Making sure my seat stayed light, I squeezed my seat bones gently, allowing him to move forward. This time I felt a surge of power flow through him. It was unexpected, and almost scary, but I breathed to relax and allowed myself to flow with him into a slow but powerful trot.

This is wonderful, I thought, opening my eyes slowly to find us circling the outside of the ring. His pricked ears flicked back toward me and he slowed, feeling the change in my concentration and I quickly shut my eyes again; it wasn't like we would run into anything. We circled the whole ring and I slowly opened my eyes, this time making sure not to let anything else change. I switched our direction through the diagonal. He was stiffer going this direction, but he still powered along happily.

I wonder if he knows any lateral work? I thought, but of course he probably did; every horse I'd seen Bryce and the boys ride had solid training. On my next pass, I moved him down the quarter line and asked him for the slightest of inside bend. I shifted my weight slightly and, without missing a beat he softened his rib cage and drifted back to the outside wall in a leg yield. I tried it again down the other quarter line with the same result.

"Good boy," I told him happily, "let's try the other way."

We did it a few more times in both directions, and at each pass he felt more supple and relaxed.

"What else can we try?" I asked him, thinking back to my lessons with Claudia. The next part in Quarry's warm up would have been shoulder-in but I wasn't sure if I remembered the aids. I closed my eyes again, trying to visualize guiding his shoulder gently off the rail.

Your hips follow his hips, your shoulders follow his shoulders, I whispered to myself softly. I felt the gentle shift in his body as he moved onto three tracks and then a little more bend as he moved onto four tracks, then back to three and then back to the wall again. I smiled and breathed out a happy sigh and switched directions. It wasn't as easy for him this way, so I kept it short and then brought him down to a walk, leaning forward to wrap my arms around his neck.

"What a good boy, Red, what a fantastic boy. Thank you so much."

He turned his head around and touched the tip of my boot with his nose.

"Well, that was unexpected," Kade said quietly.

I looked up, surprised to find that I wasn't alone with Red in my own private bubble anymore. I'd completely forgotten they were there. "Wasn't he wonderful?" I said excitedly. "I can't wait to ride him again. He reminded me of Quarry a little. Do you think I did an okay job with him? Did he look happy?"

"Uh, yeah, he looked happier than I've seen him since Trent's accident."

"You did fine," Justin said with a smile, "just keep doing what you're doing, ride him as much as you like."

I slid down and hit the ground with a thud, my jeans sticking to my legs with sweat, dirt, and horse-hair. That peaceful feeling I'd captured while riding Red stayed with me as we put the horses away and shut up everything for the night. I gave him a light brushing and put his blanket on, making sure to give him a hug and an apple before I closed his stall door.

"Do you need a ride back to the house, Astrid?" Justin asked. He'd stayed behind in the ring to put a few more minutes of riding on Doc.

"No, Aunt Lillian trusted me to drive her truck for some reason. I parked it over by Folly, at the broodmare barn."

"You're okay walking over there by yourself?" He led Doc to his stall and gave the stallion an affectionate pat on the rump.

"Yeah, I don't mind. I have my headlamp."

"Okay, goodnight."

"Night."

It was clear and crisp outside, and I was glad I'd put Folly's blanket on earlier.

"Wow." I tilted my head back to look at the night sky. The blanket of stars splashed against the blackness looked so close I could almost reach out and touch them. Everything was startlingly clear in a way I'd never seen at home. There were millions of stars here.

And to think that most of those stars are suns, maybe even with their own planets and moons in orbit. It was strange to think that I was just a tiny speck in a vast universe. I felt very small and insignificant, but also connected, too. It was a strange feeling and I made the walk back to the truck in a thoughtful daze, craning my head to take in all the sky.

Folly was asleep when I reached the truck, oblivious to the fantastic show going on over her head. I slid onto the cold vinyl truck seat and headed for home.

Chapter Fifteen

"Do you think anyone will come?" Lincoln asked nervously, looking at the open door to the little archery range above the gym. He shifted his bow nervously on the table, his face creased with worry.

"Sure," I said. "I put fliers up everywhere. I'm sure we can round up at least ten people."

I looked down at the small stack of battered bows, aluminum arrows and paper targets that we'd scrounged up from the storage unit behind the gym. Most of it was usable and it wasn't like we needed anything fancy to get started, but I couldn't help but think longingly about the equipment room at the range back home. I hadn't realized how lucky I'd been to have access to such nice stuff before.

I'd printed off dozens of inspiring archery posters that I'd made up on the computer the night before and taped them up on the walls; images of people shooting in different countries all over the world and pictures of grinning athletes holding up gold medals. I'd even found some horse archery photos to put up after doing a search online. That distraction had cost me two hours of sleep the night before, since once I started researching I could hardly bear to stop.

"Hey"—a mousy blonde girl stuck her head inside the door, looking anxious—"is this where the archery try-outs are?"

"Yes," I said delightedly, "it sure is. Here's the sign-up sheet. You just have to put in your information and we'll start shooting as soon as a few more people get here."

"Okay," she said shyly, writing her name on the sheet and then drifting away to look at the posters.

More people trailed in, some I recognized from class, and the rest were vaguely familiar strangers. Everyone seemed interested, though; they picked up the bows and arrows and other equipment and looked at the photos. When another ten minutes passed, and we, thankfully, had more people than we even needed, I went down to the end of room and started my speech.

"Thank you so much for coming, everyone. Welcome to the best sport on the planet."

It was a blur after that. There was scattered applause when I finished, and I quickly moved on to a short demonstration on how to hold a bow safely and how not to shoot your own hand off. Then I supervised while everyone took a turn shooting at the targets.

The whole time I couldn't keep the smile off my face; as much as I loved shooting, I'd always enjoyed teaching, too. My old coach Earl had usually chosen me to help the younger kids and new recruits because I was so patient with them and he knew I liked introducing people the sport I loved so much.

A throat cleared behind me and I turned around to see the scary girl, Mara, standing a few feet away just scowling at me with her arms crossed over her chest.

"Do you want to try?" I asked, trying not to look nervous. To my surprise, her face broke into a tentative smile that made her look much different than her usual sullen self.

"Sure," she said. "I've done it a couple times before." She took the bow from me slowly and I noticed the easy way she stood, calm and centered, breathing slowly before she drew her arm back in one smooth stroke and let her arrow fly. And that first arrow hit the target dead in the center.

"Mara!" I said in delight, "you're a natural."

"We had archery at summer camp every year," she said, shrugging. "I always liked it."

"Then sign here," I said excitedly, holding the sheet toward her. A few more hidden talents like this and we might have a shot at placing in this competition.

In the end, we had twelve people sign up, and Lincoln and I proudly took the sheet down to the office.

"Now can we have our space back?" I said, smiling at Mrs. Renning winningly.

"I can't see why not," she said. "But please go take those posters down so the janitor doesn't have to do it. They're everywhere."

"Thank you!" I said, dragging Lincoln back into the hall. "We did it," I squealed, grabbing him an exuberant hug that he fought off weakly. "Now, we just have to find a better place to practice. Those distances are too easy. I wonder if we could set the targets back up outside."

"It's almost winter," Lincoln said, "you won't want to shoot outside in February."

"Good point. Let me think about it."

"Astrid," Lincoln said, "you know you're a bit amazing, right? In a driven, pushy sort of way."

I stared at him in surprise. I'd never been called driven or pushy in my life; I was always the one getting shoved aside by other people. I chose to take it as a complement.

"Thanks," I said, "let's go get lunch. I'm starving."

Aunt Lillian was beyond excited when I told her the great news. "Good for you, Astrid," she said, "I knew you could do it. Go do your horse chores and I'll make us a pie to celebrate. How about blueberry?"

"Thank you!" I said, running out the door. We whizzed through chores but just as Justin and I were leaving the training barn, I happened to glance over at the little run-down storage building right next to the hay barn. I'd never paid it attention before, but for some reason this time it caught my eye.

"Hey, Justin, what's that building over there?"

"That one? Oh, it used to be an old milking parlour; now it's just used for storage. Why?"

"Oh, no reason, just curious. Do you think anyone would mind if I looked inside?"

"I can't see why; it's just full of old junk. It probably should have been cleaned out ages ago."

Hmm, I thought, *interesting.*

It didn't take me long to slip over there and take a quick look inside. When I was satisfied I headed up to the house for dinner as fast as I could.

The smell of spaghetti and garlic bread met me at the door and my stomach rumbled happily in response. I washed my hands quickly and helped Aunt Lillian set the table.

I told her all about my day as we ate, but part of my mind was occupied by what I'd seen in that old barn.

"Aunt Lillian?" I asked finally.

"Mmm?" she said, glancing up.

"Do you think I could have a friend over after school tomorrow? He's on the archery team and I was hoping that we could work on a project."

"Oh, a *boy*?" she said, looking way too interested. She put her fork down and grinned at me, eyes twinkling.

"Well, technically yes, but we're just friends. It's about finding a place to practice."

"Of course, he can come over. Have Kade bring him home, he can stay for supper."

"Oh, I don't think—"

"Nonsense, I can't wait to meet him. This is so exciting. I'm so glad I get to be here for this important stage in your life."

Oh, no, I groaned internally. *Please stop.*

"Um, okay," I said, not wanting risk jeopardizing my plans. Best to let her keep thinking I liked Lincoln for now; at least she'd be in a good mood when I asked her a favour tomorrow.

*****

The hardest part of my plan was convincing Lincoln to come over. When I asked him at lunch the next day he hemmed and hawed and came up with every excuse he could think of before finally giving in and agreeing to come to dinner that night.

"It's not like it's a date," I finally said, exasperated. "I just want to show you this barn."

"Ooh, she wants to take you home and show you her *barn*," Malcolm said, making kissy faces at us.

"How is that helping?" I snapped at him. "Do you want a place to practice or not? And why do I feel like the one doing all the work?"

Luckily, Kade and Casey were already arguing when we got to the truck, so I was spared any smart remarks from either of them. They both fell silent the second the door opened, and Kade spent the rest of the drive grimly focused on the road, not saying a word until he dropped us off at my front door.

To my surprise, Casey got out, too.

"I hope it's okay," she said, looking almost timid. "Kade's on a date tonight and Justin won't be back until late, so Lillian invited me over here."

"Sure," I said, not wanting to be rude. She still looked awful, and maybe being around Lillian would cheer her up. I hadn't told her yet that her nemesis Mara had joined the archery team and that I'd actually started to like the girl.

Aunt Lillian was nowhere to be seen, so I quickly dropped my school stuff off and changed my clothes. I wanted to show Lincoln the barn while it was still light out.

"Can I come, too?" Casey said, looking forlorn.

"Um, sure," I said. "I haven't cleaned the backseat, though, so there will be dog hair."

"That's okay." Casey followed us to the truck and pushed the mound of dog blankets aside without hesitation.

I stopped to quickly throw Folly her hay and then drove past the training barn and parked in front of the little storage barn I'd surveyed the day before

Lincoln raised an eyebrow skeptically. "This is what you wanted to show me?"

"Oh, come on, Lincoln. Don't knock it until you've seen inside. I checked it out already; I know you'll love it."

Before he could argue, I stepped forward, struggled with the latch and then threw open both big doors.

Lincoln stared into the dimly lit barn and gave me a doubtful look.

"Oh, for heaven's sake." I marched inside, flicked a switch on the nearest wall, and the whole place was bathed in light from a row of hanging, overhead lights. Despite that they were covered in cobwebs and grime, they still cast a huge glow.

"Oh, wow," Lincoln said, impressed. "What is this place?"

"It's an old milking barn," I replied. "It would be perfect if we cleaned it up. What do you think?"

"I kind of like it."

Lincoln walked to the middle of the barn and stood with his hands on his hips, like he was considering the possibilities. He turned to look at me, a smile tugging his lips. "This could work, couldn't it?"

"Yeah, if we spruced it up, I think it would be perfect."

"Let's pace it out. I bet we can shoot Olympic distances in here."

Casey snorted. "You think any of you is going to the Olympics?"

"Actually," I said coolly, "that was the plan up until last year."

"Oh," she said, looking mildly impressed. "Sorry."

Lincoln was already at the far wall, and I left Casey to join him. We slowly paced, toe to heel across the dusty floor, counting out our steps. When we reached the end, we turned to each other and smiled.

"It's about 70 feet," Lincoln said, "that's definitely over 18 meters, that's perfect."

"We'd need to do a lot of clean up, though; it would be tons of work," I warned him.

"That's fine if it means we get to shoot inside all winter. The rest of the team would help, I'm sure."

I was happy to see that he looked genuinely excited for the first time.

Casey snorted. "Aren't there, like, two of you?"

"Thanks to Astrid there are now at least twelve of us," Lincoln said. "Didn't she tell you?"

"I guess not," Casey said. "How did you manage that?"

"Didn't you see all the posters for our archery club try-outs? I plastered them over the whole school. It was the prize money for the competition that lured them in, I'm sure. But, whatever works."

"Oh, sorry, I didn't notice any posters," Casey said quickly.

"How could you have not—"

"I've been busy," she snapped, wrapping her arms around herself protectively.

Lincoln and I exchanged a puzzled glance. I'd literally covered that entire school with posters. Nobody could have missed them. What on earth was going on with Casey?

"What did your aunt say when you asked her if we could use the barn?" Lincoln said, turning to me.

"I haven't asked yet," I confessed. "I wanted you to see it first."

"Oh, you probably don't even need to bother her," Casey muttered. "I'm sure you could just go ahead. That's what I would do. Adults just say no to anything that matters and ruin your whole life."

"Well, in this case we have to ask," I said firmly. "I'm not spending all sorts of time cleaning out a disgusting barn and setting up equipment only to get kicked out the next day. Right, Lincoln?"

"Right, I don't want to sneak around. This place would be perfect, though. I hope she says yes."

Casey shrugged angrily and dropped her gaze to the ground. "Fine, don't say I didn't warn you, though. Don't blame me if she says no for no good reason at all and dashes all your dreams."

That's a little dramatic, I thought, looking at her sullen face. Her lower lip trembled like she was trying not to cry, and I felt a sudden stab of sympathy for her.

We trooped back to the truck, each lost in our own thoughts. Now that the time had come to put my plan into action it suddenly seemed like an impossible thing to ask of my aunt. Who was I to show up here and ask her to let strangers troop around on her property shooting things? She would probably hate the idea. And then I would have dragged Lincoln all the way out here and gotten his hopes up for nothing.

There's still no harm in asking, a tiny voice said in my head, *at least you tried. And you never know, there's a chance she might say yes, that barn is practically standing abandoned.* I felt a spark of renewed hope rekindle inside me.

The smell of food wafted out from the kitchen and I kicked my boots off hurriedly and led Lincoln inside. Casey stomped in behind us, still simmering in her bad mood.

The counter was strewn with ingredients and Aunt Lillian

herself was covered with streaks of flour.

"Aunt Lillian, this is my friend Lincoln. He's part of the archery club at Triple Hills."

"Well now, Lincoln, it's a pleasure to meet you. Are you Steven Howard's boy?"

"Yes, ma'am, one of them."

"Your dad's a good man. He helped me sort out some of the legal issues when my husband died. What a mess that was."

Her smile dimmed and then lit up again as she focused on Lincoln; at least he'd made a good first impression on her. I hoped she liked him enough to let him shoot up the inside of her barn.

"How nice you could come over," she beamed at both of us. "You're just in time for dinner. I made a roast."

"Thank you for inviting me, ma'am, it smells delicious." Lincoln sat down and shot me a grin when I raised my eyebrows at him. *Ma'am?*

I helped set the table and everyone sat down; my aunt at the head of the table, Casey on one side, and Lincoln and me on the other. There was a glistening roast, potatoes, biscuits, and some sort of buttery fried mushroom dish that looked a bit scary but ended up being completely delicious.

Aunt Lillian was on her best behaviour, asking us questions about school and archery, and making no hidden comments about Lincoln being a boy.

When the time seemed right, I cleared my throat. "So, Aunt Lillian, the archery team at Triple Hills is looking for a place to practice this winter."

"Oh?" she said, looking up with interest.

"We have a small area to use at school, but if we're going to have a shot at the NFSC challenge, or any competition at all, then we'll have to find an indoor place to shoot longer distances."

"Sorry, what competition?"

"It's called the Northern Flight School Competition, but everyone just calls it NFSC," Lincoln said. "It's for schools in the mid to northern BC and Yukon areas, and it's sponsored by one of the mining companies. It's supposed to give people from rural areas a chance to compete and give their schools some incentive to sponsor them. The prize money is crazy. We did well there last year so we already have an invitation; we don't need to qualify. And now, thanks to Astrid, we have a shot at forming a team. We just need a better place to practice." He looked over at me and nodded.

"So," I cleared my throat, "we were thinking that maybe we could set up that old barn, the one that used to be for milk cows. We could clean—"

"Well now, Astrid," Aunt Lillian interrupted, "I don't know about shooting arrows around willy-nilly when we have all this livestock wandering about. And what about Jake? He could get killed."

"Oh, we'd just shoot inside, ma'am," Lincoln interrupted quickly. "We'd set the barn up properly and follow all the standard safety rules. We're a very serious club. And we make everyone sign a safety waiver."

Safety waiver? I almost started laughing out loud. *Serious club? Most of the members hadn't even handled a bow before this week.*

"Hmm," she said less doubtfully. "I suppose it couldn't hurt to try it out. I'd want a list of all those kid's names, though; I need to know who's coming and going."

"Of course," Lincoln said quickly. "Anything you need. We'd mostly come on the weekends and once in a while during the week."

"Well, as long as you and Astrid are there to supervise," she beamed at him. "You will be there at all times?"

"Definitely," Lincoln assured her.

"That old barn is full to the brim of stuff. It would take a lot of hard work to clean it out properly. But, I guess if you're up for that challenge, then I can't see any reason not to at this point. You could at least do a trial run to see if it suits everyone."

Lincoln and I beamed at each other, hardly able to believe our luck. Even Casey smiled.

"Thank you so much," I said, "I promise you we won't be any trouble at all."

"Well, if you're all finished here, then come on in the living room for some tea and cookies."

Casey grabbed some for herself and took them upstairs to finish her homework while the rest of us went to the living room.

"Mind you don't get burnt. This batch just came out of the oven." Aunt Lillian set the piping hot cookies down on a plate in front of us and, despite scorching our fingertips and having to blow cold air to cool them before every bite, we dove in.

Headlights shone in the window, and Lincoln rose hastily to his feet. "That's my dad. He said he'd pick me up."

"Well, let me pack you up some cookies to go then. Can't have you starving on the way home."

"Thank you, ma'am, but that's not—"

"Nonsense, it will just take me a minute."

Aunt Lillian opened and slammed a few drawers, rifling through the tumbled contents until she found a plastic container and a lid that fit it. "There you are," she said, piling cookies right to the top and squishing down the lid. "You can just bring that back next time you come over."

"Thanks again," Lincoln said, "having a place to shoot means a lot to the team."

"Well, we'll see how it goes. Tell your dad I said hello."

"Will do, bye, Astrid, see you later."

And with that he was gone.

"Well, Astrid," she turned to me and clasped her hands together, "that's a very nice, polite young man you brought home. I'm so glad to see that you're making friends so soon."

"He does seem nice," I said, "and he's going to be a good archer once he gets more practice."

"Friends are invaluable pillars to lean on in times of trouble," my aunt said, sighing. "I don't know what I would have done if Bryce's family and Florian hadn't been here when your uncle died. I was completely lost without him."

"I'm sorry," I said, not knowing what else to say. I grabbed another cookie and stuffed it in my mouth just to have something to do.

"It was a sad season, that's for sure. But, it did get better as time went on. He was just so much a part of my life, you see. We did everything together and he was the heart and soul of this ranch. I worked hard, but he was the visionary who had all the brilliant ideas. You would have loved him, Astrid. He was funny and outgoing and larger than life; everyone loved him. But me most of all."

She fell silent and looked down at the table, scratching at a spatter on the wood with one fingernail.

I sat there, nervously plowing my way through the cookies, not sure how to deal with all this sadness. I didn't have much experience with comforting others. All the excess emotion in our condo was taken up by my dad's anger; it didn't leave room for much else except for fear. I usually just found someplace to hide until it was over. And Marion rarely shared anything she felt.

"Well, that's enough of my whining." Aunt Lillian laughed and smiled at me. And right then I wished I was the type of person who could easily hug her or know the right things to say.

"So, tell me how that horse of yours is getting on."

"Oh, she's great," I said, relieved the subject had changed. "She's so much happier here. I meant to ask you which vet I should call. I'm supposed to have her checked over again before we start hand walking her."

"Oh, sure, you'll want Bert to look at her. He's the best in this area and has a special interest in lameness. I'll call him tomorrow and see if he can make some time to come out."

"Great, thanks." I took a gulp of tea and then stared at the milky surface, gathering my thoughts. "Aunt Lillian, how much money are you asking for Red?"

"Red?" she asked in surprise. "Why? Is there interested in him?"

"Well, sort of, I'm just wondering how much he'd cost."

She peered at my face closely and then shook her head.

"Oh, Astrid." She sighed. "Of all the fantastic horses here, why would you be interested in that strange creature?"

"Because he's wonderful," I said simply. "He's kind, and

gentle, and he takes care of me. And I think he's a bit lonely, too; he needs me."

"But he'll never be a dressage horse. He's slow as molasses."

"I'm not sure," I said, slowly, thinking of those few recent glimpses of power I'd felt in him. "But I know that he makes me feel safe and that he'd be my friend. I honestly think that's what I'd want most in a horse."

She smiled and shook her head. "Fair enough. I guess I'd be asking around six or seven thousand. He's well-bred and well put together, and he'd make a nice horse for someone who could figure his pea-brain out."

Seven thousand, I thought, my heart sinking. I knew it was a completely reasonable price for a well-trained horse. Folly had cost my dad like six times as much, and she'd been considered a bargain, but it was still out of my reach.

I can't ask Liza much money for Folly; especially if she doesn't end up sound. If I found the money I wonder if my dad and Marion would even pay for board once I got home? Can we afford that once the lawsuit is settled? We might not even have a home to live in, let alone money for horses. I guess I can't exactly dip into my money for school. Dad said there was a fund set up for training. I wonder if I could use any of that money?

"Astrid?" my aunt asked, bringing me back to earth. "Don't worry about it now. You have a whole year to ride him and enjoy him. Hopefully by then you'll come to your senses and pick someone else."

She tapped my knee good naturedly to show she was kidding.

That will never happen, I thought, smiling back at her, *there will never be anyone more sweet and interesting than Red.*

Chapter Sixteen

With Bryce away, all the riding and most of the barn work fell to Justin and Kade. Aunt Lillian sometimes helped with cleaning stalls, and it was she who worked with the foals and yearlings before they left, but I noticed that she wasn't exactly the type to stay on task. She'd clean half a stall or start to sweep the aisle in the training barn, and then she'd just get this funny look on her face and disappear back into her office or to the house without any explanation.

Casey helped to feed in the mornings before school and she sometimes rode the roan mare, Kitty, who had been Aunt Lillian's horse. Casey told me that Kitty's price was set way too high, and she thought that secretly my aunt didn't want to sell her at all.

Saturday morning was supposed to be the day everyone slept in but, when you're used to getting up at 5:30 every morning it's hard to break the habit. I was up at the crack of dawn to feed and work with Folly before heading over to the training barn to help care for the horses there, too.

After breakfast, Justin and I brushed Folly, and he practiced some light walking work with her inside the corral; just some forward, some stopping, and a few steps of backing up.

"Wow, it's like she's completely cured," I said excitedly, watching her follow him around like an obedient puppy.

"She is who she is, Astrid," he said, laughing. "There's nothing challenging about what I'm asking her today so she's happy to go along with the program. It's when she wants something else and can't have it that you'll see the old Folly emerge. She'll always be a horse you'll have to be somewhat on guard around. Still, I'm real happy with her progress. We can start taking her for longer hand-walks as soon as the vet okays it."

Still, after a few weeks of full-time turnout, eating the lower-energy feed and having her manners worked on at least twice a day, even Aunt Lillian had to admit that Folly was a much different horse.

"Well, I'm relieved to have been proven wrong," she said, shaking her head. "There's hope for her yet."

Folly hadn't lost her attitude completely, of course; she could still be bossy, but that murderous edge she'd been refining had been dulled down into something much more manageable. She often nickered when she saw me, and her ear pinning moments weren't quite so dramatic.

Grooming for Justin on a Saturday was much more relaxing since we didn't have to cram in all his sessions in just a couple of hours. He took longer rides and took time to do ground work with some of the younger horses.

"Why are they all so good?" I asked him as he paused between rides to grab a bottle of water.

He looked at me in surprise and then cracked a grin. "Genetics, partially, and the rest is management and good, consistent handling. We don't let them leave the ranch until we're sure they're bomb-proof."

It was a nice enough day that he said yes when I asked him about a trail ride. I wanted to take those photos of the horses for the website like I'd promised Aunt Lillian, before winter came.

I filled my backpack with snacks and the ancient digital camera Aunt Lillian had loaned me and climbed onto Red with much more confidence since our last, amazing ride together. I also had unpacked my helmet and made sure to use it whenever I rode, even if Casey did make fun of me.

I left the reins loose on his neck while he plodded along, content to follow Badger and only pausing to grab a few bites to eat when he saw something particularly tasty.

We started with the broodmares and I took tons of photos of each horse, trying to find the most flattering shots to use for the website. I had a notebook in my backpack that I used to write down descriptions of each horse and their location so I could figure out their names with Aunt Lillian later that night over dinner. After that we did the foals and yearlings and then the two- and three-year-olds before moving on to the older horses.

It took longer than I'd expected, but in the end, I felt like I had taken photos of everyone except Folly and the horses in the training barn.

Aunt Lillian was delighted when I showed her the pictures that night. I went through the descriptions with her, getting her to fill in their names and pedigrees so we could have everything on the website. Sometimes even she didn't know who they were, especially the yearlings and two-year-olds who changed so much from season to season. When that happened, I made a star beside each name and put their photo in a special album on the computer. I'd have to consult with Justin and Kade to try and figure out who the mystery horses were.

Chapter Seventeen

The next morning the ground was covered in a thick layer of frost that made the whole world look like a lacy topper for a wedding cake.

My truck didn't appreciate the cold very much, though. It wheezed and snorted and finally started with a roar.

Folly looked adorable wrapped up, warm and toasty in her thick plaid blanket. She pawed impatiently when she saw me and tossed her head, but she stood politely with her ears pricked when I came out of the barn with her breakfast.

"Good girl," I said, "you're such a smart girl."

I jogged over to the training barn to help Kade and a grumpy, yawning Casey feed breakfast and give Red his morning apple. By the time I was done I was shivering with cold. I really needed to add some winter gear to my shopping list. I ran back to my truck to keep warm and drove that coughing, sputtering beast slowly back up to the house, ready for my own breakfast.

To my surprise, even though the sun was hardly up, Lincoln was waiting at the kitchen table already tucking in to a heaping plate of food when I got back to the house. He looked up, grinning, and stuffed a huge bite of pancake into his mouth.

"Astrid, you're back," my aunt said, practically skipping around the table. "Just in time for breakfast. Wash your hands and pull up a chair."

I dutifully scrubbed my hands at the kitchen sink and sat down across from Lincoln, filling my own plate with pancakes and bacon.

"Here's your coffee, dear," Aunt Lillian said, setting a milky cup in front of me, "Lincoln's been telling me about your plans for the barn. That thing has been neglected for years so I can't wait to see it all cleaned up."

"Yeah, you must be excited if you got here before sunrise," I joked. "I thought we were starting after lunch."

He blushed and cleared his throat nervously. "Sorry, I might have been overly excited. My mom thought I was insane to ask her to drive me here this early. It *is* okay, isn't it?"

"Sure," I said, "I don't know how much help I'm going to be with cleaning and lifting, but I'll do my best."

"I thought I'd come early to help get everything organized. Everyone else should be here around ten or eleven." He looked quickly up at my aunt. "I can call and cancel them, though, if it's going to be too much of a bother."

"Oh, you won't be a bother," my aunt said. "The more the merrier. Just set all that junk outside the barn for now and I'll come look it over to see if there's anything worth keeping. I doubt it, though, that barn has sat for so long the rats have probably gotten to everything."

Great, I thought, *dirt, rats, and heavy lifting. Just how I wanted my Sunday to start.*

Lincoln finished before me and he sat there twirling his coffee cup on the table and staring at my unfinished plate as if he could telepathically will me to eat faster. The second I was done he shot up and helped me take my dishes to the dishwasher.

"Thanks so much for breakfast, ma'am," he said to Lillian. "It was delicious. Come on, Astrid, let's get a move on it."

"Okay, okay," I grumbled, following him to the door.

The truck protested loudly when I started it back up from its nap, and I drove it slowly, avoiding the pot-holed short cut and taking the smooth road to our new archery range. At least the sun had melted off most of the frost already.

I hadn't been to the barn since the night we'd looked at it with Casey; the space had seemed fantastic at the time, but now, as we swung open the large door and flicked on the light, it just looked like a lot of work.

"Wow," Lincoln said. "I don't remember there being so much stuff crowded in here."

"Yeah, or all this dirt."

Everything inside was caked with about three inches of thickly layered dust particles and half-moulded hay.

"I don't even know where to start," I said, shoulders sagging. "It will take us weeks to do all this by ourselves."

"No, it won't," Lincoln said straightening his shoulders, completely undaunted. "We just have to chip away at it one step at a time."

I walked slowly inside, skirting around the piles of junk. Cardboard boxes, their sides sagging from years of sitting, were piled in orderly stacks on one side, their contents neatly labelled in black marker. Cattle 1995, one said, although I doubted it was full of cows. When I pulled back an edge I could see stacks of paper pressed neatly together. So, it was probably accounting or records about everything that happened with the cows back in that year. I hadn't even been born yet.

Another one at the edge of a stack read *Beezy First year* and I eased it out and carefully lifted the lid. "Oh," I said, pulling out a fistful of brightly coloured ribbons. "They must be from old shows." I flipped one over and read *Champion, Yearling Halter*, and the next said, *Reserve Champion, Yearling Halter*.

Wasn't that big, raw-boned, chestnut broodmare named Beezy? I thought I could remember Aunt Lillian pointing her out to me in the pasture when we'd dropped off hay. She had a wide blaze and socks, and she was probably in her twenties now. These must have been from when she was a baby. Sure enough, when I dug further into the box I came up with a faded photograph in a tarnished, gold frame. It showed a young blonde woman with a huge grin on her face accepting a ribbon from a smiling judge.

Someone had written at the bottom: Lillian and Beezy triumph again.

Wow, I leaned closer; was that really Aunt Lillian? She looked about sixteen in the photo, although I knew she had to have been older at the time. Long blonde hair fell in curls around her shoulders and she beamed up at the judge.

The little horse beside her didn't look much like the adult Beezy, either; this yearling was stunning with a refined head and a solid, well-muscled body. She was craning her delicately arched neck to reach a tall young man who stood next to her shoulder, one arm draped proudly over her neck.

I squinted at the photo. That must be my Uncle Trent. This

photo must have been taken when they were just starting out on the ranch. I took in the familiar lines of the horse and suddenly it dawned on me, she looked exactly like a younger version of Red, she must be related to him somehow.

I put the picture carefully away and dragged the box gently to one side so I would remember to take it back to the house to show Aunt Lillian.

We came up with a system where I would open a box, quickly survey the contents, and then put it either to the left or right. Stuff on the left went to the truck to be taken to the barn office where Aunt Lillian could see if it needed to be kept or not. Anything extra interesting like photos or ribbons I planned to take up to the house. Furniture or garbage would just stay piled in front of the barn.

Lincoln was a serious worker and not much of a talker. With me out of commission he had to do most of the carrying of things out to the truck.

By the time the mini-van full of back-up labourers arrived, he was red-faced, sweating, and had decades worth of barn dust and cobwebs clinging to his clothes and hair.

"Hey, Linc, Astrid," Gage said, jumping out of the truck, closely followed by Malcolm. An older blond guy with a goatee slid out of the driver's seat. He didn't look like a high-school student; maybe in his mid-twenties. Although it was hard to tell since he was dressed in some sort of forest-green outfit with a wide leather belt and knee-high brown suede boots. He basically looked like Robin Hood, minus the long-bow and the pointy hat.

"Hey," Lincoln said in relief, dropping another box into the back of Aunt Lillian's truck. "You made it. Hey guys," he added as three more people slowly climbed out of the truck. Two of them were Mara and Allison, and the last person was another Robin Hood. This one was wearing a darker green outfit than the first guy but still with the wide belt and the boots, and he *did* have the pointy hat to match the outfit. He had red hair and wide green eyes that took in the dairy barn appreciatively.

"Nice spot," he said, "this is going to be great."

"Guys, this is Astrid," Lincoln said, waving a hand to where I sat surrounded by a pile of boxes. "This is her Aunt Lillian's barn. Astrid, that's Gage's older brother Bill and his friend Martin, they're the organizers of the Triple Bar Society for Creative Anachronism group."

"M'Lady," Bill said, sweeping into a low bow.

"Greetings, Princess," Martin said at the same time, twirling his arm as he made a similar bow.

"Oh, hi," I said, startled. Then I added, "but I'm not a princess. And the society of *what?*"

"Creative Anachronism." Martin raised an eyebrow. "It's very popular. We research customs of the Middle Ages and Renaissance, and then we have all sorts of tournaments, including archery. It's real fun. And, you *could* be a princess if you wanted. We're always looking for new members. You could be a warrior, too, on horseback maybe, if you're into that. Or, if LARPing's more your style we have a group, too. Then you could be an Elf or pretty much anything you like, actually. You could just make something up."

"You know, if I hear one more word about *elves*," Mara said, looking at him darkly, "someone is going to get hurt."

"Mara, hi," I said. "I'm glad you and Allison could come."

"Are the weirdos going to be on the team?" she said rudely. "Because if they are then I'm out."

"Hey, that's not nice," I said. "They came to help us. Why are you being mean?"

She stared at me in astonishment, her mouth working and then she suddenly sagged. "You're right. It's this *place*," she said, frowning. "I haven't been to the ranch since last spring. Since the thing with…with Dinah happened. It's making me a little sick to be here. I'll be fine, though. Let's just start shooting."

"Casey's not here," I said quickly. "She went to town with Kade."

"Don't worry, I won't beat her up when I see her," she said, sounding more sad than angry. "There wouldn't be much point."

"Okay, let's get to work everyone," Lincoln said quickly, interrupting us. "We're all here for the same thing. Astrid, the local SCA, and LARPers are hoping that they could come to some practice sessions, too; they're a very fun group and they don't have a place to practice, either. Don't worry, they're not weird at all."

No, not weird at all, I thought, raising an eyebrow at their uniforms. "I'm sure it would be fine as long as we don't get too many people."

"Right," Lincoln said. "So that's everyone introduced. Let's get everything moved out of here."

Seven and a half people working on a project was much faster than one and a half, and by late afternoon, the inside of the barn was finally clear of everything besides dirt, old hay and spiders.

Now that the space was opened up, I could see again how much potential it had. The lower half of the walls were made of the same concrete as the floor; only the upper half and the roof was made of wood. It would be easy to get this space looking good; especially if Aunt Lillian let us paint it.

I looked around, wondering what other changes I could make, while I slowly dragged my rake through the debris on the floor, gathering piles toward the door for someone else to pick up later.

"All right, kids, time for lunch," Aunt Lillian called. I hadn't even heard her truck pull up. My stomach rumbled in anticipation of lunch as I hurried outside.

Aunt Lillian had dropped her truck's tail-gate down and was handing out sandwiches and drinks to the group surrounding her. "Astrid, come on before they've eaten it all."

She didn't have to tell me twice. I grabbed a plastic-wrapped sandwich and gratefully let her pour me a cup of steaming hot chocolate from the big thermos she'd brought along.

"Well, you, er, kids," she said, eyeing up Martin's outfit suspiciously, "have certainly made a big dent here. Now, I guess I have to find a place to put all this junk. I guess all this old furniture will have to go to the dump."

"Couldn't you sell it online?" Lincoln asked, "I'm sure someone would take it."

"Oh, I wouldn't have time to figure out something like that," Aunt Lillian said. "That computer is not my strong point. It would be easier just to throw the stuff out."

"Well, what if we sold it for you? We could put out some ads and then split the money with you fifty-fifty. We could use the money for paint and targets to set up the range properly. And we need more equipment, too."

"Oh," Aunt Lillian said thoughtfully. "Or, how about you sell all this junk and keep a hundred percent of the money to get started."

"Oh no, we couldn't do that."

"Of course you can. I don't want this old rubbish; you'd be doing me a favour. If you think you can sell it quickly then you can stick it in the corner of the big hay barn for a bit. There's a space to one side that's open. Astrid can show you where to stack it."

She strode into the old dairy barn and stood looking around, her hands on her hips. "Now, this is impressive. It's so nice to see such hard-working kids; some of my grown-up working students wouldn't have been able to accomplish half as much. Anyway, all the accounting stuff and paperwork can go to the office in the barn. I'll have to sort through it to see what I need to keep and what I can burn. I can't wait to see what this place looks like when it's all finished."

Between the two trucks it only took us four trips to get all the old furniture over to the hay barn and safely tucked in one corner. Before each piece was loaded we quickly cleaned it up with some rags and lemon-scented cleaner and then took pictures so Lincoln could post them online later.

We moved all the boxes of old paperwork to the office in the training barn, and I had Malcolm load the boxes of photos and ribbons I'd found into the back of my pick-up truck.

By that time, we were all exhausted and decided to call it a day. I stood back and surveyed all our hard work proudly. If we could get it swept, washed, and de-spidered this week, then we might be able to start painting next weekend.

"Do you think we'd have time to quickly see the horses?" Allison asked tentatively. "We live in town, so I can't have one, but I really like them."

"Sure. Does everyone want to come?"

There were some half-hearted yeses from everyone except Mara, so I led the way. Mara didn't say a word, but she trailed after us as we headed to the training barn.

"This is Doc," I said, standing back so everyone could admire him. And then we moved from horse to horse. Allison's eyes shone as she stroked their noses, even though she seemed afraid of them. She made sudden high-pitched squeaking noises whenever one of them moved too quickly and jerked away when Red lipped gently at her jacket. But the look in her eye didn't fade.

When we reached the end, and everyone was marvelling at the enormous indoor, I turned to see Mara leaning over Kitty's stall, stroking the mare's neck.

"Did you know her?" I asked, "from before?"

"She's Dinah's sister," Mara said. "I've ridden her a little, too. She's a great mare."

"Oh, Aunt Lillian said Kitty doesn't like very many people. You're lucky she likes you."

"Yeah, me, Lillian, and Casey were about the only ones she approved of." Mara laughed. "Mares are weird sometimes."

"Tell me about it, you should see my mare, Folly, when she has a tantrum. What's your horse like?"

"Chief. He's great. He's in his twenties now, so he's really slowing down, but we can still trail ride and potter around. Just no speed work. I really loved barrel racing and games. Casey and I grew up doing that stuff. Dinah was perfect at it; she was so fast that nobody could outrun her." Mara looked down and kicked her boot lightly against Kitty's door. "I guess that's why she sold for all that money."

"I'm sorry, Mara," I said. "I heard about that."

"Yeah, well, it's over with now."

"You know, if you're through beating up Casey, then maybe you could come over and ride Kitty sometime. Casey only rides once in a while, and I'd love to go trail riding or play in the ring. I'm riding Red."

"Really? You're riding *him*?" Mara said in a tone that made me instantly want to take back my invitation. "I thought he was sort of messed in the head."

"No," I said sharply, "he isn't. He's perfect."

"Okay, okay," she said, raising up both hands. "Sor-ry to offend you." And she turned and walked away without looking back.

We all trudged wearily back to the van and I couldn't help yawning every few steps. I was exhausted. "Bye, Astrid, nice to meet you," Bill called out as he pulled away. "Make sure you look up our SCA group online. We'd love to have you."

"Okay," I said, laughing. "I'll check it out."

During the four hours we'd spent cleaning the barn and moving heavy furniture together, I'd gotten to know him and his friends, and it turned out they were real nice guys; not as weird as I'd originally thought. He'd told me all about the groups he belonged to and had also backed up what Kade and Justin had told me earlier; Horse Archery was most-definitely a thing.

I knew I could never do anything like that on a horse like Folly, but maybe Red would be steady enough to try.

"My dad will be here soon," Lincoln said, looking at his watch. "We should head back up to the house."

We drove back in a comfortable silence, both tired and lost in our own thoughts.

"Oops, he's already here. We must be late," Lincoln said, but when we reached the black SUV parked in the driveway, it was empty. "Huh, he must have gone inside."

We trudged inside, the warm air full of the smell of Aunt Lillian's chocolate chip cookies just fresh from the oven.

"Wow, she's a good cook," Lincoln said. "You're lucky to live here."

"I know. Tell her that, though. She thinks she's terrible compared to her old cook, Florian."

We found Aunt Lillian and Lincoln's dad sitting together at one end of the big wooden table drinking coffee and laughing like old friends, which I guessed they were.

"Oh, kids, you're back just in time for cookies," Aunt Lillian said. Her cheeks were flushed, and her eyes sparkled. She looked happier than I'd seen her since I'd arrived here. It made her look about ten years younger, more like the photo I'd seen of her earlier. It was the first time I'd seen her with a friend her age.

Lincoln's dad looked up just as he stuck half a cookie in his mouth. He didn't look much like Lincoln; he was round-cheeked with black hair flecked with grey, and he lacked his son's serious expression.

"Oh, you two are filthy," Aunt Lillian said, laughing at us.

"No, don't come any closer, you can have your cookies after you go and shower, Astrid."

"I know, I think there are spiders in my hair. Oh, Aunt Lillian, I almost forgot, there are some boxes of ribbons and pictures that I brought back to the house in the truck. We left them outside, though."

"Well, I'll bring them in when we're done here. Find anything interesting?"

"Yes," I nodded. "Some really old pictures. There's one of your old broodmare Beezy when she was young. She's winning a prize."

"Oh," she said in delight. "I'd love to see that. Beezy was the very first filly we bred ourselves. That girl won everything back in the day, and she's given us a spectacular foal every year since she became a broodmare. This will be her last year, though. Even though the vet says she's in fantastic shape, I can't condone breeding a twenty-seven-year-old horse any longer. She'll have to retire after this one."

"Is Red related to her?" I remembered to ask.

"Well, certainly, she's his mother. Trent took one look at that day-old foal and knew it was destined to be his horse." Aunt Lillian sighed and picked up her coffee mug, turning it slowly between her hands. "We were so young when we first started out; we were only nineteen when we got married, you know. We knew we wanted to work with horses. Trent had grown up with them, of course; Triple Bar was his granddad's place and he used to spend the summers working here. He never thought he'd inherit it, since Grandpa was such a cranky old goat who hated everyone. But for some reason, he took a shine to Trent and it became ours.

"I'll never forget that day we moved in. One thousand acres, complete with horses and a herd of cattle; and us not having a clue where to start. To say we were overwhelmed would be an understatement. Plus, of course, everything was so run-down. Most of the buildings were from the original homestead that had been built over a hundred years ago. We had to work hard to keep the whole place from falling down on our heads."

"But you did a fine job," Lincoln's dad said. "The two of you turned this place around and made it shine."

"Oh, thank you," she said, shaking her head. "I just wish I knew which direction to go in right now. I'm sorely tempted to sell the last of those cows and stick with horses. It's a risk, though, and I hate taking chances. I wish I could see my way through it."

"It will come to you," Lincoln's dad said reassuringly. "I have faith. Now, we'd better be heading home. Thanks for the hospitality, Lillian."

"Oh, anytime," she smiled and stood up to show them to the door.

I waved to Lincoln, snagged a cookie quickly off the plate and then ran upstairs to have a long, hot shower.

Chapter Eighteen

The next week passed in a flurry of activity. With so many people signed up for the archery team, the school caved in and paid for our entries to the Northern Flight School Competition. That was all they could offer, though; we were going to have to fundraise for everything else including equipment and transportation.

We didn't have to declare our team members yet, just promise that five of us would show up. I had a faint hope that I'd be able to be on the team, but realistically there was a good chance that my arm wouldn't be strong enough by then.

On Friday night, Bryce's truck was parked in front of Aunt Lillian's when we got home from school.

"Dad's home!" Casey shrieked, opening the door and tumbling out of the truck before it had even stopped. She ran inside ahead of us, her face lit up like a candle.

"What a kid," Kade said, shaking his head. "She acts like she can't stand him when he's home. I guess I should come in and say hello."

The smell of pasta and garlic met us at the front door and my stomach rumbled eagerly in answer.

"There they are," Aunt Lillian said happily. "Come on in, everyone, this lasagna's ready way too early and we have to eat it while it's hot. You kids can work with the horses after an early dinner."

Casey stood next to her dad with her arms around his neck, clinging to him like she never wanted to let go.

"You're thin, kid," Bryce said, frowning as the put his hand around her bicep and gave it a squeeze. "Have you been eating at all?"

She straightened up, pulled away, sitting down on the chair beside him.

"Course I have, Dad," she said, crossing her arms protectively over her chest. "I'm fine, stop fussing."

"We're so glad to have you back home, Bryce," Aunt Lillian said. "I was thinking of bringing the broodmares in on Sunday. I know it's a bit early, but I think it's going to be a cold winter."

"Your aunt just misses her big ladies," Kade joked, expertly dodging the glare Aunt Lillian sent him.

"Well, I *do* miss them," she said. "It will give me something to focus on. I'll confess that I'm feeling a little lost this year."

There was a long silence, and everyone looked down, focused intently on their food.

Bryce smiled at her kindly. "Probably a good idea to get them in early this year, Lillian. Some of them are looking on the thin side. Beezy and a couple of the older girls are starting to look their age. It will be tough for them to stay in condition if they stay out much longer."

As soon as the talk shifted, inevitably, to bloodlines there was no getting a word in edgewise. I half-listened, but my main focus was in piling as much of Aunt Lillian's delicious food into me as possible. I always felt like I was going to be dragged from this place at any moment and I had to eat as much as I could while I still had the chance.

*****

Lincoln, Gage, and Malcolm came back on Saturday so we could finish sweeping the barn, and power wash the walls and floor, and get rid of all the spider webs that clung overhead on the lights, windows, and in every available corner.

We'd already figured out a colour scheme for the paint. As soon as the walls dried, and as soon as we sold some of the old furniture and had some money, we could start painting. Lincoln's dad had found us a source for the thick, industrial foam that we could use to the line the far end of the range. We would put the targets up against the thick backdrop, so our arrows had something to bite into.

*****

Sunday morning, I woke up early to feed Folly and, to my surprise, Aunt Lillian was already in the barn, going from stall to stall shaking out golden flakes of straw in thick layers. She hummed and sang snippets of old songs under her breath as she worked, and looked happier than I'd ever seen her.

"There," she said in satisfaction, "all ready for them. They'll be so pleased to come in. And this space on the end is for your girl, if you think she's ready to come in and behave."

Her excitement was contagious and the whole morning took on a festive feeling. Even Casey looked happier, still trailing her dad around as if she were afraid he'd disappear again.

After breakfast, everyone except Aunt Lillian saddled up the horses and off we rode at a sedate walk, down into the bowl pasture toward the lake.

Red walked along at a brisk pace, easily keeping up with Badger, Doc, and Kitty. Fox, of course, strode on ahead on his long legs, prancing in excitement.

The mares were already crowded at the gate, ears pricked; they must have heard our horses coming from a long way off.

Old Beezy stood at the front, her head up and her nostrils quivering at the strange horses approaching her herd.

"Hey, Beezy," Bryce called to her, "how are you doing there, old timer? Ready to go in and live a civilized life this winter?"

She bobbed her head a few times as if she understood him and we all laughed. Bryce instructed us to stand to one side while he leaned down from the saddle to open the gate and swing it wide.

Beezy didn't hesitate. She trotted slowly through the open gate, her big belly swinging, and her tail arched up over her back in excitement. The other mares followed her lead, heads craning around in all directions to check out the new territory.

"All right, keep them moving slowly," Bryce said, "nice and easy up to the barn; they know the way, but keep them from making side trips."

It went smoothly; only once did Kade have to trot up to the front of the group to steer a wandering bay mare from heading off by herself. She tossed her head at Fox and gave a little squeal before heading back to her herd of ladies. She was already very pregnant so had no interest in cheeky stallions.

Red marched along beside Kitty, cheerfully trotting when the other horses picked up speed, and then dropping down to a slumbering walk as soon as the pace went back down. He was a fun and relaxing ride. I never had to worry about him doing anything silly, and he liked to expend just as much effort as was needed and no more.

Aunt Lillian stood by the gate that led to the make-shift paddock behind the barn, both gates to it standing wide open. We were to push the mares in there to settle down, and then we'd halter them and take them into their stalls in twos and threes.

The mares trotted past her, shaking their heads and snorting in excitement. Folly called from her paddock out front, and a few of the new horses answered back, voices high-pitched with the exhilaration of the day.

"Hey, girls," Aunt Lillian said in delight, shutting the gates quietly behind them. "So good to have you all back inside. Settle down now and we'll get you all tucked into your nice, warm stalls."

Beezy broke out of the herd and trotted over to Lillian. She wasn't due for months, but her sides were absolutely huge; she looked ready to give birth any day.

"Hello, sweetheart," my aunt said affectionately, stroking Beezy's greying forehead, "you don't need time to settle, do you? You're ready to go in."

To my surprise, she unlatched the gate and opened it just enough for the old mare to slip through, then she turned her back and walked toward the barn, Beezy trotting in her wake right into her own stall.

"Wow," I said, "that's amazing."

"Well, she's done this trip about twenty times." Kade laughed. "She knows the drill by now."

"It's still amazing to me." I knew Folly would probably never follow me willingly if she was loose, but would Red? He had the same sweet temperament as Beezy.

Gradually, the milling mares settled down, and Lillian and Bryce walked gently through the herd, putting on halters and then leading them two by two into the barn until they were all tucked away neatly in their stalls.

Only the one on the end was empty, the one meant for Folly.

"Ready to bring her in?" Justin asked, appearing beside me with her halter already slung over his shoulder.

"You think she's ready to be a civilized horse?"

He shrugged. "No way to tell without giving it a try. But, honestly, I think she'll be fine."

I'd been gaining confidence leading Folly around in her pen and practicing her exercises, but I didn't think now was the time to test my skills. She stood stock still with her eyes bugging out and her tail flagged over her back.

"She's just excited," Justin said. "She'll be fine."

And she was; she pranced alongside him, her feet snapping up off the ground like they were on elastics. But she stayed obediently at his shoulder and kept her nose level with his arm. It almost looked like she'd tucked herself in behind him as a shield from the strange new horses who had invaded her territory.

He walked her into the barn and let her pause to take in all the new residents. She snorted and nickered under her breath, bobbing her head up and down in excitement.

Finally, he led her into her stall and slipped off her halter. She dove for the hay in her manger, dragging a mouthful of it over so she could eat while craning her neck out of the door, peering anxiously down the aisle.

Beezy was right next to her and Folly nickered under her breath in a way that sounded friendly to me. Which was surprising because she'd never seemed very interested in other horses, even back at Claudia's.

Once everyone was settled, I went back to where Red was tied and was surprised to see Aunt Lillian standing a few feet away, just staring at him with her arms crossed over her chest.

My stomach lurched; there was no way to tell what she was thinking while she watched him, but something protective rose up inside of me and I moved quickly to stand between them, patting his neck reassuringly.

"He looks good, Astrid," she said slowly. "I watched you ride him in. He's happier now then he has been in years."

"He's great," I said, still petting Red's shoulder. "He's more interested in ring work, too. I ride him bareback and he's more forward than he was before."

"Well, he might make a ranch horse yet," she said cryptically and strode back into the barn.

I led Red over to the stump we used as a mounting block and slowly climbed up on him, feeling uneasy. *Does that mean that she's thinking of selling him as a ranch horse or keeping him here as a ranch horse?*

I couldn't see my way through to buying him right now, but there had to be a way.

Chapter Nineteen

It was a good thing we'd brought the mares inside because when the snows came, they fell with a vengeance. One day, it was just a crisp smell in the air, grey swirling clouds overhead pressed low to the earth like they were too heavy to float. And then the next morning, a few inches of white covered the ground. I was glad to have Folly tucked safe inside.

All the other horses on the ranch had been moved from their hillside grazing to smaller pastures with huge lean-to shelters that weren't too far from the big barn. It would be easier to bring them hay and water that way, and to keep an eye on everyone.

That first morning, I drove down to the broodmare barn, my heart thudding in preparation of what I might find there. I half expected to find that Folly had destroyed her stall and attacked all the horses around her.

To my delight, she, and all fifteen of her new best friends, nickered happily when I came in, eager for their breakfast.

"Good morning, Folly," I called to her. "I'm sorry I'm late. I had to drive extra carefully in the snow."

I threw her hay in first, and then fed Beezy and the rest of the girls. The broodmares weren't getting grain yet, just hay, but every last one of them knew what the sound meant when I started mixing up Folly's grain. Fifteen sets of eyes followed the progress of the bucket to Folly's stall.

"Sorry, girls," I said. "I'll mix it up more quietly next time."

I waited until Folly had stepped back and was standing politely by her feed tub before I went in. Justin had warned me that she might be confused when her routine changed and revert to some of her old behaviours, but this morning she stood perfectly while I dumped in her food, and I stroked her neck while she ate; something I could have never dreamed of doing a month ago.

I walked to the back of her stall where the door to her paddock stood open. The snow was trampled down in a big circle a few feet outside and on the other side of the fence there was the same pattern. It looked like she and her neighbour Beezy had spent some time standing side by side out there.

"Are you making some friends, Folly?" I said, leaving her stall and going to the tack room for her lighter blanket. I pulled off the heavier one she wore at night and replaced it with the lighter, breathable one. If it warmed up during the day, then she wouldn't overheat.

On Monday, I got to miss school, and Kade drove me to Williams Lake to the hospital, which was where the nearest X-ray center was.

I didn't have to wait at all, and it took them about five minutes to X-ray me and hurry me off to a closet-sized exam room. A young doctor with a harried look on her face breezed in and sat down on a stool in front of me, her white lab coat billowing out around her.

"X-rays look good," she said briskly, taking my arm in both hands and poking the exposed skin at the bottom of my cast. Then she did the same thing with my shoulder. "Any pain?"

"No," I said honestly, "but it itches. I want it off so my life can get back to normal."

"I bet you do; it's been on a long time."

A nurse came in with a little saw-like tool.

"Don't worry, this won't hurt you at all."

I winced as the saw whirred up and down my arm, but it didn't hurt and finally, the cast cracked apart like magic and I was free.

"Ew," I said, looking down at my pale, lifeless-looking arm. It didn't even look like it belonged to me. There were some grey, scaly bits clinging to the skin, like I was a reptile or something. "Is that...*is that fungus?*"

"No," the doctor said with a laugh, running some damp, soapy gauze up and down my arm where the cast had been. "It hasn't seen the light in months; give it time to recover. I'm going to get you set up with a splint to wear to give it some extra protection. You'll need to have the limb re-X-rayed in one week, and you'll need some physiotherapy, too. You live in Triple Hills, right? There's a good physiotherapist in town. Go see her soon so she can give you some exercises to get that limb back in shape."

"Okay," I said, nodding happily. I would do whatever it took to get back to normal again. "When can I start archery again?"

"Hmm," she said, bending my arm slowly at the elbow.

"We'll see what next week's X-rays say, but I'm guessing a month or two? As long as you don't overdo it. Your bones might have healed, but the muscles themselves have atrophied. It takes a long time to build your strength back up. So, off you go, and we'll see you next week."

"Thanks," I called out, but she was already moving down the hall at a rapid trot. The technician fit me with a loose splint that I could take on and off whenever I liked and showed me a few simple exercises just to get the basic range of motion back. I thanked her and headed for the truck, practically skipping like kid because I was so happy to be nearly done with this whole awful accident.

"Looking good," Kade said when I made it back to the truck. "How should we celebrate?"

"With lunch," I said, smiling happily, "and a visit to the tack store."

Chapter Twenty

We stopped at Triple Hills to have lunch at the diner, and so we could both check our messages.

Astrid, Hilary's text said, *have you talked to Marion yet? You need to call home right now.*

What about? I typed back, but there was no response.

That's weird, I thought, sending a quick text to Marion and then another to Rob.

It was probably nothing, but just in case, I pressed Marion's number and listened to it ring and ring before going to voicemail.

"Marion," I said, "can you call me? I got a weird text from Hilary."

I ate my lunch and drank my chocolate milkshake quietly, trying not to worry. It wasn't like it had to be a bad thing. Maybe it was a good thing they had to tell me.

We invited everyone over to the house for dinner that night to celebrate my cast coming off. Lillian made stuffed manicotti with extra cheese, and we had garlic bread and Caesar salad to go with it. All the flavours I liked best.

We were just starting on the pecan pie when the phone rang.

"Marion!" Aunt Lillian bellowed down the line as if my step-mom was calling from the other end of the world. "How are…oh, yes, she's here. I see." There was a long pause. "Okay, Marion, I'll put her on the line now."

Aunt Lillian motioned me over and handed me the phone, a strange look on her face. "It's Marion," she said, pointlessly, giving me a pat on the shoulder.

"Hello," I said tentatively, gripping the phone like a lifeline. I knew that the news had to be about my dad. We'd all known he might have to spend some time in jail. The question was when and how long. The final sentencing must have come through.

"Astrid, darling, are you alone?"

"No," I said, looking at the table, "not at all. But tell me what's happened with Dad? Is he okay? Did we lose the condo?"

"No, Astrid, it's nothing like that. Your father is fine. We're still waiting to hear what happens next. But, in the meantime, he's taken up squash."

"Like the vegetable?"

"No, darling, it's a game, like tennis. He's finding it a very therapeutic outlet for all his tension."

"So, that's good. Isn't it?"

"Astrid, sweetheart. That isn't why I called. I'm afraid I have some very bad news."

Immediately, my heart sank, and I knew what she was about to say before she said it.

"Darling, I'm afraid it's Claudia; she passed away today."

There was a rushing sound in my ears and I had to lean up against the wall to stay upright.

"That can't be true," I said, even though I knew it was. "She was getting better."

"She was in remission long enough to enjoy some precious time with everyone she loved. Liza was right by her side the whole time, darling. Claudia didn't have any regrets except for leaving this world too soon. The end was very peaceful."

I was crying hard now, tears running down my cheeks and soaking the sleeve I rubbed hurriedly across my face.

"What about Cole," I choked out. "Did he get to see her?"

"He flew in early this morning. She wasn't very lucid by that point, but he sat with her and got to say his goodbyes."

"I should have been there, too." I sniffled. "I didn't get to see her."

"I know it's hard, darling. But Claudia knew you loved her and she was so proud of you, Astrid."

I couldn't do anything but cry for a minute. "How's Liza?" I asked finally.

"She's very sad, dear. But this visit to Holland will do her a world of good. She worked so hard, and worried about Claudia so much, it will be good for her to get away."

"Holland? Wait, what are you talking about?"

"Didn't she tell you? Claudia arranged it for her months ago. She's going to train with a friend of Claudia's for a while."

"But what about Quarry and Marcus? What about the other horses?"

"Quarry and Marcus will move to Rob's farm, darling, that's what Claudia arranged with them before…before she passed. I'm not sure where the other horses will go once Mud Lark is sold."

"Mud Lark is being *sold*?" By then I was sobbing hysterically. Behind me, I could hear chairs scraping back and boots moving hurriedly over the floor as everyone left the kitchen.

"You know it was what Claudia had planned, Astrid. Marcus and Quarry will stay under Liza's care, but she'll board them with Rob while she's away. Claudia left the horses a piece of her estate in the will, so they'll be taken care of forever, no matter where they live. The farm belongs to Cole and he's decided to sell it."

"What about Liza, though? She's more like Claudia's kid than Cole ever was, why doesn't *she* get the farm?"

"I don't think it works that way, Astrid."

I was silent for a long time while I tried to process this information. "So, when's the service going to be? When do I come home?"

There was a long pause and then Marion cleared her throat. "I'm so sorry, Astrid. They decided to just do a quick service this weekend for friends and family. I'm afraid there wouldn't be time to make arrangements to get you home and back again."

"You mean I can't go?"

"I know you're disappointed, Astrid."

Disappointment was not a word that defined the black pit opening in my stomach or the roaring ocean of noise that filled my head. I was numb and on fire at the same time. I wanted to run and curl up and hide and hit someone and be hugged all at once. I leaned up against the wall, not able to speak.

"Astrid, darling, I know you cared for Claudia very much…."

I stopped listening, her words jumbling together. Claudia had been like family to me. Sure, I'd only been at Mud Lark for the summer, but she'd taught me so much in that short time. She'd let me ride Quarry, and had taken me to my first show; she'd believed in me. I couldn't comprehend that Marion didn't know how important Claudia had been to me.

"Sweetheart, can you hear me? Are you still there?"

Her words sounded sharp and metallic in my ear and suddenly, I couldn't stand there listening to her anymore.

"I have to go, Marion," I said.

"Astrid," she started to say, but I'd already hung up before she could finish my name.

I leaned my forehead against the wall, pressing hard until all I felt was that one point of pain. It didn't make the awful buzzing in my head go away, though, and it didn't stop the ripping of my heart.

"Astrid?" my aunt asked gently. "Sweetie, are you okay?"

"No," I said weakly. "I don't know what I am."

I felt her hand touch my shoulder, but I couldn't face her right then. I pushed past her and ran for the barn as fast as I could.

I went past Folly without stopping, even though she nickered as I ran past. I loved Folly, but she wasn't the type of horse you could throw your arms around and cry on; at least, not for me.

Instead, I made a beeline for Red's stall and walked right in, not even bothering to shut the door behind me before I buried my face in his mane and started bawling like a little kid.

Red's head lifted slowly, and then I felt him gently bending around me until he'd wrapped my body in a hug with his neck. There was no other way to describe it; it was like he *knew* and was comforting me. It was just for a minute, and then he turned back to his hay like nothing had happened.

"You lost someone, too, didn't you, Red?" I sniffled, running my fingers through his mane to straighten it. I slid down to the ground and sat with my back to his manger right next to his front feet. Bits of hay fell on my shoulders, but I didn't bother to brush them away.

My mind was caught between the shock of losing Claudia and the betrayal of Marion not caring enough to get me back in time for the service. I wondered if maybe I could buy my own ticket and be back in time. Aunt Lillian would probably drive me to the nearest bus station. I could be home by the weekend for sure. Marion hadn't even *looked* into it. She hadn't cared at all.

I didn't know how long I sat there, just staring into space. Red ate his hay, only moving over to peek out his open door once before coming quickly back to me again.

He reached down and whuffled his breath into my hair, and I touched the silky tip of his nose with my fingers.

Chapter Twenty-one

When I finally went back to the house it was dark outside. Lillian had waited up for me and was sitting at the kitchen table. I slowly went in to join her, sitting down heavily across the table from her.

She set a steaming cup of tea down in front of me, and I reached out and wrapped my hands carefully around it, soaking the heat into my cold hands.

"I don't know what to do," I said finally.

"Sweetheart, you don't have to do anything at all. Grief is its own process and you just have to let it happen naturally. I'm so sorry about your friend Claudia, though. I know how much she meant to you."

That's all it took, and I was balling again. Aunt Lillian came around to my side of the table, wrapped me in a strong hug, and let me cry on her shoulder until there was nothing left.

"I know, honey," she said softly. "I know just what it feels like. I'm so sorry."

I sat up and wiped my eyes, taking the handful of Kleenex she offered me.

"I'm so sorry you lost Uncle Trent, Aunt Lillian. We should have come to the funeral."

"Oh, baby, don't worry about that. I only wish that your uncle could have seen you all grown up. He would have been so proud of you. You've turned into such a wonderful young lady."

"I don't feel wonderful." I sniffled, and then stopped. I had been about to say that I always felt fat and stupid, but before the words left my mouth, I had a sudden realization: I actually didn't feel that way here. I hadn't in a long time.

"Well, I'm your aunt and I know better," she said, squeezing my hand. "You are the spitting image of your mom, and she was one of the most beautiful, talented, intelligent women I knew."

I thought about that, about how everyone said my mom was this fantastic person, and that I was just like her. But in the end, she'd let everyone down and pretty much killed herself.

My aunt was watching me closely and she must have seen the struggle on my face because she reached out and gave me another hug.

"She was a wonderful person," she said firmly, "and she was flawed just like every single one of us is flawed. You're your own person, Astrid. You don't have to make the same mistakes she did."

I sighed, and she squeezed my hand again. "It's nearly ten o' clock, kiddo. You must be exhausted."

Suddenly, I realized how tired I was. And I had to get up early tomorrow morning and drag myself to school somehow.

I said goodnight to my aunt and trudged up to my room. To my surprise, Jake leapt up as soon as I pushed my chair back and followed me closely upstairs, not listening when I told him to stay out in the hall.

"Fine," I said, "you can come in, but you're not sleeping in my—"

Too late; the big dog leapt up onto my comforter and curled himself into a not-so-little ball at the end of my bed.

"You're not staying," I said, although I knew he wasn't going anywhere. I gave him a half-hearted nudge before giving up. Then I shucked off the day's clothes, threw on pajamas, and crawled into bed.

*****

The rest of the week went by in a fog. Aunt Lillian let me sleep in until noon on that first morning after, and she let me stay home the second day, too. But I decided that I had to go to school on Wednesday. I would go crazy if I spent one more day wallowing in my own misery.

Everyone at home and my few friends at school treated me carefully, respecting that I needed my space and didn't want to answer any questions.

By the next weekend, when Lincoln and some of the rest of the club came to paint the range, I felt a little more like my old self.

The furniture that we'd sold for Aunt Lillian had paid for the paint and for a bunch of backing for the targets, and we'd decided to paint the concrete floor as well as the walls, just to freshen everything up and get rid of the smell of mildew and rats that lingered in the corners. It took us most of the day, but by the end we could stand back and proudly survey our brand new range.

*****

Thankfully, the vet was able to come on a Saturday when Justin could be there, too. Folly was much better with me, but I wasn't sure if she'd listen to me while a stranger handled her.

Amazingly enough, she behaved perfectly while the vet felt her all over, only snarling at him when his careful hands hit a sore spot, and only offering to kick a couple times.

She grudgingly trotted in hand for Justin, going back and forth in front of the broodmare barn so the vet could watch how she moved. I alternated between watching the mare and watching the vet's face to see what he thought. To me, Folly looked like she was moving decently. Only a few head bobs and lurches; much better than it had been before. The vet, though, was frowning.

"So, I watched the video from her previous vet," he said thoughtfully, "and, while there's been a lot of improvement, she's still quite sore in that shoulder and front leg. She should be further along than this in my estimation. Still, she's markedly more comfortable at the walk, you have my okay to start increasing her work load. Walk. Just stick to easy terrain right now and keep it short. Sometimes in these cases a bit of light exercise is actually beneficial, but we'll see how it goes. I'll be back in a few weeks to see how she's doing."

Chapter Twenty-two

The painful void that had lodged in my heart when Claudia died gradually eased but never fully went away. It lay there like a vague, dull ache that only raised its head in those unguarded hours when I fell into bed late at night, exhausted but unable to sleep.

I fell automatically back into my old routine, grateful for the daily structure that meant I could operate on autopilot without having to think too hard. Wake up, get dressed, feed Folly and the mares, go say hi to Red, eat breakfast, and go to school. When I got home from school, I would grab a snack and then run down to take care of Folly and do a short training session with her. Then head to the training barn to help Justin and, if there was still time, ride Red.

The light was already fading now that winter was almost here, so Folly's after-school hand-walking sessions had to be done in the indoor arena. At first, she'd been overwhelmed by having to walk past the stallions and all the new horses but, by the end of the first week, she could follow Justin confidently into the ring.

We started just hand-walking her, and then added short

sessions of trot on the lunge line. Every night she waited eagerly for her session, happy to get the praise and treats that came with it.

"She's not sore," the vet said, palpating her shoulder the next time he came, "but something still isn't quite right there. Hopefully she just needs to build up some strength. You can try hiking her up in the mountains and see if hill work helps. Heck, if she's comfortable, you can even ride her up there, but just at the walk."

As soon as he was confident that she was relaxed with her sessions in the indoor, Justin tacked her up with the western saddle and bridle to see what she'd think.

I'd thought she would pitch a fit, but she didn't. She just looked around in a half-interested way, seeming happy to be back in work.

After that, Justin incorporated her into his riding schedule every other day or so, riding her in slow careful circles around the ring, and on the weekends, we took her on short trail rides, which she took to right away.

After Justin's training sessions were done, I usually took Red out and played with him. Sometimes, I free lunged him in the ring and let him play, and sometimes, I slipped on his back and rode him around the arena, just enjoying spending time with him. Justin had shown me how to ask him for spins in both directions, which was something Red already knew how to do. Compared to the spins and slides that Justin and Kade did, mine were in slow motion, but the feeling was still like flying.

I'd gone online to find some training videos of more lateral movements to help free up Red's shoulders and help him move better. Half-pass, Haunches-in, Haunches-out; I studied each movement carefully and, with Justin's help, gently guided Red to stretch and strengthen his body.

Chapter Twenty-three

With the range all finished and looking professional, we'd set up a practice schedule of a couple hours on Saturday and Sunday. Not everyone could come both days, of course, but usually somebody showed up besides Lincoln, Mara, and me. Mara had thrown herself into both weekend and school practice with a vengeance; she was definitely one who would be on the final team with Lincoln. We just had to weed out the other three entries.

Casey avoided coming anywhere need the range when other people were around. She never said as much, but I assumed it was because Mara was usually there, and Casey was afraid.

"She's not going to beat you up, Casey," I'd told her, but she'd just turned away, refusing to talk to me about it.

I hadn't found out where she disappeared to in school. I'd never seen her in the library or the lab or any of the other places that seemed good for hiding. I could only assume that she stayed back in class to help a teacher somewhere.

On Wednesday, Aunt Lillian actually left the farm to drive me all the way back to Williams Lake to have my arm X-rayed again.

"Might as well do some winter shopping at the same time. You're going to need some warmer clothes, Astrid."

When Casey heard I was getting to miss a day of school, she begged to be allowed to go, too.

"Fine," Bryce had said, looking at her worriedly. "Whatever makes you happy."

We'd already booked an appointment for me online at the X-ray clinic, so all I had to do was run in and get it done while Aunt Lillian and Casey waited in the truck. I only had to wait a few minutes for the X-ray before being shepherded off to an exam room where the same young doctor as before stopped in to talk to me.

"Looking good, young lady," she said with a smile. "I'd say you're good to start back to your normal routine. Remember to go to physio. Just start slowly; don't overdo it."

"I'm okay to start archery again, then?" I asked hopefully.

"Sure, you can try. But, like I said, take it very slowly and listen to what your body tells you."

"I will, thank you!" I said, and I happily tossed my splint in the garbage on my way out.

"All right, girls," Aunt Lillian said once I'd gotten back to the truck. "I'm going to brave the mall with you ladies so we can get you some winter clothes. I hate crowds, so let's not linger. Just stick to your lists. I'd like to get back home by dinner."

We didn't have a lot of time to just browse; Aunt Lillian herded us from store to store, going down her list of essentials to make sure we got only what we came for. I ended up with two thick, warm coats—one for the barn and one to wear to school— socks and sweaters, two warm pairs of winter boots—one for the house and one for the barn—three pairs of thermal gloves, and a few nicer shirts and jeans for school.

"Casey?" I said outside the change room door where she'd been holed up for an eternity, "I'm all done and we're going to go get lunch. Are you almost finished in there?"

No answer.

"Casey?" I knocked again and to my surprise the door swung open.

"What?" she said sleepily from where she lay curled up in the corner of the change room floor, her head propped up on the bench.

"Oh my gosh," I said, hurrying to her side. "Are you hurt? Did you fall?"

"No." She stumbled to her feet. "I'm fine. Just tired, that's all. I needed to have a nap."

"A nap? Are you kidding, Casey, we're, like, in public. That's not normal."

She was wearing just a thin t-shirt with the tags still on and through it I could see just how thin she had become. She was practically skeletal.

"Casey, you need to tell me what's going on right now or I'm telling Aunt Lillian and your dad, and whoever else will listen, that there's something wrong."

"Astrid, you're being crazy. I'm just doing a ton of extra school work so I'm not getting enough sleep. I'm taking a bunch of extra credit classes. You're right, though, I need to find a better balance."

She looked so reasonable that I almost believed her. Almost.

"I'm just going to finish trying on these shirts and then I'll be right out. I'm looking forward to lunch."

She shut the door in my face before I could say anything else and she looked so normal for the rest of the day that I decided to hold off on telling anyone. Maybe she was just doing extra school work like she'd said.

But, as the days went on and the winter winds began to blow in earnest, Casey didn't look better. She looked worse and worse every day.

One day it was just Kade who showed up to take me to school.

"Casey's home sick with the flu," he said. "She's staying in bed today."

"Okay," I said. "Did she want me to pick up her homework or anything? She must be panicked about falling behind."

"Hmm, I don't know, she didn't say."

"That's okay, I'll stop by the office and let them know she'll be away."

I went to the office first, my new boots squelching on the slippery school floors. I was glad I had them; having to change footwear five times a day was much better than spending the day in soaking wet socks.

The secretary looked up with a smile. "Hello, Astrid. What can I do for you this morning?"

"Hi, I just came to tell you that Casey's home sick for a few days. I can take her homework back to the ranch, if she has any."

"Casey?" She frowned. "Well, honey, she does *all* her schoolwork online now. That's how the home-learning program works. I hope the extra work load hasn't made her ill. She's such a hard worker."

"Home learning program?" I said in confusion. "I don't understand. Casey goes to school here."

She stared at me, eyebrows raised. "Technically, she does. But she doesn't come to class; she does her work from home."

"Oh," I said, my mind whirring. "Right, um, of course. I must have forgotten that. Well, thanks for your help."

I opened the door and backed quickly into the hall before she could say another word.

"Wow," Lincoln said at lunch, when I told him what had happened. "So you think she's been showing up for school but then not going to class? What's she doing all day, then?"

"I don't know, but I'm guessing that her dad doesn't know about the online learning thing."

"I know where she goes," Mara said from the other end of the table. She'd taken to eating lunch at our table, but she usually just sat there in silence, concentrating on her food. We'd forgotten she was even there.

"You do?" I turned to her in surprise. "Why didn't you say something?"

"It was none of my business." Mara shrugged. "But I can show you where she goes."

We finished our lunch quickly, grabbed our coats and winter gear from our lockers and followed Mara out into the snow.

"I followed her once," Mara said as she led us around the back of the building and across the playing field, our feet sinking in the wind-blown drifts.

"Why?" Lincoln asked, puffing with exertion.

She shot him a side-long glance. "I'm not going to lie. I wanted to pick a fight with her. I was still angry back then, and she'd been so awful to me after that summer. I might have forgiven what had happened with Dinah if she hadn't been so mean to me afterward. She was so nasty in class all the time, always saying something about me being stupid…and I got angry. It wasn't just me; nobody liked her. She was a stuck-up snob."

"So, what happened?" I asked.

"I followed her, and I found her hiding spot. She didn't know I was there, but when I saw her she just looked so sad that I didn't bother her. I just went back to school and didn't tell anyone. I figured that she knew what she was doing. Casey always knows everything."

We'd entered the thick woods at the back of the school, and from here I could see a well-worn path through the snowy underbrush.

"I'm surprised she hasn't been caught before this," Lincoln said, as we pushed up the narrow trail. "This trail would be completely obvious to anyone who came close."

After about ten minutes, we came upon a small, crumbling, brick building with a hole where the door had once been.

"I think this was an old well-house or something," Mara said, "from before the new school was built."

"It looks creepy," I said. "You mean Casey's been spending every day in here?"

"Looks, like it," Lincoln said, peering inside. There was a blanket in one corner and a small pile of empty granola bar wrappers and wadded up sheets of paper beside it. There was even a pile of burnt kindling that looked like she'd tried to start a fire.

"Come on, let's go," I said, turning away sadly. How desperate had Casey been to spend every day here in this damp, lonely place instead of in school? She must have been freezing out there.

That night I had no choice but to tell Aunt Lillian.

"Oh, that poor girl. I knew something was wrong. I just wish she'd have told us how miserable she was."

"I guess she tried in her own way," I said slowly, thinking of how upset Casey had been when she didn't get into Redmond.

"I'll call Bryce," Aunt Lillian said, but she shooed me outside to work with the horses so I couldn't eavesdrop.

The next day, Kade announced that when Casey was better, Bryce was taking her to California for Christmas vacation to visit her mom and Olive.

"What did Casey have to say about that?" I asked, thinking of how little she seemed to think of her mom.

"She's okay with it, I think. She cried a lot. Dad was really upset that she hadn't told him what was going on. I think he feels guilty for not cluing in earlier. She's been miserable for a long time."

"Is she going to have to go back to school?"

Kade shook his head. "I doubt it. She's acing her online classes. I think he's going to talk to mom to see if she'll help pay for private school next year. Her slimy boyfriend's loaded and it's her fault Dad doesn't have any money right now. She took him to the cleaners in the divorce and he just gave away everything without putting up a fight. He really loves her, and he can't see how manipulative she is."

"Oh," I said. It seemed like everyone's life was complicated these days. At least it wasn't just my family who was messed up.

Casey was up and about in less than a week and the first thing she did was drop in to one of our archery practices. She still looked pale and thin, but the dark circles under her eyes had faded and she looked more peaceful than I'd ever seen her.

"Hi," she said shyly, standing in the open doorway.

"Hey, Casey," I said in delight, "come on in."

"Oh, it's okay," she said quickly, "I wanted to talk to Mara, if that's okay."

She sent Mara a tentative smile. "Can you walk with me to the barn?"

Mara blinked at her a few times and then nodded. "Okay, sure. I guess so."

She put on her coat slowly and followed Casey out into the snow. They were gone a long time and when Mara came back, alone, her face was blotchy with tears, but she was smiling.

"What happened?" I asked, dying of curiosity.

"She apologized," Mara said simply. "And so did I. We both made mistakes. And…well, she offered me Kitty."

"Kitty?" I said in astonishment. "But she's Aunt Lillian's horse."

"I know. I guess they talked it over and decided that I would make the best home for her. They offered me a really good price, and said I could make payments and everything. I can come and ride her any time."

"Wow, Mara," I said, grabbing her into a hug before I could stop myself.

She stiffened and pulled away, but at least she didn't hit me.

"It's amazing news," she said, smiling. "I can't wait to tell my parents."

*****

Casey and Bryce left for California a couple weeks before Christmas. Which was great for them but made double the work for the rest of us. Luckily, Justin was on winter break from school, although it wasn't very relaxing since we spent most of our time just trudging through the deep snow, keeping the horses clean and fed and chipping ice out of their water buckets.

The night before their departure there was a knock at the door and Bryce stood there grinning, trailing a gigantic tree behind him.

"Astrid, I almost forgot to bring you this," he laughed. "I told your aunt that we'd get you an honest to goodness tree this year."

Earlier, I'd confessed to them that I'd never had a real Christmas tree at home. Sometimes Marion set up a miniature, plastic tree on the kitchen counter. But normally it was a holiday only recognized by solemnly exchanging gift cards and going out for a silent dinner at an expensive restaurant. Upon hearing this, Bryce had sworn that he would cut down a tree for us when he got the one for his own house.

Now the giant tree stood in our doorway, so big that it took all of us to haul it through and drag it to the living room. Bryce had made a nice wooden stand that fit a water bucket perfectly in the center for the tree to sit in.

"There, now I'll leave you to the decorations," Bryce said, brushing his hands together in satisfaction. "That's not my department."

We hugged him goodbye, and the next morning he and Casey were gone before the sun even came up. I hoped she had a good time.

Aunt Lillian dragged all her decorations out of storage and piled them in the living room for me to sort through. It took me two days, but in the end, I'd decorated my very first Christmas tree and made the whole living room look like a winter wonderland.

Chapter Twenty-four

"Astrid, come on down, they're here."

I was already halfway down the stairs by the time my aunt called. I'd been waiting at my bedroom window, pretending to read but really checking outside every thirty seconds. I'd already seen the big, shiny black rental car pulling carefully up the snowy driveway.

I thudded down the stairs and hit the bottom step just as Jake woke up and started to bark at the sound of car tires crunching on gravel. I threw open the front door without even bothering to put a coat on, dancing up and down on the cold wooden porch in my socked feet.

"Astrid!" Hilary jumped out of the car before it had even stopped and ran up the icy pathway toward me. She bounced up the porch steps and wrapped me in a big hug, at which I promptly burst into tears.

"Oh, don't do that," she said and burst into tears, too. We both pulled back at the same moment, and I looked up to see Rob standing right there, grinning at both of us. I couldn't help the surge of excitement that shot through me. *He looks the same*, I thought, taken back by his dark hair and eyes, *he's beautiful.*

Before I had the chance to feel shy, he'd stepped forward and wrapped me in a tight hug. "Astrid," he whispered, still laughing so his breath tickled my neck, "your dad is intense."

"My dad?" I froze, looking back and forth between them.

"Yeah." Hilary laughed under her breath. "He started arguing with the guy across the aisle from him about politics. It was a very long flight."

"Oh no," I groaned. "I didn't even know he was coming. I hope he didn't say anything awful."

Before I could dwell on it anymore, I saw Marion getting out of the car and my heart gave another little leap of excitement.

"Darling, you look wonderful," Marion said, tripping up the driveway in a pair of thin, knee-high leather boots. She let out a sudden shriek as Jake pushed past me and bounded down the porch steps, barking wildly.

"It's okay!" I called out. "He's harmless."

Marion stood rooted to the ground in fear, eyes closed and face white. She had her hands clenched at her sides and I thought she would pass out. Before I could move, Rob trotted down the porch steps to rescue her, his mouth curving upward in a smile as he reached down and grabbed Jake's collar, ruffling the big dog's fur.

"Come on, giant dog," he said, laughing. "You're all talk. I know your type."

I paused, studying his face as he came toward me through the falling snow, pulling the reluctant dog behind him. He *had* changed a bit in the few months since I'd left. His face was more angular, and he looked like he'd filled out. His eyes were still the same, though, warm and smiling, full of fun.

"Well now, this is nice," Aunt Lillian said, appearing behind us in the doorway, "It's good to see this girl finally smiling. Marion, come on in, you must be freezing out there. Bruce," her voice faltered slightly, "what a surprise. You look…well."

"Lillian," he said in a lukewarm voice, "likewise."

My breath caught in my throat as I saw my dad for the first time since I'd left. He was tired and thin but, when he looked my way, the small smile he gave me was genuine.

"Astrid." He came up the porch steps, and for a moment we just stared at one another, neither of us seeming to know what to do. We settled on a quick hug and then broke apart almost instantly, both looking down the porch, rendered speechless by this overwhelming display of affection.

"Oh, my goodness, Astrid, you've grown up so much," Marion said, wrapping me in her own soft hug. I leaned into her, inhaling her familiar scent. She was the closest thing to a mom I'd ever had, and I'd missed her tons since I'd been away.

"Come on, everyone," my aunt said briskly from the door. "Don't stand outside in the freezing cold, come on inside. Astrid, show your friends to their rooms. I'll take Marion and your father upstairs to their room. Jake, you lie down there; nobody needs your help."

Rob and Hilary ran back to the car to grab their bags and Hilary came back carrying a suspiciously familiar looking parcel covered in red wrapping paper and ribbons.

"Don't peek," she said, "it's supposed to be a surprise."

"Um, okay," I said, confused. Because that looked suspiciously like a saddle and, as rich as Hilary was, I was pretty sure she was not going to randomly buy me a saddle when I didn't even have my own horse.

"Here, Rob, this is your room." I ushered him into one of our nicest guest rooms, decorated in green and gold plaid.

"Wow, Astrid, this place is great," Rob said, looking around admiringly at the exposed wooden beams. "I love log buildings." He dropped his oversized backpack on the bed and followed us next door to where Hilary was staying. "You must love living here. You're never going to want to come home."

"It's a beautiful place," I said, "and the people and horses are fantastic. But I still want to come home. I miss you guys."

"Okay," Hilary said, hardly able to contain herself, "I can't stand it anymore. Open your present, Astrid."

"For me?" I said, "but, Hilary, I can't let you buy me a—"

"Just open it, silly."

I looked over at Rob and he nodded encouragingly, so I sat down on the bed and carefully took the loosely wrapped saddle out of Hilary's arms. I peeled the paper back slowly and then exhaled my breath all at once, tears springing to my eyes.

"Do you recognize it?" Hilary asked softly, laying a hand on my shoulder.

"I do." I sniffled, then pulled the familiar burgundy saddle-cover off and looked down at the beautiful saddle underneath. I ran my fingers tentatively over the buttery, soft leather that I'd grown to know almost as well as my bow. "It's Quarry's saddle."

"Claudia wanted you to have it. She was so proud of you, Astrid, and she knew how much you loved Quarry. He won't need it now that he's retired, and it's fully adjustable, so you can get a saddle fitter to adjust it to your next horse."

My next horse, I thought, *will there even be a next horse?*

"Wow, I don't know what to say. Thank you."

"There's a couple more things that go with it," Rob said, "since we're opening presents early. Hang on."

He disappeared back to his room and came back with two presents. "These are still from Claudia and Liza. You can open your real presents from us on Christmas."

I took the first present from him wordlessly, too overwhelmed to do anything but sniffle and gulp back tears. I couldn't believe that Claudia had even been thinking of me when she was sick. What an amazing person she'd been. I wished I could have known her so much longer.

"That first one is from Claudia. The small one is from Liza."

I unwrapped the larger of the two, a bulky package covered with green paper and gasped as I pulled Quarry's bridle from the packaging. I ran my fingers down the supple reins, and then, like a weirdo, I leaned down and breathed in the well-remembered smell, hoping to capture any memories of Quarry and Claudia that still clung to it.

Luckily, I was in the room with two horse people; they understood completely.

"Last one," Rob said, handing me a small square. "Careful, it's fragile."

I peeled back the paper and smiled tearfully. It was a beautiful framed photo of Quarry, standing loose in his paddock, head thrown up and mane blowing in the wind. He looked like a unicorn, all proud and regal. I traced the lines of his face with my fingers and sighed.

"Astrid!" my aunt called, "we're having tea and cookies in the living room. Come on out."

Aunt Lillian had set out tea and my favourite lemon cookies

on the low table in the sunken living room and we all sat down on the big couches that were only used for formal occasions. I squeezed in with Hilary and Rob on the big couch and passed around the plate of cookies. "You have to taste these," I said, "Aunt Lillian is an amazing cook, she's teaching me how to make some stuff, too."

"Oh, I'm nothing compared to what Florian was like," Aunt Lillian waved her hand in the air dismissively, "but Astrid is getting to be quite the baker, too."

I looked over to see Marion watching me closely, a puzzled look on her face. She sat perched on the edge of her cushion, clutching her tea cup as if she would leap up and bolt at any minute.

"Have a cookie, Marion," my aunt ordered, "you look as though you could use some fattening up."

"Oh, no thank you." Marion jumped and then laughed nervously, glancing quickly at my dad.

"Right," my dad said absently, blowing on the top of his tea to cool it down, "we don't eat sugar or carbs in our home."

I almost choked on the cookie I'd stuffed in my mouth and Aunt Lillian shot me a look.

"Well, luckily you're not home then. Eat up."

"Tea's fine for me," Marion insisted, "maybe later."

There was a long, awkward silence while everyone stared at the table and tried to think of what to say. I was dying to get back alone with Rob and Hilary so I could ask them all about home.

"So, Astrid," my dad said, clearing his throat, "how is that horse of yours?"

"He's great!" I said, and then stopped, realizing that, of course, he meant Folly and not Red. "I mean, uh, she's much better. She's letting me handle her and we're taking her for walks and stuff. Justin's tacked her up and has started riding her lightly."

"Hmmph." His gaze drifted over the window and he sighed. "Good," he said vaguely, as if he were thinking about something else entirely.

Marion and I exchanged a quick glance and she shook her head ever so slightly.

"But I've been riding," I said, suddenly. "Aunt Lillian has this great horse named Red; he's really quiet. And, Dad, you have to see the indoor range we built."

I faltered to a stop, not sure if he was even listening to me, he looked so far away. I'd forgotten how disconcerting it was to have my dad around, how I'd always felt on guard and ready to defend myself. Until those last few weeks at the hospital, we'd never even so much as had a conversation and I wasn't sure what to expect.

"Range?" he said, coming out of his fog and looking interested. "You're back practicing already? I thought the doctor said—"

"It's fine, Dad, I'm going to physio and everything. They said that it's okay as long as I take it easy."

"Oh, well, that's reasonable then, I guess. But I wouldn't put too much stock in what these small-town doctors say. I'll get Marion to set up an appointment with a specialist. You don't want it to heal badly and wreck your career. Be careful."

"Okay," I said, gulping nervously, wondering if he'd always spoken of Marion as if she was merely his secretary. "I'll be careful. But, don't you want to see the range?"

"Yes," Aunt Lillian said, glaring at my dad. "The kids worked so hard to clean it up and get it ready. Surely, you want to be somewhat supportive of your daughter."

"Don't start with me, Lillian," he snapped, "I don't need advice—"

"Okay." Marion stood up so quickly she nearly spilled her tea. "Time for everyone to get some fresh air. We'd love to see the horses, wouldn't we, dear? Astrid, why don't you take us all on a tour?"

Rob and Hilary were watching all this silently, eyes wide. I knew Hilary had never liked my dad much and she was staring at him now as if he were a rattlesnake rising its head up out of the grass. She fingered the little cross necklace at her throat and I knew she was reminding herself not to judge him. I hope she had better luck with that than I did.

We dressed in our winter gear and filed outside, Aunt Lillian and Marion making high-pitched small talk to fill in the silence.

I was overflowing with things to tell Rob and Hilary, and even Marion, but I'd gone completely mute in the presence of my dad. I was a much different person than the one who'd left home three months ago, but I still was tongue-tied around him.

"Astrid," my aunt said quickly as I automatically headed toward the battered farm truck I thought of as 'mine,' "we'll take my truck."

Right, maybe now's not the time to reveal that I've been driving illegally all fall. I swerved toward the other truck and we all squashed inside. Marion and my dad sat up front, and I had to quickly push aside Jake's yucky dog blankets so the rest of us could fit in the backseat.

Marion wrinkled her nose against the smell of dog and farm, but she didn't say a word. My dad just stared out the window, frowning distractedly.

Aunt Lillian didn't take the short-cut; she drove carefully down the road to the broodmare barn while she politely asked Marion about how things were going back on the Island.

"Wow, what a neat barn," Hilary said, staring up at the stacked log broodmare barn. "It matches the house."

"Yes, Trent loved log homes. When we moved from the old homestead we had the house and this barn built at the same time."

I rolled back the big outer door and a row of horse heads poked out of their stalls, looking at us with interest. Folly, stationed closest to the door, bobbed her head up and down and nickered when she saw me. She stretched her nose out, wiggling her lips, clearly expecting a carrot. I was proud of the way she just looked like any other friendly horse.

"Oh, there she is," Hilary said happily, recognizing Folly right away. "Hang on, I'm going to take pictures for Liza." We paused while she snapped about a hundred shots of Folly leaning over her stall door and then finally could walk over.

"Hey, girl," I said, stroking her neck to reassure her, "you have a fan club."

"She looks happy, Astrid," Rob said quietly.

"Oh, she is, she's so much better, but, Dad…no, be careful."

My dad had been trailing behind us outside and now he'd marched up close to Folly and stuck out his hand to abruptly pet her nose. Her ears flattened, and she whipped her head sideways, snapping her big teeth in the air right next to his face.

"Arrgh," he yelled, flailing his arms around wildly and jumping back before she could hurt him. He moved backward until he bumped up against the wall, glaring at her.

"It's okay," I said, moving quickly to the stall door to stand between them. Folly had retreated to the back of her stall, and she stood there glaring balefully back at him just as hard. "She was just scared. She needs time to get to know people first. If you give her a minute, then she'll be okay."

"Humph," my dad said, "she's a piece of work, isn't she?"

I took a deep breath. "She's a difficult horse," I said carefully, "but she has a good side, too. She just needs to be handled in a specific way. We've come a long way with her, though. She's starting to trust us."

I turned to lean over Folly's door. "It's okay, girl," I said, "nobody's going to hurt you. They just want to say hello. Would you like a carrot?"

Folly's pinned ears slowly unfolded, and she made a low whuffling sound under her breath when she saw the carrot I'd pulled out of my pocket. She moved forward through the deep straw and stretched her neck out until she could reach her treat. I let her take a bite and then moved backward. "Come on, Folly, these are your friends."

She crunched the carrot thoughtfully and then took the last few steps forward to the stall door. She nosed happily at Rob and Hilary while they fed her treats and then, when she'd exhausted the food supply, she moved back to her hay.

I glanced at my dad, but he had moved down the aisle to look at the other horses.

"She looks much better, Astrid," Marion said encouragingly.

"I remember how she acted when we visited her at the veterinary hospital; you've done a good job with her."

"Thanks," I said gratefully. "I'm learning so much about horses here; about how they think and the body language they use. I really love it. Justin's like some sort of horse training genius; they'll do anything for him."

"Who's Justin?" Rob asked casually.

"Oh, just one of the trainers here. You'll get to meet him later. He's brilliant."

We walked up the aisle, meeting the other broodmares who wanted their share of treats, and everyone laughed at their fat, low hanging bellies. We piled back in the truck and drove to the training barn.

Everyone oohed and ahhed over Doc and Fox, admiring their exotic good looks. And then I pulled them over to meet Red. "This is him," I said proudly. Even though it was the middle of the day, we'd clearly woken him up and he blinked at us sleepily before shuffling over to greet everyone.

"Oh, isn't he sweet?" Hilary said, scratching him behind the ears. Even Marion came over to gently stroke his velvety nose.

"Do you want to give him a carrot, Dad? He's super nice."

My dad had looked grumpy ever since his run-in with Folly, but he came over and stuck the carrot I offered under Red's nose.

His mouth curved in a slow smile when Red lipped the carrot from his hand.

"This is the horse you're riding?" he asked, sticking his hand out abruptly to pet Red on the neck. He meant well, but he patted him way too hard; it was like he was slapping him. Those kinds of pats would have driven Folly nuts, but Red just closed his eyes and concentrated on his snack.

"Yes, he's wonderful. He's so much fun to ride, we can even canter around bareback. I can show you later...if you like."

"Sure, that sounds impressive. He's a fine-looking animal. Should we check out that archery range of yours?"

He was obviously bored of the barn and ready to move onto something else.

"We can come back after the tour," I told Hilary who was busy snapping pictures of everything. "Aunt Lillian said we can ride while you're here, too, if you like. If the weather's okay and the snow's not too deep, we can go on a trail ride."

"Sure," Hilary said enthusiastically. "I've never ridden western before. Astrid, I love it here, it's fantastic. And these horses are so beautiful."

We drove up to the dairy barn, and I felt a shimmer of excitement as I threw open the big double doors and led everyone inside. Lincoln and I had worked hard, and it showed. The floor was spotless. The walls painted white and the targets still looked brand new. It looked almost professional.

"Hey," my dad said, "this looks great. You did this all yourself?"

"Yes, well Lincoln and everyone from the archery club helped. We practice here a couple times a week, sometimes more."

"I can't think of a better use for this old barn," Lillian said, "the kids worked so hard."

"Who's Lincoln?" Rob asked beside me.

"Oh," I said, blushing, "just this guy from school."

"Astrid, you'll have to invite him up while your friends are here." Aunt Lillian turned to Marion. "Lincoln spent nearly every weekend here getting this ready. He's a wonderful boy; so thoughtful and polite. Isn't he, Astrid?"

"Um, yeah." I looked down at the ground. "He's great."

"Well, he can't be nearly as good as you are, Astrid," my dad said unexpectedly, misunderstanding the conversation. "You should see this girl shoot, Lillian, I don't think she ever misses."

I stared at him, stunned at the compliment. He'd probably said five nice things about me in my entire life, usually only when I'd won something big. To hear him casually toss out a compliment was shocking.

"Oh, I believe it," my aunt said. "I'm hoping to see her in a competition one of these days."

Chapter Twenty-five

Later that afternoon, we left my dad and Marion holed up in the library and headed back down to the barn. I took my truck this time, after carefully nestling my new saddle and bridle in the backseat. I couldn't wait to try everything out on Red.

"Thank goodness, we're alone," Hilary said, as soon as the truck door slammed, "I've been dying to tell you the good news. You have to swear not to tell anyone, though. The sale hasn't been a hundred percent finalized yet."

"What is it?" I said, taking in her flushed cheeks and sparkling eyes.

"My dad finally cracked," she said, not sounding sorry at all. "He stepped down from running his company and we sold our house; we have to be out of it by spring."

"You're moving?" I wailed, then slammed on the brake just before I veered into a snowbank. I carefully put us back in the center of the road and kept my eyes pointed straight ahead. "Hilary, you can't move just as I'm coming home. I'll miss you too much."

"Astrid, you're not listening. I said we're selling our house, not that we're leaving the country."

"Okay, where are you moving to then," I said, keeping my eyes on the road. "It had better be good."

"It's not good, it's great. We bought a farm."

"No way, seriously?"

"Yes, seriously. If the deal goes through then it's on sixty acres in Cedar, right by the ocean and everything. It's on a little bay where we can moor the boat. My dad's decided he's going to completely change his life. He wants to run a working farm with a bed and breakfast and a private restaurant. You know how much he loves to cook; he's already designing the commercial kitchen."

"Oh, Hilary, that's amazing. You're so lucky."

"I know, I could hardly believe it when he told me. I still pinch myself to prove it's really happening. Anyway, I still haven't told you the most amazing part. It has an old farm house that my mom is already making plans to renovate, and a decent-sized barn. There's room for at least eight horses plus all that pasture space. There's even a ring, although it's going to need a lot of work to make it usable again."

"Wow, that's awesome. Are you going to get another horse to keep Jerry company?"

"That's what I wanted to tell you. My dad's completely into this "learn by doing" thing so we're all doing our part to make it a working farm. Mom's organizing the renovations and decorating, dad's going to grow his own food and animals for the bed and breakfast, and I'm going to board horses. Sadie and Pender have already said they'll move their horses over when it's ready. And I want you to come, too."

"Oh!" I felt a shiver of excitement rush up my spine. "Yes, I'd love that, that is if I still have a horse then. I'm not sure what will happen with Folly...or Red."

"Oh, I'm sure it will all work out," Hilary said in her breezy way. "There isn't room for Folly over at Rob's place anyway, not with Marcus and Quarry staying there. So maybe Liza could keep Folly at our place, and you can work with her."

"Sure," I said, keeping my voice light. In the back of my mind, I couldn't help being a bit worried, though. As much as I'd grown to love Folly, I knew she wasn't the horse for me. I couldn't see myself spending the rest of my life taking care of her. I wanted to hand her over to Liza when she was all healed up, but there was a good chance that I'd wouldn't be able to get another horse; not while I was in school anyway.

Still, it was selfish of me not to be happy for Hilary. It was wonderful news. We pulled up in front of the training barn, and I reached out and gave her a hug.

"Hilary, this is wonderful. We need to celebrate."

"It needs a ton of work so, if we even get it, we don't move in until summer anyway, so you'll be home in time to help get things set up. It will be so much fun."

"Is Liza going to stay and teach, then?"

Hilary frowned, and she and Rob exchanged a glance.

"What?" I asked. "What's going on?"

"Well, Liza's not quite sure what she's going to do next. She's pretty unhappy right now. She's having a great time in Holland, and she's afraid to come home in case Cole starts harassing her and making her life miserable again."

"Cole? Why? He got the whole farm, didn't he?"

"Yeah, but he's contesting the will. He wants Marcus and all the money that Claudia left Liza to take care of the horses."

"Can he do that? I mean, it's Claudia's will, isn't it?"

"Well, he can try. My mom says there's probably no chance he'll win, but he's making Liza's life miserable right now. Cole fired her the instant his mom passed away. She had to move the horses out the same day as the memorial service, and she was too scared to be alone at her apartment just in case he showed up, so she stayed with Marion and your dad for a while.

"What?" I said incredulously. "I didn't know that."

"The scene at the barn was horrible. Rob's dad had to come and get the horses right after the service, and Cole showed up, drunk, and it was awful."

"Oh my gosh, you're kidding. I had no idea."

"Yeah, it was scary. Cole freaked out and I called my parents because I was afraid that he'd hurt someone. They were so mad at him that they made me move Jerry right away, that afternoon. Rob's dad came back for him as soon as he picked up Liza's horses."

"Wow, that is horrible."

"Luckily, Rob had enough room to squeeze Jerry into his barn, but everyone else is still stuck there. Ally, Sadie, and Pender say that it's not too bad; Cole hired some young girl to do the feeding and mucking out, so at least they're well cared for. Cole himself hardly shows up, even to ride his own horses, and when he does show up he looks hungover. Claudia's death hit him hard; he just has an awful way of dealing with it."

I frowned, and opened my door, letting cold air pour into the truck. I felt a bit sorry for Cole. He was a spoiled, stuck up brat, but he hadn't been all awful; just most of the time. All that he'd wanted was to have money and horses, and now that Mud Lark was his, it seemed that he couldn't handle it. Claudia had been one of the best people I'd ever met, and I imagined that she'd been a wonderful mother. So how had Cole turned out so selfish and spoiled? And how could he be so mean to Liza when his mom had cared for her so much?

"Anyway, I think Liza might need a long-term change of scenery. She was talking about maybe taking Marcus back to Holland to ride with her trainer there."

"But what about Quarry?"

"Don't worry, he'll stay with me," Rob said quickly. "He's doing great at our place. He and Artimax get along really well. He's a good influence on Arti. They go out on pasture together and gossip about poor Ferdi."

He cracked a smile and, despite my anxiety, I couldn't help but smile back. Being around Rob always made me feel like things were going to be okay somehow.

I pulled my saddle and bridle out of the backseat and we walked slowly toward the barn.

"Hey, big guy," I called, "we're back already. I have a present for you, but I have to clean you up first."

I put my new tack carefully in the tack room, stacking one of the old, beat-up saddles on top of another one to make room. They didn't mind that here, lots of saddles were piled two or three deep. If they ever decided to have a yard sale they'd probably make a fortune selling mostly unused tack.

"Hey, Astrid," Justin called out.

"Whoa," Hilary said, staring up at him with her eyes wide open, her mouth curved in a half-smile. "Hello."

"Hi," Justin said, striding up and reaching out to shake her hand in greeting.

Hilary watched him with a silly smile on her face, cheeks faintly blushing.

Rob didn't seem quite so taken with him, but he shook his hand politely and gave him a tight smile.

"I don't suppose you'd mind if I put you guys to work," Justin said with a laugh. "Astrid's already told me you two are ace riders so there's no backing out of it now."

"Sure, we'd love to ride," Hilary said, "we're up for anything, right, Rob?"

"Okay," Rob said, looking more interested.

"Well, I'll show you who's on the schedule for today and you can let me know what you think." Justin led them down the aisle to show them some of the newer four-year–olds that had come in.

"I'm trying to focus on these older guys first, since we have so many three-year-olds coming up behind them. I want to find these guys homes as soon as possible. What do you think?"

"Ooh, can I ride this one?" Hilary asked, stopping in front of Jane, the little palomino.

"Sure, she's a good choice. She has a few people coming to look at her next week, but you're welcome to ride her. She's green, but solid. She has her basic walk, trot, canter down, and we're working on some light lateral work."

"You event, right?" he said, turning to Rob.

"I do, Eventing and Dressage," Rob said quietly. He was studying Justin as if were not quite sure if he liked him or not.

"Would you take a look at this one then for me? I think this one's a little leggy to be a western horse, but she'd look mighty fine in English tack."

Rob leaned over the stall door smiled when the saw the little buckskin mare inside. "Sure," he said, "she's cute."

"I told Lillian she should send a bunch down with Astrid when she goes home this summer. It's much easier to sell horses closer to Vancouver. It's a long way for people to come up here just to try a horse out. Although, some people do make the trip, of course."

"You did?" I said in surprise. "She didn't tell me that."

"She's not completely sold on the idea. We'd have to find a place to board them down there and that costs money. If they didn't sell quickly then we'd be out of pocket. And then there's the commission to the trainer down there, of course."

I saw Rob and Hilary look at each other, eyebrows raised. I wondered if some of the horses could go to Hilary's place to be trained and sold. Maybe that was a way for me to have a horse to ride; although, I didn't have any experience training young horses.

I brushed Red carefully and smoothed his mane and tail until they felt like silk. I wanted him to look good now that we had an audience. I didn't have a real dressage pad, of course, so I had to take a thin western Navajo saddle blanket and fold it lengthwise until it fit under my saddle.

"I'll make sure I get you a proper set of saddle pads for Christmas," I promised Red, "but at least the saddle looks like it fits you." Red was much rounder than Quarry and I had to put the girth on the second to last hole in order to do it up. "It's probably because your winter coat's so thick," I reassured him, "you're just fluffy."

He sighed and reached for another mouthful of hay as I led him to the door.

Even with the makeshift saddle pad, he still looked handsome in his new dressage tack. I'd had to adjust the bridle, but I thought the whole outfit suited him very well.

"You're so handsome, Red. I can't wait for everyone to see you."

I could already tell that Rob was completely in love with the little mare, Possum, and the feeling was mutual. He led her around the ring a few times, just to get to know her and then brought her over to the mounting block and carefully swung up. The mare turned her head to look back at him, as if asking what on earth he was doing up there, and then obediently moved across the ring.

It took both Rob and Hilary a few minutes to get used to the western tack but soon they looked like they'd been born riding the range.

"Put a few more hours on these guys this week," Justin said, "and we'll take them for a trail ride before you go. They'd like that."

"Okay, big guy," I said, taking a deep breath. I led him over to the block and stepped gently into the saddle.

But, instead of immediately relaxing and stretching down like he usually did, Red chomped on the bit nervously and tensed his back before sticking his nose out and letting his ears flop to the side. He looked like he'd fallen asleep.

"Um, Red?" I said, but his head only drooped lower.

I took a few seconds to pet his neck and give both of us time to get used to the new saddle, focusing on aligning my position and allowing my breath to flow evenly. But, when I asked him to walk he didn't listen at all. He stubbornly stood rooted to the ground.

I looked around, embarrassed, to see Rob and Hilary watching me.

I closed my eyes and tried again, but Red still didn't move. I actually had to give him a little kick with my leg. He jolted a bit and then, reluctantly, moved into a shambling walk.

"Come on, buddy, what's wrong?" I tried everything I could think of to get him to relax and be like his old self, but nothing worked.

"Everything okay, Astrid?" Justin said quietly.

"No, something's wrong with him," I said, feeling tears of disappointment sting my eyes. "I don't think he likes the saddle."

"Well, hop down and let's take it off. We'll see how he goes without it. Maybe it just doesn't fit him."

I jumped down and we pulled Claudia's saddle off and Justin took it over and hung it on the in-gate. As soon as the saddle was gone, Red gave himself a mighty shake, as if he'd woken up from a deep sleep and followed me eagerly to the mounting block.

This time when I got on, he was right back to his old self, ears pricked and a spring in his step. I still took the time to regulate my breathing and center myself, but I could tell right away that the rest of our ride would be great.

"Wow, Astrid, he's a different horse now," Rob said as I moved Red easily through some trotting serpentines. "He's a really nice mover."

"Thanks," I said, "I love him. But I'm sad he doesn't like his saddle."

"Give it some time," Justin said thoughtfully. "That's the same thing he's done to us whenever we tacked him up. We had his back checked, and his teeth; the vet's say there's nothing wrong with him. It might be more psychological, just be patient with him."

After their ride, Rob and Hilary were both bubbling over with enthusiasm for their project horses for the week.

"You fill your boots," Justin said with a laugh, "that gives me two less horses to ride this week."

I was happy Red had been back to his old self by the end of our ride, but I was curious about why he was so different under saddle. It was like he became a different horse when he was all tacked up. How was I going to figure out what was going on in his head?

Chapter Twenty-six

"Snowshoes?" I said doubtfully.

"Yes, your father wants to spend some time alone with you. It will be fun, you'll see. He's getting ready on the porch."

"Okay." I sighed, getting into my winter gear and trudging outside. It was just after breakfast and I'd been looking forward to getting back to the barn, but my family had other ideas.

I figured since they had come all the way out here to visit with me, I should spend at least *some* time with them.

"Hey, Dad," I said tentatively, coming up behind him.

"Hey, Astrid," he said, smiling. "I used to snow-shoe all the time when I was a kid. We should give it a try."

"Okay." I gulped, sitting down to strap on the old-school wooden snow shoes. They were like flat woven baskets, shaped like tennis rackets with a place in the middle to attach my boots.

To my surprise, they were fun and easy to use. Aunt Lillian had told my dad about a trail behind the house that I didn't even know about.

"She says she goes hiking back here sometimes," he told me, which was complete news to me. I'd never thought about what she did all day when I was at school.

The sun was bright against the snow, and I found myself unexpectedly having a good time. We talked about archery and Red, and my dad told me about the squash tournament he had been in, and won, of course.

"Rob seems like a decent young man," my dad said unexpectedly as we crunched through the snow. "Hard working," he added.

"He is," I agreed. "I really like him."

"I had my doubts at first, what with him being Native and all. I couldn't believe that Hilary's father would let his daughter date him."

"What?" I said in shock, stopping in my tracks.

All the bright sunshine surrounding us seemed to bleed out of the sky in one swoop, leaving me surrounded by a dizzying field of white. I faltered, almost tripping into the snow. My dad didn't notice; he just plowed along, not looking back.

"As long as it doesn't get too serious, of course, I can't see how he could object. That kid isn't like the rest of those people. He's going places. And his dad's a respected business man. Of course, I wouldn't be so tolerant if it were *you* dating him."

He said it casually enough, but there was an underlying threat in his voice.

Bile rose in my throat. It wasn't my dad's blatant racism that struck me first. I'd grown up with the man, of course, and had heard him say much worse than that. He hated pretty much all races, religions, and people who weren't exactly like himself.

But what was that about Rob and Hilary dating? I thought back to all their shared smiles and inside jokes. She was boarding Jerry at Rob's farm; that meant they saw each other almost every day. And here I was stuck thousands of miles away. Hilary was beautiful and funny and smart; I was just an average girl squeezed into too-tight pants who could barely stay on her horse. If it came down between the two of us, I knew Rob couldn't possibly choose me.

"Come on, Astrid," my dad called from up ahead, "you're falling behind. You have to keep up in this world or it will plow you over."

Oh no, I thought, trudging through the snow behind him, *please don't spend the rest of this hike giving me bad life lessons.*

"You know, Astrid, I approve of your initiative in building that archery range. That shows some ingenuity. That makes up for you slacking off on your fitness goals."

"What?" I felt my face flush. The shock I'd felt when he'd made that stupid comment about Rob turned instantly to anger. Who was this man to show up every few months just to ruin my life and lecture me? What did he know about anything, anyway?

"I didn't want to say anything," he called over his shoulder, "because you're doing so well here. But you've plumped up a little. You'll never get ahead if you don't have any will power."

My anger propelled me forward across the snow until I'd caught up and then passed him. I tromped down the trail with my back stiff and my jaw set in a hard line. Despite having my own truck I'd been doing a lot of walking to and from the barn this fall and winter, and I played with Red in the ring almost every night; my legs were strong, and I wasn't about to slow down. Somewhere behind I could hear his laboured breathing.

I glanced over my shoulder to see if he'd given up, but he was still marching along, cheeks glowing red with exertion and a determined look set on his face. His eyes looked right past me, fixated on the trail ahead.

I turned around and pushed on harder, my snow shoes whisking me across the snow. I was almost running, but for some reason I'd decided that there was no way I was going to let him pass me.

I looked over my shoulder again to see that he'd managed to make up a lot of ground, he was moving in long-legged leaps up the trail, and I whipped around fast and started to run; as much as a person can run in snow shoes anyway. For a second, I thought he was going to catch up to me, but his pace slackened, and he gradually fell behind. I kept going, moving fast, even though I was overheating inside my down jacket. When the house came in sight again, I almost sobbed with relief. My muscles ached, and I felt like I'd run a marathon.

I dropped down in a snow-drift beside the porch, unzipped my jacket as fast as I could, and lay there panting in great gasps.

After a few minutes, I heard a thud beside me and found my dad sitting in the same snow-bank, his face shiny with exertion.

"Good job, kid," he said, once he could talk without gasping, "you sure made me hustle."

"Thanks," I said flatly, staring up at the blue sky overhead. *But, it shouldn't be like that,* I thought sadly, *a girl should be able to take a nice walk with her dad without it becoming some life lesson or a competition. I don't want it to be like this. How do I change it?*

"This was fun, Astrid," my dad said, slapping my shoulder briskly. "We should do it again tomorrow. I'm heading in for a shower and some lunch."

Great, I thought, lying back in the snow with a thump, *that sounds great.*

Chapter Twenty-seven

I watched Hilary and Rob carefully but, as far as I could tell, my dad had been wrong about their relationship. I wasn't sure where he had gotten that from, but they seemed to treat each other exactly as they always had.

I almost asked Hilary about it a few times but in the end, I decided to let it go. She was such an honest person that I doubted she'd ever keep a secret like that from me. She knew how much I'd liked Rob.

The rest of our visit passed way too quickly. We did our Christmas a few days before the real date because my dad and Marion wanted to be safe at home before the crazy mass of travellers crowded the roads.

No matter the day, it was the best Christmas I'd ever had. The food was amazing, and the presents were perfect.

I got a fancy new grooming set from Hilary.

"They're made from ethically sourced horse hair," she said, beaming in excitement, "and they're specifically made for brushing chestnut horses," she said. "I ordered them from England for you ages ago so it's a good thing you're still riding Red."

"Yes." Aunt Lillian shook her head and sent me a wry smile. "I can't seem to pry her away from him. Although, really, any other horse would do."

I stuck my tongue out at her playfully, knowing full well she was mostly kidding.

Rob had gotten me a fancy new blue saddle pad with gold braided trim, and Aunt Lillian had found me some DVDs on training and even one on horseback archery which I could hardly wait to watch. My dad and Marion had given me a big gift certificate to an online tack store, and I was already plotting all the things I would buy.

All in all, it was a wonderful visit and I had tears in my eyes when I hugged everyone goodbye.

"Come home soon," Rob whispered, hugging me tightly. And right then, I knew that my dad had been lying to me.

"I will," I said. "See you this summer!" I called to all of them.

Chapter Twenty-eight

When Casey and Bryce came home, she was about ten pounds heavier and tanned from the California sun. She'd had some purple streaks added to her dark hair and looked a million times happier.

"I'm going back to school," she told me, "and I'm joining your archery club, too."

"Wait, what?" I sputtered. "Why?"

"Because I need some sort of extra-curricular activity on my records if I'm getting into Redmond next year. They want to see a well-rounded student. I hate sports, so I figure that if I join archery, at least you'll have to be nice to me and make sure nobody makes fun of me."

"Nobody will make fun of you." I laughed. "Especially now that you have Mara back on your side; nobody will be brave enough to bother you again."

We made sure to save a space for her at lunch and keep an eye out for her at study hall, but nobody bothered her, and she made sure to keep her sarcastic comments about people to herself. After a couple weeks, it was like she'd always been there.

She wasn't a good archer at all, but she was quiet and respectful and helped to keep stuff organized, so it was nice to have her there.

Chapter Twenty-nine

"I just have to check the mail on the way home," Kade said, a few weeks after Christmas. He swung into the pullout in front of the block of communal mail boxes at the side of the road.

We'd gotten our official invite to the NFSC that afternoon, and Casey and I were huddled together in the backseat so we could read it.

So we hardly noticed when he got back in the truck, or that he didn't start it right away. He just sat there looking at the envelope in his hands.

"Kade?" I said uncertainly when I finally looked up and saw how pale he was. "Are you okay?"

The large envelope looked strange between his calloused fingers. It was made of thick, cream-coloured paper and had scrolled writing on the outside. The stamp had a running bull on it. It looked expensive.

Kade tore it open wordlessly, and unfolded more thick paper, his hands shaking. A photograph fluttered out and landed on the seat beside him.

I reached over and picked it up carefully, smiling at the

picture of a dark-haired girl holding up a smiling toddler with curly blonde hair. They were standing outside what looked like a café, on a busy, cobblestoned street.

"Is this one of the working students?" I guessed.

Kade looked over and snatched the photo from my hand. He held it up close to his face, devouring the image with tears in his eyes.

"Kade?" Casey asked uncertainly. "Are you okay?"

"Florian," he said brokenly, "and my daughter. That's my daughter, Estelle."

"Ooh," I said quietly, things suddenly clicking into place. Casey leaned forward to gently squeeze her brother's shoulder and he didn't pull away.

"I didn't want to tell anyone that they wouldn't let me see her. I went to Spain as soon as I knew why she'd left. I wanted to be there for her and for the baby. But her awful family wouldn't even open the door. They tried to pay me to go away. As if I'd ever take their money. And, when that didn't work, they called the police."

"Oh my gosh, Kade. That's awful."

"The thing is, I loved Florian, and I would have been a great dad. She just panicked when she found out she was having a baby. And then she was so afraid of what her family would think; she thought they'd disown her. They're very traditional."

"But she's writing you now."

"Yeah," he said, his face breaking into an incredulous smile, "she is."

"Kade, why didn't you tell your family and Aunt Lillian any of this?"

"I was embarrassed. Florian was so upset when she found out she was pregnant, and she just took off back home without saying a word. All she left me was a crappy note. Everyone just assumed we'd had a fight, and since it left us short-handed at the ranch everyone said it must have been my fault that she left. Lillian was so mad at me. She depended on Florian for everything."

"That's awful."

"Yeah, it was. It is. I'm not sure what to do."

"Well, what does the letter say?" Casey asked.

"Not much, it just says she misses me and how Estelle is growing up fast. Then she talks about the weather and stuff. And about how her brother's stable is looking for a trainer. It's stupid."

"Kade!" Casey cried, "she's saying that she misses you and that there's a job opening nearby. And that her brother, her *family*, is willing to maybe hire you. Read between the lines!"

"Huh?"

"Do I have to do everything? Write her back, right now. Text her or email her. Whatever's faster. Let her know that you're coming to visit."

Kade looked down at the letter again, his brow crinkled in confusion, almost as if he were actually looking between the lines. "Hmm," he said, his face clearing. "Well, maybe I could just write her a quick email."

"Yes, but you need to make it a good one," Casey commanded. "Come on, let's go home and I'll help you write it."

Things happened quickly after that. Florian must have written him back right away because he had his ticket and was on a plane the next week. He was gone for two weeks and came back glowing, all tanned and happy and toned from riding horses all day in the sun.

"It was great," he told us when he picked us up from school as a surprise and we were done squealing and hugging him. "Florian's brother breeds Andalusians and those horses are stunning. He needs someone to help start the young guys and he was quite impressed with my mad skills. He offered me a job right away, and there's an apartment included that's just a few miles down from where Florian and Estelle are living with her parents."

"Wait, you're going all the way to Spain, but you're not moving in with her?"

"Not right away," Kade said seriously. "She broke my heart and took my daughter away from me. It takes a man a while to get over something like that. We're taking it slow and getting to know each other again."

He pulled out his phone and let us flip through the photos of him in the fantastic Spanish countryside. The horses were beautiful, and Estelle was completely adorable.

"When do you leave?" I asked.

"Not until late spring. I'll wait until all the foals are done and help Lillian find a rider to replace me. Dad and Justin are going to need some more help. Either we need to hire someone locally, or get back into the working students. We have all that apartment space up above the broodmare barn going to waste, too. It's time for Lillian to pull her bootstraps up and make some decisions about this ranch."

*****

The winter passed in a blur of horses, archery, and cold, snowy weather.

We finalized the team for the competition. I'd known all along that I wasn't going to be strong enough to compete, but it was still a bitter pill to swallow when the time came.

To ease my disappointment, I threw myself into coaching them for all I was worth. Our final team was comprised of Mara, of course—she was by far our best shooter—then Lincoln, Allison, Gage, and a thin boy who went by the unlikely name of Pudge.

They all practiced diligently, and by the time we had to send in our list of names, I felt fairly confident that we had a chance.

My birthday came in the middle of winter and, despite the chill in the air, we had a celebration with the whole team at our range at home. They presented me with a new set of beautiful wooden arrows and a cake big enough for us all to have about four pieces each.

Aunt Lillian took me on a miniature shopping spree to the city, and we even went to see a movie in a real theatre. Something I hadn't done in years.

Kade came back just in time for the first foal to drop in the broodmare barn, and then another, and another. First, it was just full of increasingly cranky fat ladies, and then the foals were born one by one like clockwork.

Nobody would let Casey and I be on foal watch during the week, no matter how much we begged.

"No," Lillian said firmly. "I won't have you exhausted in school all day. You can stay up and help on Friday and Saturday."

Luckily, that was the night that Jewel, a pretty buckskin mare, decided to drop her tiny dark filly. Casey had seen mares deliver foals dozens of times, but it was brand new to me.

I huddled just outside the stall in the semi-darkness, practically holding my breath the whole time while Jewel lay on the floor, grunting and straining. And then, after one prolonged push, a little bundle of slimy foal lay motionless in the straw. Jewel struggled to her feet and then turned around to sniff at it.

"It's not moving," I whispered, gripping the edge of the stall anxiously. "Aunt Lillian, we have to do something."

"Just be patient," she said, laughing quietly under her breath. "Nature usually knows best."

In another few minutes, the little foal sat partway up and Jewel began the long job of licking it clean. She wasn't too careful about it, either, she washed the baby so hard that it staggered under her care, sometimes even falling over only to bob back up instantly, struggling against this rough treatment.

"That gets its circulation flowing," Aunt Lillian said, "mama knows what she's doing." Once the foal was mostly clean and had laid back down in the straw, exhausted, my aunt walked carefully to the door and slipped inside the stall. "Good girl, Jewel," she said, offering up a bucket of warm water.

Jewel sniffed and then stuck her nose deep into the bucket, taking long, grateful gulps of water. Her eyes were half-closed, long dark eyelashes fluttering against her buttermilk coat, and when she finished her drink, she heaved a deep sigh and turned back to her baby, dribbling rivulets of water across his damp fur. Lillian patted the mare's neck softly and then moved in gently beside the foal and crouched down beside it.

"He's a little colt," she whispered softly, "you'll have to think of a good name for him, Astrid."

She took a small bottle out of her pocket and carefully painted his umbilical cord with betadine to prevent him from getting an infection.

Jewel snorted at the strange smell and touched the little foal's head to make sure he wasn't being harmed.

"He's perfect, Jewel," Aunt Lillian said, giving her a reassuring scratch behind the ears. Then she carefully but firmly rubbed her hands all over the tiny colt's neck, sides, and legs, and even gently opened his little mouth and touched his teeth. She cupped its doll-sized feet one by one, gently restraining the little hooves when the colt tried to pull away. Finally, she stood up and brushed her hands together in satisfaction.

"We'll do that every day when they're young," she explained. "That makes our job a million times easier when it comes time to start training them for riding. They'll have absolutely no fear of the process. We imprint ourselves on them so that they'll instinctively trust us right from day one, just like they trust their own mothers."

I didn't get to bed until the sun was coming up again, but when I'd finally done morning chores and Aunt Lillian had ordered me to go get some rest, I still couldn't sleep. My mind kept turning over and over the glorious thing I'd just witnessed.

I saw a foal born, I marveled to myself, *a whole life was created out of nothing. The universe is amazing.*

I finally sat up and grabbed a pen and paper, rubbed my bleary eyes and wrote down my list of possible names for the tiny colt. His mom was Jewel and his dad was Doc, so first I tried a list of different gemstones, but nothing sounded quite right. And medical terms certainly weren't very suitable for such a fantastic baby.

What about something related to archery, I thought. *Bullseye, Quiver, Flu-flu, Target, Bolt.*

No, none of those seemed right and I dropped back into bed, stifling a yawn. I wasn't the creative, imaginative type at the best of times, and especially not on zero hours of sleep.

Well, what about Arrow, I thought drowsily, *arrows are strong but flexible just like Jewel's colt, and it has a nice ring to it.*

"Arrow," I said out loud, testing the word. *Arrow. Yes, I think that's it. I should go tell Aunt Lillian right now. Maybe after I just rest my eyes for a second.*

My eyelids flickered shut and I fell blissfully into sleep.

*****

Arrow lived up to his strong name, growing bigger and cheekier every day. More and more foals were born, and the aisles rang with the tiny, demanding baby whinnies at every meal time. Soon Arrow had a whole barn full of little cousins to play with. Finally, there was only Beezy left to give birth.

"I was sure you were going to be first," Lillian said to her, "and here you are, last."

Beezy looked at her unconcernedly. Stoically eating hay and ignoring all the drama around her.

And, like the professional she was, she dropped a beautiful, chestnut colt twelve days later. The morning of the archery competition.

"I'm so sorry I can't come, Astrid," Aunt Lillian said. "I just don't want to leave her so soon after birth. I'm going to have the vet out to check on her, just in case."

"Don't worry about it," I said, "it's not like I'll be shooting anyway, and we won't be back until late."

"But, you worked so hard. I wanted to cheer on your team."

"You've helped us enough by lending us the space to practice," I said. "I'll take lots of pictures."

Lincoln's dad had agreed to drive us all the way up north to McLeod Lake where the competition was being held. We all piled into his mini-van. Lincoln, Mara, Allison, Gage, and Pudge (whose real name was Everett), and then Casey who had managed to weasel her way along as equipment manager. With all our gear and snacks on board, we barely had room to move in the van.

When we got there, the hall was teeming with people. A harried-looking entry secretary took down our names and handed us each an entry packet filled with information on the competition.

It was a variation on a standard tournament format. Each team set up opposite a specific target and, one at a time, we would take turns shooting at the same time as when the other teams shot. Each archer had two minutes to shoot three arrows at the 18meter distance. Points were counted for each round and tallied together. The team with the highest score was the winner.

"Don't be nervous," I told them, looking around anxiously. "Just do exactly what we do at home. Everything will be fine. Just fine."

I must have sounded like I was about to have a breakdown because Mara raised her eyebrows at me skeptically. "Who's nervous?" she asked, shouldering her pack and heading to our spot. "Look at these losers; we're going to clean up here."

Oh no, I cringed, seeing a few people look up in surprise as she pushed roughly past them, *I've created a monster.*

But Mara's bravado wasn't misplaced; she was a steady, fearless shooter, completely unfazed by the chaos around her. She slammed her arrows home one after another. Lincoln and the others started off shaky, but gained confidence round by round.

In the end, it was, unbelievably, *us,* who took the top of the podium.

Even though I wouldn't get to share in the money, watching them climb up to the top of the wooden platform, made me cry with pride. I felt more emotional watching this team, that I'd helped create, succeed than I ever had when I won on my own. There was something incredibly satisfying about coaching.

We went out for pizza to celebrate and then drove the long way back home.

Even though it was late when we arrived back, I did a last-minute drive back to the barn to check on the horses. All was well in the broodmare barn. Folly nickered to me happily when I passed by to check on Beezy and the new baby. They were fine. The baby was passed out in the straw and Beezy stood over top of him, her head hanging just a few inches over his little body and her lower lip drooping with exhaustion.

I frowned as I ran my gaze over her. All the mares tended to look thin and hollow after giving birth; most of their fat bellies had really been made up of growing baby after all. But Beezy looked extra skinny. Her hipbones stuck out and I could see all her ribs.

Someone had left a giant pile of alfalfa in the corner, so I hoped it was just a matter of time before she recovered.

"Goodnight, everyone," I whispered, moving quietly from stall to stall.

I drove to the big barn to quickly visit Red and found him already standing at the front of his stall, looking alert.

"What is it, buddy?" I asked. "Did you know I was bringing you a snack?"

He lipped the apple half-heartedly off my hand and stared out into the darkness, his whiskers quivering.

That's strange, I thought. *I've never seen him not totally interested in food before. I wonder what he's thinking about.*

After a few minutes, he went back to his hay and I drove slowly back to the house.

Chapter Thirty

I woke up from a deep sleep to the sound of movement in the hall. 4:15, said the red numbers on my alarm clock.

"Aunt Lillian," I said sleepily, coming out into the hall in my pajamas to see what all the noise was about. "What is it? Is it one of the mares?"

"It's Beezy," she said shortly, "she's in trouble, the vet's on his way. Go back to bed."

I went obediently back to my room and sat on the edge of the bed, waiting for the fog in my brain to clear. Then I went to my dresser, pulled out jeans, a sweatshirt, and fuzzy socks, and went downstairs as fast as I could.

My aunt was already gone and so was Jake. The blinking light on the microwave said it was 4:30 am. I flicked on all the lights downstairs so the whole place was lit up and went to the kitchen to make coffee, just like we did on nights we had to wait up for a mare to foal.

Part of me knew that I should be freaking out over what was happening with Beezy. It wasn't like my aunt to panic, and that had been definite dread in her eyes. But I felt like I'd been wrapped in a thick cocoon of calm. My aunt was with her, the vet was coming, and everything would probably be fine.

I yawned sleepily while the coffee maker chugged away, filling the kitchen with that sweet, tangy smell of freshly brewed coffee. I filled the big thermos full to the top, put it in the canvas bag we'd been using for foal watch, and then threw a handful of granola bars inside as well.

Aunt Lillian had taken my truck for some reason, so I was stuck walking, but I didn't mind; the air was cold, but it was clear out and I was bundled up tightly in my winter coat and boots, with a wool hat pulled down over my ears and a long scarf wrapped snugly around my neck.

The sky overhead was covered in a blanket of stars so thick I could hardly see any black spaces between them. I stood with my head thrown back, just gazing upward in awe. I came back to earth with a sigh and continued down the well-worn road, the beam from my head lamp bobbing along.

The first thing I saw as I neared the barn was that someone had moved Folly from her nice warm stall to the snow-covered paddock out front. She whinnied when she saw me, striking the gate with an outraged front foot to let me know that this situation was *not* to her liking.

"What happened, Folly?" I said, reaching up to scratch her neck reassuringly. "Why did you get kicked out? Hang on, I'll go get you some hay and see what's going on."

The lights in the broodmare barn were blazing, streaming across the snow in a wide path. My truck was there, parked half in a snowbank, and Bryce's, Kade's, and the vet's. A group of people stood in the aisle, and I walked hesitantly toward them, suddenly afraid of what I would find.

Bryce looked up wearily and rubbed his face. I was horrified to see a smear of blood across his cheek.

"Where's Aunt Lillian?" I asked, looking from face to face.

The vet just shook his head. "She's saying goodbye to an old friend, Astrid. Beezy prolapsed, I'm afraid she's gone."

"Oh no." Tears welled in my eyes and I put a hand over my mouth. "Can I go see her?"

"Better not, kiddo. Beezy had a rough time and it got bloody. You don't need to see all that. And Lillian needs some time alone with her."

I had a sudden thought. "And…the baby? Did the baby die, too?"

"Nope," Kade said, "come look."

He turned to Folly's old stall and I went to look over the half door. There, curled up in the stall was Beezy's small, red colt, smears of half-dried blood covering his shoulder and neck. He was curled up in a tiny ball with his nose resting on his rump. A shudder ran through his body as if he were cold, even with the thick bed of straw.

"Poor little guy," the vet said. "He had a scary time of it. His mom was pretty panicked, so she knocked him over a few times. He's feeling miserable right now. He's probably hungry, too."

"What's he going to eat?" I asked, remembering how often the mares called their babies to their sides for a drink.

"Excellent question," Bryce said. "I guess we'll have to see if any of the other mares will take to him. We'll have to wait until everyone settles down from all the excitement before we give it a try, though. We have to, uh, move, Beezy first. Astrid, you don't want to be here for that. You'd best go up to the house."

"But I want to help," I said. I was a part of this family, too. I'd cared about Beezy, too.

"Can you go feed the training barn horses for me then?" Bryce said wearily. "And is that coffee in there? We could use some of that right now."

"Okay," I said, handing him the bag of coffee and snacks. "I just have to feed Folly." I started toward the hay stall, but Bryce laid a hand on my arm.

"I'll get your mare fed," Bryce said, turning me to the door and escorting me outside. "I promise. Now go on so I don't have to worry about you. Check all their waters, too, and make sure nobody's blanket is rubbing."

"Fine," I sighed, trudging off toward the far barn, ignoring Folly's outraged nicker. I had to trust that Bryce would remember to feed her. They clearly wanted me out of the way, but I guessed that putting up a fuss wasn't going to be helpful at that moment.

The horses in the big barn nickered sleepily when I came inside.

"Hey, everyone," I whispered, "it's just me. We're going to do breakfast early this morning."

I filled the big wheelbarrow with as many flakes as I could fit and towed it down the aisle, throwing some into each stall for the surprised, but appreciative, residents inside.

Finally, I went into Red's stall and sat down at his feet, listening to contented chewing. *Beezy's gone,* I thought, leaning back against the wall, *just like that. Life is so fragile.*

Red paused between bites and reached down to ruffle my hair with his top lip in that affectionate way he had.

"Oh, Red, she was your mother, wasn't she?"

That was all it took; my throat closed, and the weight on my chest broke and I began to cry softly. Red sighed deeply and grabbed another mouthful, dropping bits of hay over my head and shoulders in a gentle rain.

Chapter Thirty-one

The little foal needed to be fed many, many times both day and night. He'd moved into his own stall, the old one he'd shared with Beezy, and Folly had been allowed back inside again. She'd followed me indignantly into the barn, pawing at her straw bed and sniffing every corner of her stall for signs of the intruder.

We took turns feeding him. At first, it took two people; one to hold him in place and another person to hold the bottle that was a poor replacement for a missing mother. He didn't want to drink, but Aunt Lillian squirted a few drops of the milk replacer onto his tongue and then his hunger took over. Once he understood where his food came from, he drained each bottle dry, stomping his little hooves and demanding more.

The vet had tried unsuccessfully to get one of the other mares to accept him. They either tried to kick him or bite him, and no amount of encouragement would get them to take him on. So, in the end, it was decided it was safer for the baby to just live on his own and be fed by hand until he was big enough to be integrated with the other horses.

Saturday morning came too early. I yawned and rubbed my

eyes, the brisk morning air not enough to break through all my sleep deprivation as I stumbled into my clothes and drove slowly down to the barn.

Casey and I were scheduled to be on duty all weekend, since we couldn't help much during the week, and I was already exhausted.

I flicked on the dim light on the wall, not wanting to blind everyone so early in the morning.

"Morning, Folly," I mumbled, glancing over at her.

She wasn't at the front of her stall, eagerly demanding food like usual. She stood in the back corner with one back leg propped up, looking half asleep. She nickered to me under her breath.

"You're still asleep, too, girl?" I said, walking past her down the aisle past the mares who were rumbling eagerly in their stalls. I slid the hay room door open and filled the wheelbarrow and dragged it down the hall, tossing hay into each manger.

"Morning, baby." I leaned over to peek in at him and then froze. The stall was empty.

"Oh no." I looked at the half-open door to his paddock, the one that should have been tightly closed, and shut my eyes. I was sure it had been locked last night, there was no reason to have it open. Had he gone downhill in the night and passed away and nobody had woken me up to tell me?

Heart thudding in my chest, I slipped into the stall and moved quickly through the open back door into the paddock, shining my headlight over every inch of space. No little foal lying in the snow. It hadn't snowed last night, so surely, I'd see him. I searched it carefully just to be sure, walking the fence line twice just to be positive. No, definitely no baby horse.

But there. I shone my headlamp carefully onto the ground, where a set of tiny footprints had ploughed up the snow. What had happened to him?

There was a low nicker from Folly's stall and then a tiny answering one in return.

No, I thought in disbelief, *that's not possible.*

I walked back inside and went next door to check on my horse. There he was, stretched out on the straw, lounging like a young sultan without a care in the world. Folly stood over him, looking down lovingly as if he were her own.

"Oh, Folly," I whispered, "did he climb through the fence to get to you? You saved him."

She looked up at me, her eyes shining bright with a contentment I'd only seen from her a handful of times.

I stood there for a long time, just watching them, sharing in this magical moment that was just for the three of us.

"Wow," Aunt Lillian whispered quietly, coming up behind me. "I would have never guessed this in a million years."

"Can she keep him?" I asked anxiously. "Could we leave them together?"

"I don't see why not. We'll have to bottle feed him still, of course, but the main thing is that he needs a horse to nurture him. If she wants the job, then I don't see why she can't have it. We'll have to make sure she doesn't reject him later, though."

Looking at her and her new son, I really doubted that she'd ever reject him.

Chapter Thirty-two

"She's here, Folly!" I called, bouncing up and down on the hay bale I'd been sitting on to do my homework while I waited. "Liza's here."

Folly glanced up from her hay when she heard her name and then went right back to eating, unconcerned.

Justin's truck crunched up the gravel driveway to the barn, and I could just make out Liza's familiar face behind the glass. A shiver of anxiety rolled up my spine. The last time I'd spoken to Liza in person, she'd been very angry with me; she'd practically hated me. Sure, we'd texted back and forth since then, and we'd spoken on the phone at Christmas, but I wasn't a hundred percent sure what to expect.

"Astrid," Liza said warmly as soon as she got out of the truck, "it's good to see you. You look fantastic."

"I do?" I laughed, getting up and going to meet her. I'd put on clean jeans and brushed my hair, but I still looked like a barn rat.

"Yes, you're all grown up," she said, pulling me into a tight hug. "Okay, I can't stand it anymore, where is she?"

"Come on," I said, grinning, "you're not going to believe this when you see it. You didn't tell her, did you, Justin?"

"Nope, I left it all to you."

"Hey, Folly, you have a visitor," I called and smiled when she nickered in response.

"Wow." Liza raised her eyebrows, impressed, as Folly stuck her head over the stall door, bobbing her nose up and down in her eagerness to see everyone. "Is that Folly?"

"Just wait, it gets better."

Folly's eyes widened when she saw Liza, and she froze, ears swivelling in all directions as if she was trying to figure out what was happening. Suddenly, she let out a high-pitched squeal and pressed forward against the door, banging her front hoof against the wood.

"Oh, Folly," Liza said, moving forward to touch the big mare. Her fingers brushed the shining copper coat and then she burst into tears as Folly buried her head against Liza's chest.

Tears welled in my own eyes and I had to look away. Of course, I was glad that I'd reunited these two, but I was also aware that it was my fault they'd been separated so long.

Justin put a hand on my shoulder and squeezed it gently. I knew he understood completely.

"Folly, I've missed you so much." Liza pushed herself upright and wiped her tears away impatiently. "Astrid, she looks fabulous."

She still hadn't noticed the surprise, but when I didn't answer she turned to look at me questioningly.

"Go look," I said, pointing at Folly's stall. I put my hand over my mouth to keep back the laughter and I could hear Justin chuckling beside me.

"What the heck?" Liza's eyes widened as she peered over the stall door to see the big red colt laying at Folly's feet. "But how? With who?"

Justin and I both burst out laughing; I just couldn't keep it in any longer.

"Surprise! Folly's a mom; well, not a real mom, a surrogate mom. We still have to bottle feed him, but she takes care of everything else. Do you want to meet him?"

"She won't get too protective?"

"Nope." I shook my head. "She's been an angel."

Liza slid open the stall door and slipped inside to stand next to Folly and the little colt who'd scrambled to his feet as soon as a stranger came into his stall. Gently, she stroked Folly's neck and then held out her hand for the little guy to sniff. He rocked backwards for a second, as if to run away, and then his boldness took over and he took a big step toward her, sticking his nose in her armpit.

"Oh my gosh, he is adorable. What's his name?"

"We were thinking of Figaro," I said. "What do you think?"

"Oh, that's perfect. Astrid, I have to say that you have done a fantastic job with Folly. She's a new horse."

"Well, it wasn't all me," I said. "Justin taught me a lot. And he's the one that rides her, not me. I hope you don't mind that she's going Western."

"She looked so happy in the pictures," Liza said quickly. "She's going on trail rides?"

"Yes, she's still not happy in the ring, the vet doesn't think she's totally sound yet, but she's still so much better. She's fine on the trail, if you don't mind her spooking all the time."

"She's a lot of horse." Justin laughed. "Lots of power there, for sure."

Liza smiled at him and he met her grin with one of his own.

"We were originally planning to take you on a trail ride," I said, "but I don't think that would work with little Figaro here."

"Oh, that's okay, I've been riding a ton of horses back home. I don't mind a break."

"You're the only person I've met who comes to a ranch to get a break from riding." Justin laughed.

"I know, but I've been riding like eight horses a day for the last few months. And the only thing people want me to ride right now are silly, young horses. I have bruises layered over bruises."

"I feel your pain. Too bad, though, Lillian's been itching to get you to test out some of her horses."

"Oh?" Liza raised her eyebrows, looking interested. "Why?"

"She wants to see if any of them would make good amateur dressage prospects."

"Sure, I'm not an expert or anything, but I can look at them for you. You have some prospects in mind?"

"Yeah, about thirty of them," Justin joked. "Come on and see the training barn."

"Yes," I said, dancing up and down eagerly beside her. "I want you to meet Red."

I'd left the battered old farm truck in front of the broodmare barn, and I got to enjoy Liza's look of surprise when I jumped into the front seat and started the ignition.

"Look at you, driving like a pro," she joked.

"Yeah, farm kids are just more advanced than city kids, I guess," I said, quoting Aunt Lillian. I carefully maneuvered in front of the training barn, excited to show her the love of my life. "Thanks again for sending me Quarry's tack. That meant a lot. I hope we can figure out how to get him moving better under saddle. I love riding bareback, but it would be nice to use tack sometimes."

"I'm sure we'll figure it out, Astrid. And Claudia was so happy to give you that saddle. She knew how much you loved Quarry."

"Here he is," I said, bypassing the first two stalls and moving right to Red.

"Aww, Astrid, he's adorable. Look at his fuzzy coat. He's like a big pony."

"Yeah, it's too cold to clip him much. He's shedding now, though; he's losing handfuls of it every day. My clothes are always covered in fur."

I watched as she reached out and absently scratched his neck, her gaze wandering down the aisle, settling first on Doc, and then Fox.

"Wow, those are your stallions?" she said, giving Red a final pat and moving toward Doc. "He's a gorgeous guy, isn't he? Look at those eyes."

Justin opened the stall door and they went inside, petting Doc and going over his bloodlines and accomplishments.

I stayed by Red, trying not to feel let down. Of course, he couldn't compare to fancy horses like Doc, but I was proud of him and I'd been looking forward to showing him off; I had been so sure that Liza would like him.

"Well, I like you best, Red," I whispered to him as he nuzzled the zipper on my jacket. "I think you're fantastic."

"Wow, now this guy is something," Liza said, moving from Doc's stall and stopping in front of Fox. "He's built like a tank. And look at those stockings. I bet he's flashy under saddle."

"Yep, it's mostly his offspring that Lillian wants you to look at. They're built powerful like him and have longer, more elastic gaits."

"Okay," Liza said, looking interested.

"I'll show you some of the young horses we've been working with," Justin said, leading Liza past me. His eyes sparkled, and he didn't even glance at me as he passed by. Liza's cheeks were flushed, and she watched him closely as he talked as if she was memorizing the lines of his face.

I had the sinking feeling I wasn't going to be seeing much of her this week.

They walked up and down the barn, discussing each young horse, and then went to stare in at the indoor.

"Wow," Liza said, "this is amazing. You're so lucky to have something like this to work in. Rob's place is nice, but I miss that indoor at Mud Lark like crazy. It's hard to ride your horses consistently when those monsoon rains hit."

"Yeah, we're lucky here, for sure. Hey, we should go out on a trail ride this afternoon and see some of the other young horses. We have some pastured three-year-olds up and coming that Lillian wants you to have a look at. And I know Astrid wanted you to see her buddy, Red, in action."

"Oh," Liza said, suddenly remembering I existed. She turned to smile at me. "That would be great. Thanks so much for inviting me to visit this place, Astrid. It's fabulous."

I trailed the two of them back to my truck listening as they talked eagerly about the horses.

*****

The spring run-off had rutted the shortcut into a series of potholes chained together by heaps of mud. We bounced and shuddered our way down the road, the old truck heaving itself from side to side.

"For heaven's sake, Astrid." Liza laughed. "What kind of shortcut is this?"

"Sorry," I said, gripping the wheel tight in both hands. "It wasn't this bad last night. Everything is melting."

We finally made it to the house in one piece and Aunt Lillian threw the door open excitedly.

"Come in, come in," she called. "Lunch is on the table. Justin, you're welcome, too, of course. Looks like you two have already gotten *acquainted*." She ushered them inside and raised an eyebrow at me.

"Astrid, show Liza where to put her things, and then wash up and join us at the table."

"Sure, come on, Liza. I put you in the same room I put Hilary over Christmas. She loved it."

"Oh, I'm sure it will be perfect. This entire place is amazing."

She sighed happily when she saw her room and sat down on the bed with a flounce. "Honestly, I don't know why you'd ever want to come back home after living here. Won't you miss it?"

"I will," I said slowly, "but I miss home, too. And there's no archery coach for me here. Earl was really, really good, and I'm going to start working with him again this summer to see if I can get my strength back."

"Oh yeah, I forgot about the archery thing. You're such a

good rider that I forget that you do other stuff, too." She laughed, not noticing my incredulous stare.

"*Good rider*," I sputtered. "You're kidding, right? You said I was awful."

It was her turn to stare at me. "Awful? When did I say that? You're a beautiful natural rider, Astrid, you have an inborn feel and timing that most people have to work very hard for. Not saying that you didn't work hard, of course, it's just that some stuff comes more naturally to you than it does for others. You're lucky; it's a gift."

"But Folly—"

"Is a difficult, temperamental horse that needs a professional to handle her. Yes, you had no business ever getting on her back, but that doesn't mean that you're an awful rider."

"Oh," I said softly.

"Stop being so hard on yourself, silly," she said, reaching out and tapping me gently on the arm. "Come on, let's get some lunch."

Aunt Lillian flitted around happily, making sure everyone's plates and cups stayed full and listening to the conversation with interest. I could tell that Liza was making a good impression on her.

"So, what did you think of our horses so far, Liza? Are they much different than what you're used to?"

"Oh, no, I ride all sorts of horses," Liza said. "Right now, I'm mostly starting babies for clients and tuning up a few mid-level horses. Marcus is the only upper level horse I have going right now."

"And Astrid was saying that you teach lessons, too?"

"Yes, when I'm not riding, I'm teaching and sometimes I do both at the same time." She laughed and shook her head. "I love the work, but half the time I don't know whether I'm coming or going. This winter was hard without the indoor. There were lots of days we either had to trailer somewhere or just skip lessons and training for the day. It sets things behind schedule."

"Oh, I can imagine. And what are your plans now?"

Liza looked down at her plate and took a deep breath. "I don't know, to be honest. I loved my time in Holland, and part of me wants to go back. But then I'd have to go through all the hassle of exporting Marcus. And I have to consider Quarry, too."

"And Folly," I said quietly, watching her face.

"Yeah…" She sighed. "About that, Astrid. I'm not sure it's a good idea."

"What?" I said incredulously. "You don't want her?"

"I love her, Astrid, but I don't own my own place. I'm barely making ends meet."

I stared at her in shock. My whole year with Folly had been planned around this moment. I was supposed to hand Folly triumphantly back to Liza and get on with my own life.

"But, I did exactly what Claudia said. She told me that I had to get Folly better and give her back to you; that's what she wanted most of all. That's what I've been working toward all this time. Here."

"What's this?" Liza stared at me, her eyes glistening with tears. She took the envelope I'd pulled out of my hoodie pocket and slid down the table toward her.

"Go on, open it."

She opened the envelope with trembling fingers and then put a hand over her eyes.

"It's her registration papers," I explained. "And a bill of sale marked for one dollar. I don't want any money for her. She's all yours."

"Oh, Astrid," she said tearfully. "I honestly don't know what to say. Thank you. But...but...what am I going to do with all these horses?" And she suddenly burst into tears.

Justin and I exchanged bewildered looks, but Aunt Lillian shot to her feet. "Go on outside for a bit, you two. I want to have a talk with Liza alone."

Justin and I went outside and sat on the porch swing, lost in our own, silentthoughts.

"Well, I'd better start working my horses," Justin said finally, when nobody came out to tell us it was okay to go back in. "You want a lesson on Red?"

"Sure," I said with a sigh and followed him to the truck. So far, this visit was not going how I'd planned.

I was just putting Red away when Aunt Lillian pulled up in front of the barn with her truck.

"Family meeting," she called from the driver's seat, "get in. Tell Justin to follow as soon as he can."

"Okay," Justin said when I went to the tack room to let him know that Aunt Lillian had lost her mind. "Sounds interesting. I'll be up there in a sec."

Aunt Lillian didn't say much as we drove, but a little smile kept flickering across her face, so I knew that the news couldn't be that bad.

Bryce, Kade, and Casey were already at the table, sitting beside a tear-stained Liza. Justin came in a few minutes behind us and sat down slowly at the table beside me.

"All right, everyone," Aunt Lillian said, setting the inevitable pot of tea down in the center of the table and passing out mugs. "I have some things to say.

"First of all, I want to apologize to all of you for my behaviour since Trent passed away. Yes, yes, I know I was grieving and that's okay, but it's no excuse for me to let this ranch slip into disrepair. That was the last thing Trent would have wanted. He loved this place.

"However, his vision and my vision are slightly different. For example, I hate cattle. I didn't like them before his accident and I liked them even less afterward. So, my first step will be to sell them off as quickly as possible."

She held up her hand as Kade opened his mouth to say something.

"None of that. I'll give you all plenty of time to add your input later. And, speaking of you Kade, darling, I am so happy that you are going to be closer to your daughter and Florian. I'm going to miss you, but I agree that it's the best thing for you right now. You know you're welcome back here anytime.

"But, that means, of course, that we have a big space to fill here. Not many people could fill Kade's boots. But, I hope, that Liza will be able to do just that."

I looked up, not entirely surprised at Aunt Lillian's announcement, to see Liza smiling shyly around the table.

"You all know we're severely over-horsed here. I've let our program slide badly and, as a result, we've lost many potential clients. I have some ideas to branch off in a few different directions. So, we're going to try an experiment this summer to test the waters."

She looked around the table, judging everyone's reactions. "Bryce and Justin will continue on their excellent training program. There is no need to alter anything there. Liza is going to hand-pick a few potential horses to start our new amateur dressage horse program. These are quality horses; we should be able to find a good market of people who value temperament and overall athleticism above extravagant gaits."

"So, you're moving up here?" I asked slowly. "What about your horses and Folly?"

"I…I guess I'm bringing Marcus and Quarry up here," Liza said, as if she didn't quite believe it herself, "and Folly can stay, of course. I'll work off their board here."

"It'll be included in your contract," Lillian corrected, "along with your apartment. That brings me to the second part of my plan. Astrid, listen up, this is where you become involved."

"Me?" I said nervously, looking around the table.

"Yes, Liza has told me some interesting things about the situation at home. Namely, that your Claudia worked out a deal with Rob's family regarding board for two horses."

"Oh, yes, she gave them a good price on Ferdi if he agreed to board Quarry and Marcus there for free."

"Right, I know. So, I need you to help convince him and his father to accept my proposal."

"Proposal?"

"Yes, I want to go into business with him. I want those two stalls full of my horses as long as Liza doesn't need the space. Rob can work them for me, show them, get the Triple Hill's name out there, and take a nice commission off every sale."

"Oh," I said, remembering how much he'd liked the little

buckskin mare, Possum, "he would probably like that. He likes training young horses."

"That's what I suspected. So, if you can handle that aspect for me, and perhaps see if your friend Hilary might take one or two on as well, then I would appreciate it. It would help free up some room in the training barn here."

"Of course," I said, "I'll call them tonight."

There might even be something I can ride, I thought excitedly, *maybe Hilary and I can work on a project together.*

"Now, I know you don't have much experience with young horses, and I don't want to push you when you're just starting to enjoy riding again. But, I do have a proposition for you, too, Astrid."

"Oh, what?" I said, my curiosity rising.

"I don't want to sell Red," she said abruptly, "he was Trent's horse and he would haunt me if anything bad happened to that animal."

"Oh, okay," I said, fighting back the tears that sprang to my eyes. I took a deep, shaking breath, "I understand." *He's not your horse*, I told myself fiercely, *he'll have a good home here all his life. That's all you can ask. You knew this would happen eventually.*

"On the other hand, he eats a ton and he's lazy as sin for anyone but you."

A small seed of hope shivered in my chest. *Maybe.*

"So, how about if I send him down to the Island for you to ride. You take care of him, you handle his board, but I'll keep ownership of him. Would that work?"

"Are you serious?" I said quietly, hardly daring to speak. "Are you sure?"

"Of course I am. Trent would want Red to be kept in the family and he's not going to be useful here. If you want him, and your parents say it's okay, then he's yours."

"Aunt Lillian…" I rose slowly out of my chair, moved to my aunt's side and threw my arms around her neck.

"Thank you," I said, holding her tightly. "Thank you so much."

"Oh, sweetie, you're welcome. I hope you have fun with him."

"I will," I said and promptly burst into tears.

*****

The next day I finally I got my chance to show off Red to Liza.

"He looks fine to me, Astrid," Liza said from the middle of the ring as I trotted around her in circles. "He's actually a really nice mover. What are your plans with him?"

"I'm not sure," I said honestly. "I'm just going to keep playing with him, I guess."

"Well, I think you could start showing him this summer if you're interested. I know you liked it with Quarry and this guy seems like a real steady fellow. I can help you get him ready next month when I come down for my visit, if you like."

"Um, thanks, but he's only forward like this when I ride bareback; he's a totally different horse under saddle."

"It can't be that much different," Liza said.

"Hang on, I'll show you." I slid off Red's back and led him back to the gate where I'd hung his saddle and pad. He stood patiently while I tacked him up, his eyes half-closed and his head dropped down to the arena floor as he fell into his usual napping position. His nostrils fluttered, and he began to snore gently.

"Come on, big guy," I said, tugging softly on his reins.

He followed me reluctantly, shuffling through the arena footing like he was a hundred years old.

"Wow," Liza said, "that's quite the transformation."

"I know, it's what he does every time he's tacked up. Even to go on a trail ride. He perks up a little when he hits the trails, but it's nowhere near as animated as when we ride bareback."

I led him to the mounting block and swung up on him.

"Drop your stirrups, Astrid, you stiffened up right away when you got on him."

"I know, it's because it's always so awful to ride this way."

"Okay, but being tense won't help. Just concentrate on your breathing first and let your whole body drift into relaxation."

I'd been through this a hundred times on my own, but maybe Liza would see something I'd missed. I felt all my tension drain away and relaxed deeply into the saddle. Red sighed contentedly and drifted to a halt in the center of the ring, his nose a millimeter off the ground.

"Maybe that's a little too relaxed." Liza laughed. "Send him forward."

I tried, I really tried, but though Red obediently moved into a shuffling walk, trot, and even a laborious canter, all the joy had gone out of the ride.

"Can I try him out, Astrid?" Liza asked, moving to the mounting block without waiting for me to answer. Red shuffled over to her and she reached out and stroked his neck.

As soon as I swung down she pulled the saddle off and handed it to me, running her hands over his back and withers, pressing deeply into his muscles.

"He doesn't seem sore at all."

"No, the vet said that he couldn't find anything wrong with him at all. They've had him checked out a few times."

"Okay, Red, do you mind if I go for a spin?" She swung up easily onto his broad back and reached down to scratch his withers. Red's ears swivelled around, and he turned to touch the tip of her boot with his nose, lipping at the leather gently.

"You're a sweetheart, aren't you?" she said, moving him into a walk. Red arched his neck and strode off in a powerful walk, looking like a proud war-horse preparing for battle, his steps and his eyes alive with excitement at this interesting change in his routine. He moved easily under Liza, stepping eagerly into a trot and stretching down when she slowly fed him a longer rein. She didn't ask him anything too difficult, just walk, trot, canter, and some easy lateral work, and when she was satisfied she brought him back to the mounting block and jumped to the ground.

"Astrid, I love him," she said enthusiastically, "let's try him with the saddle again."

She tacked him up herself, gently smoothing the saddle pad into position before lifting the saddle carefully on to his back. She fastened the girth slowly, watching him for any signs of flinching or discomfort but he merely yawned and drooped his head to the arena dirt.

"Okay, fellow, let's see what's going on."

She put a foot in the near stirrup and swung up lightly, taking a moment to get settled before asking him to move forward. There was a long pause as his eyes flickered open and then he yawned again and shuffled into the slowest walk possible.

"Oh geez." Liza burst out laughing and leaned down to give

him a good-natured pat on the neck. "What a silly horse. Come on, you have more that than in you, buddy."

She moved him straight to a canter and then urged him to stretch out into a gallop, but he still moved like he was churning through molasses, each stride laboured. Finally, she drew him to a walk and then a halt, shaking her head.

"I've never seen anything like this, Astrid."

"I know, Justin and Kade think that it's in his head for some reason. He associates riding with the saddle with something bad. Because…because of what happened to Uncle Trent."

"Hmm, I don't know," Liza said slowly. "But there's something going on with him, that's for sure."

"Well, what should I do with him?"

Liza shrugged. "Exactly what you're doing; keep riding him bareback in the ring, since he's so happy that way. And if it were my horse, I'd do whatever I could to make work under saddle fun. So, lots of trail rides and lots of speed work; he needs to associate his tack with things that are pleasant for him. He'll probably love doing conditioning rides out on the trails. I can help you work out a program for him. Overall, though, I'd say you have a really nice horse here."

"Thank you," I said, relieved to finally know what she thought of him. "I'm glad you like him."

Chapter Thirty-three

Leaving was not as easy as I'd thought it would be. Triple Hills had grown to be a real home to me and I loved Aunt Lillian almost as much as I did Marion. Still, there was something that always pulled me back to the Island, back to the coast, back to the mountains I loved. It was like an inner magnet that constantly gave me gentle nudges in that direction.

It also helped that Aunt Lillian had sworn that we would be visiting back and forth constantly from now on.

"I let you out of my life for too long," she said, sweeping me into yet another hug. "I'm not about to lose touch with you now. Besides, you'll have to come up here to pick out horses whenever one sells. I have high hopes for this scheme of mine."

"Thanks for letting them keep the archery range," I said gratefully, "it means a lot to everyone."

I was secretly hoping that I could come back for a few weeks in the summer to visit and help them practice. I couldn't let their skills slip just because I was moving.

Liza was already ensconced in her new home over the broodmare barn. And Quarry and Marcus had happily accepted their new surroundings. The look on Quarry's face when he'd come off the trailer and seen all the green, rolling pastures spread out in front of him was priceless. It was like he'd died and gone to heaven.

Kade was en route to Spain, and I hoped that everything worked out for him and Florian. He deserved to be happy.

"All loaded up, Astrid?" Allan looked over at me with a grin.

"Yes," I said happily, glancing up at the monitor where Red was calmly eating his hay, stationed between Possum, Ellie, and Maverick. All completely unconcerned about the big journey ahead of them.

"Well, let's roll out then. We'll get you home by dinnertime."

Home, I thought, hugging my arms to my chest in delight. *I'm going home.*

The End

Acknowledgments

Huge thanks to my fabulous editor Jinxie Gervasio who always laughs and cries in the right places and is full of good advice.

Massive appreciation, in no particular order, to Heather Stewart of Sweet Water Stables, Helen Cartwright, Jennifer Warburton, and Emily Pelletier of Generation Farms for being the first readers. Your help was invaluable!

Fabulous cover design credit goes to *Cover Design by James, GoOnWrite.com*

Interior design credit goes to the wonderful folks at Polgarus Studio.

And last, but not least, many thanks to Messenger, who is the funniest, bossiest, most clever horse in the world. Thanks for putting up with me all these years, buddy.

Genevieve Mckay is a six-time novelist and horse enthusiast living with her family on the wet and wonderful West Coast. She is an excellent horse-mom but a terrible archer.

All About Books

If you enjoyed *Defining Gravity*, *Flight*, *The Horses of Winter* or any of my other books, I'd love if you'd take a moment to write a review on any of the platforms where they are sold.

Visit my website at www.genevievemckay.com
Follow on Twitter @Geners_Mckay
Or join my Facebook author page:
https://www.facebook.com/authorgenevievemckay

Astrid's Series

Defining Gravity
Flight
Freefall (coming 2018)

Short Stories

The Horses of Winter

The Strange Adventures of Carolina Brown

The Opposite of Living
An Aching in the Bone
Wayfarer's End

20433475R00208

Made in the USA
Middletown, DE
10 December 2018